LIVING FOR JESUS

LIVING FOR JESUS

Developing a Biblical Worldview for Success

Pastor Robert L. Dickie
Berean Baptist Church
Grand Blanc, Michigan

Emmaus Road Publishing, Inc.
6705 Rustic Ridge Trail
Grand Blanc, Michigan, 48439

© Robert L. Dickie

First published 2008

ISBN: 978 0 615 21537 2

To Dr. and Mrs. Del Fehsenfeld, Sr.
who taught their family to fear God, love Jesus,
and prepare for eternity

Contents

Preface

I am writing this book for the purpose of leaving my children and my children's children a legacy that will be more valuable to them than gold and silver. I want to leave them a Christian worldview that will help them and anyone else who may profit from reading these pages, a philosophy of living that will ensure that they will have a good opportunity to find success and meaning to life. A biblical worldview will teach us how to live for Jesus in this fallen world.

There are two things that we need to clarify as we begin this study: first, "What is a worldview?" and second, "What do we mean by success?" A worldview refers to the framework through which an individual interprets the world and interacts in it. Dr. Philip Johnson, Professor Emeritus of Law at the University of Berkeley in California, wrote,

> Understanding a worldview is a bit like trying to see the lens of one's own eye. We do not ordinarily see our own worldview, but we see everything else by looking through it. Put simply, our worldview is the window by which we view the world, and decide, often subconsciously, what is real and important, or unreal and unimportant.[1]

A worldview should answer three main questions:

1. Where did we come from? This concerns our view of Creation.
2. What is the source of evil and suffering? This concerns our view of the fall of man.
3. What can we do about all of this? This concerns our view of redemption.

These three questions, summarized by the key words of creation, fall, and redemption, serve as an excellent means of evaluating all competing worldviews. Every worldview has an answer to these three questions. By examining the answers, we can decide if the worldview is valid or invalid.

From a religious and philosophical point of view, a worldview involves our understanding of how the world came to be, its design, and people's place in it. A worldview includes all the beliefs that we hold about life. These beliefs, in turn, shape our thinking and direct our steps in our everyday lives. Whether people realize it or not, their worldview is the driving force behind all of their behavior and actions. In this book, I want to leave a framework or grid that people can look through when they evaluate all of the experiences of life. A worldview is a solid biblical foundation upon which we build our hopes, goals, and future dreams. I have found that most people do not have a worldview. Many people seem to pass through life as if clueless to what they should be and do. Understanding your worldview will ensure that you do not make that mistake of drifting through life while wasting precious time.

The importance of Christians having a well-thought-out worldview is stated clearly by Chuck Colsen and Nancy Pearcey in their book *How Now Shall We Live.*

A debilitating weakness in modern evangelicalism is that we've been fighting cultural skirmishes on all sides without knowing what the war is about. We have not identified the worldviews that lie at the root of cultural conflict — and this ignorance dooms our best efforts. The culture war is not just about abortion, homosexual rights, or decline of public education. These are only skirmishes. The real war is a cosmic struggle between worldviews — between the Christian worldview and the various secular and spiritual worldviews arrayed against it. This is what we must understand if we are going to be effective in evangelizing our world today and in transforming it to reflect the wisdom of the Creator.[2]

A worldview is very important. A worldview is like having a map to show us how to
live in the spiritual journey
of life. Without such a map,
people tend to wander and
stumble along without any
real purpose and sense of
destiny. The British author,
Os Guinness, raises some

A worldview is like having a map to show us how to live in the spiritual journey of life.

questions that show us why having a worldview in life is important.

> *How do we unriddle the mystery of life and make the most of it? What does it mean to find ourselves guests on a tiny, spinning blue ball in a vast universe? Is our sense of individual uniqueness backed by a guarantee, or are we only dust in the wind? What explains our grotesque human capacity for slaughtering our fellow human beings by day and listening to classical music in the evening? Is there an emergency number to call when we have vandalized our planet home like a drunken rock star on a hotel rampage? Why is birth the automatic qualification for death? How should we live, knowing that we each owe death one life, and nothing we can ever do will ransom us? What recourse do we have if we conclude that the world should have been otherwise?*[3]

A second question that is of utmost importance is, "What is success?" There is a quote in the Bible that defines success for us:

> *This book of the law shall not depart out of thy mouth; but thou shalt meditate therein day and night, that thou mayest observe to do according to all that is written therein: for then thou shalt make thy way prosperous, and then thou shalt have good success. Joshua 1:8*

Joshua would have us understand that true success is not measured by our health, wealth, prosperity, happiness, or even by what others say about us. True success is measured by what our Creator says about us. True success is knowing the will of God and doing it. True success is having the smile of God upon your life. True success is being at peace with yourself and with your God when you are near to death.

To have success in life, we need to know why we are here and what our lives are all about. For most people, there is only confusion and uncertainty with the fact of life and existence. They do not know why they are here or where they are going, or what life is all about. The person who knows the "whys" to these questions has a great advantage over the person who still stumbles along in the dark with doubts, uncertainty, and confusion. Success in the Christian life is simply, "Knowing the why."

When life for each of us is finally over, and we find ourselves standing before our God to be judged for those things done in life, what will matter most at that moment will be this — Did we live for Jesus? That is the great question of life. If we did not develop a Christian worldview, and if we failed to live for the Lord, no matter what we may have accomplished in life, we will have wasted the gift of life that God gave to us.

Introduction

The following principles are things that I have learned over the years in my ministry and life. For the most part, these principles are found in the Bible of the Judeo-Christian Scriptures. I believe it is necessary for us to develop a worldview and philosophy for living. By developing a Christian worldview, we will learn how to live our lives for the glory of God. If we live life in a casual, hit-and-miss way, we must not be surprised if we stumble along and have a hard time knowing what is pleasing to God. I happen to believe that at the end of life, the most important thing is to know that I have lived a life that was pleasing to the God that I worship.

My Christian faith influences everything that I do in life. Many of the thoughts and principles that I follow and by which I seek to mold my life, are directly connected to the laws that are found in the Bible of both the Old and New Testaments. All of us should be striving for excellence in everything we seek to achieve in our lives. These Christian principles and biblical laws will help us in that great quest in our lives. It is my prayer that this material will be of assistance to all of you and bring you a greater measure of success in your business, in your marriage, in your family, and in your daily life, and will help you reach your personal goals.

In developing a biblical worldview, we must begin with certain presuppositions. Presuppositions are starting points. Presuppositions are the foundational principles that undergird everything else that we believe and do. Before we ever come to a decision about what we believe, there are presuppositions that we hold that influence our decisions and any conclusions that we make. The basic presuppositions that I build my life and my worldview upon are these:

1. The existence of an infinite and personal God.
2. The belief that this infinite God has revealed Himself to us in the Christian Scriptures of the Old and New Testaments.
3. That God can only be known through a personal relationship with His Son Jesus Christ.
4. That everything I need to know about truth, life, who I am, and why I am here, is told to me in the Bible.
5. That there can be no real meaning and purpose in life without believing these presuppositions.

These are the presuppositions that influence most Christians. A biblical worldview, filled with these presuppositions, will give us a framework that will help us to live. How can we live and achieve success if we do not have a plan? A worldview gives us such a plan. One author put it this way:

Without a plan, you have nowhere to go, nothing toward which you direct your energies.

It is amazing how few companies have a master plan by which they chart their course and measure their progress. Even fewer individuals have constructed a plan for their lives with short term, intermediate, and long-range goals. This is a fundamental mistake…Without a plan, you have nowhere to go, nothing toward which you direct your energies. Without a plan, you can only react to circumstances.[1]

It is my prayer that this book will give you a plan for your life, and a framework to help you develop a biblical worldview. This plan will be a Christian worldview that will enable you to live for Christ and will help you to walk with God. When your life is over and you stand before God, may you be one of those blessed ones who hear Him say, *"Well done, thou good and faithful servant, enter thou into the joy of thy Lord."* Matthew 25:21

How to Use This Book

This book is comprised of three sections. Part I is going to teach us the **purpose** of Christian living. Part II will teach us the **practical** aspects of Christian living. Finally, Part III will reveal the **peace** that comes to those who live for Jesus.

At the end of each chapter, there will be a few practical suggestions on how to get started. These suggestions will focus on applying the material in each chapter to your daily life. Following the "How to Get Started" section there will be some "Thoughts for Consideration" and "Questions for Discussion."

I hope that these thoughts and questions will further challenge the reader to deeper reflection and obedience.

It is my prayer that fathers will the take the time to sit down and read this book to their families and children. Discussing the contents of each chapter will enforce the principles being taught and ensure that our families develop a biblical worldview.

Before we begin, let me give a brief description of what living for Jesus involves. A person living for Jesus should:

1. Begin each day in prayer.
2. Have a definite time each day for private Bible study and worship of God.
3. Have a brief mission statement describing the purpose and goal of one's life, and then try to follow it each day.
4. End each day in prayer.
5. Attend a Bible-believing church each week to hear the preaching of God's Word and to worship the Lord.

Following these five simple guidelines will have a profound impact on our lives.

Part I: The Purpose of Christian Living

1
Following the Instructions — the Creation Mandate

"[26] And God said, Let us make man in our image, after our likeness: and let them have dominion over the fish of the sea, and over the fowl of the air, and over the cattle, and over all the earth, and over every creeping thing that creepeth upon the earth. [27] So God created man in his own image, in the image of God created he him; male and female created he them. [28] And God blessed them, and God said unto them, Be fruitful, and multiply, and replenish the earth, and subdue it: and have dominion over the fish of the sea, and over the fowl of the air, and over every living thing that moveth upon the earth." Genesis 1:26-28

"Redemption is not just about being saved from sin, it is also about being saved to something — to resume the task for which we were originally created." Nancy Pearcey

I n Genesis 1:26-28, we see the plan of God for man as it was revealed to us in the book of Genesis. These verses are often referred to as the Creation Mandate. The word mandate means "to assign, to make mandatory." At creation, God gave man an assignment. What does this mandate or assignment from God involve? It involves man having dominion over all of the earth that God has created. God created man to exercise dominion and to subdue the earth. It is my belief that there can be no serious obedience to God and faithful Christian living apart from understanding the instructions that God gave mankind in the beginning at the Garden of Eden. This was also understood by author Nancy Pearcey who wrote:

> *How do we go about constructing a Christian worldview? The key passage is the creation account in Genesis, because that's where we are taken back to the beginning to learn what God's original purpose was in creating the human race. With the entrance of sin, humans went off course, lost their way, wandered off the path. But when we accept Christ's salvation, we are put back on the right path and are restored to our original purpose. Redemption is not just about being saved from sin, it is also about being saved to something — to resume the task for which we were originally created.*[1]

When we take a close look at Genesis 1:28, we see the heart of this mandate that God has given man to obey. I need to remind you that this command and assignment is for the believer. The non-Christian will not even take the time to read what is said here in the first chapter of Genesis. This assignment then is for the true follower of God. I used to look at this verse and assume that the wording here was repetitive of the same thought. For example we read, *"And God blessed them, and God said unto them, Be fruitful, and multiply, and replenish the earth, and subdue it: and have dominion over the fish of the sea, and over the fowl of the air, and over every living thing that moveth upon the earth."* I thought that the verbal commands to be fruitful, to multiply, and to replenish the earth were just three ways of saying the same thing. I believe that these three words and commands can possibly have widely different meanings. Let's consider what the Scriptures may mean by the five commands and instructions that are mentioned in this text.

1. *Be fruitful.* I believe that this idea can involve the concept of accruing wealth. Wealth can give us leverage and influence in the world that God has made for us to rule and subdue. Although it is not necessary to have wealth in order to have

influence with others, we do know that those who have wealth, if they use it wisely, can have great influence on those around them. This fact has been seen all throughout the Bible where people with wealth had great opportunities to influence for good or evil.

2. *Multiply.* I believe that this has reference to reproducing off-spring. The believer is to produce a godly seed that will come after them. The ungodly are aborting their influence today. This gives the Christian a greater advantage to exercise more influence in the coming future. We, as believers, should not refuse to have children. Psalm 127:3-5 says, *"Lo, children are an heritage of the Lord: and the fruit of the womb is his reward. As arrows are in the hand of a mighty man; so are the children of the youth. Happy is the man that hath his quiver full of them: they shall not be ashamed, but they shall speak with the enemies in the gate."* Never forget that a godly heritage spreads the Kingdom of God from one generation to another.

3. *Replenish the earth.* This command involves filling the earth with the beauty and the wonders of all that man can make. Man is to make this world a more beautiful and wonderful place to live. When we die, we should be able to say that we made the world a better place because of our presence here.

4. *Subdue it.* This word is from the Hebrew word "kabhash" and means "to knead or to tread."

5. *Have dominion over.* The Hebrew word for dominion is "radhah" and means "to trample down, or master."

The dominion that man is to exercise is to be over every area of life. In the Old Testament, God was working through His covenant people in a theocracy called Israel. But today, God is working through His people whom He has saved by grace. Francis Schaeffer, a Christian apologist and philosopher, once said, *"Man…can influence history for himself and for others, for this life and the life to come."* This is what we must understand here in this creation mandate. We as Christians have an opportunity to make a difference in the world, and in the way history is being played

We as Christians have an opportunity to make a difference in the world, and in the way history is being played out before our very eyes.

out before our very eyes. How amazing and challenging these thoughts ought to be to each of us.

This command to have dominion is found in both the Old and the New Testaments (Genesis 1:26 and in the Lord's Prayer in Matthew 6:10, *"Thy kingdom come, Thy will be done"*). The creation mandate was the requirement of man to subdue the earth and exercise dominion over it. There is not one word of Scripture to indicate that this command and requirement has ever been abolished.

Chuck Colson in his book *How Now Shall We Live* had this to say about Christians influencing their culture:

> *Understanding Christianity as a worldview is important not only for fulfilling the great commission but also for fulfilling the cultural commission — the call to create a culture under the Lordship of Christ. God cares not only about redeeming souls but also about restoring his creation. He calls us to be agents not only of his saving grace but also of his common grace. Our job is not only to build up the church but also to build a society to the glory of God.*[3]

The bigger picture here is that we are involved in a great culture war. What is at stake is the future of Western Civilization as we know it.

The Meaning of This Mandate

The creation mandate simply means that man, being made in God's image and as His representative, is to subdue the earth and have dominion over all of God's creation. What most modern men lack is a sense of purpose, destiny, and what it is that they were created for. Non-Christians wander through life aimlessly. This is now sadly true of many professing Christians, as well. True

Christians should know what their purpose in life is all about. The Westminster Shorter Catechism asks the question, *"What is the chief end of man?"* The answer is, *"To glorify God and to enjoy Him forever."* In Genesis 1:26 we learn that man was made in the image of God. This means that man, unlike the other creatures that God has made, has a capacity to:

1. Worship and enjoy God.
2. Make moral choices and know the difference between good and evil.
3. Exercise authority over the creation, the animals, and the earth.
4. Have an innate sense of God in his soul.
5. Be creative, productive, and use his God-given talents to make a difference in the world in which he has been placed.

The Christian mandate simply means that man, as the centerpiece of God's creation, is to exercise authority over every area of life. Man is to flex his intellectual muscles, and to use his God-given abilities to bring the earth under his control for the glory of God. Author Nancy Pearcey writes:

> [Man's] *Most effective work…is done by ordinary Christians fulfilling God's calling to reform culture within their local spheres of influence — their families, churches, schools, neighborhoods, workplaces, professional organizations, and civic institutions. In order to affect lasting change…we need to develop a Christian worldview.*[4]

Another Christian author stated it this way:

> *Everyday, millions of workers go to work without seeing the slightest connection between what they do all day and what they think God wants done in the world. For example, you may sell insurance, yet you may have no idea whether or not God wants insurance to be sold. Does selling insurance matter to God or not? If not, you are wasting your life…It is not something we do apart from*

God, as the secular world would view it. It is not something beneath God's dignity and concern, as (some Christians view it)...Work is a major part of human life that God takes very seriously. It has intrinsic value. It is inherently worth doing. Through work we serve people, meet our own needs, meet our family's needs, earn money to give to others, and through work we love God.[5]

The Christian mandate means that as Christians live their lives in this fallen world, they should seek to make a difference in every area of life. The people of God are "difference makers." Christians should make a difference economically, politically, socially, and spiritually. The gospel of Jesus Christ should impact every area of life and society through the Christian's life and witness. We must be those who make a difference, for that is the very purpose of our creation. The goal of Christian living is not to be seen as longing for an endless vacation or retreating into little ghettoes of religious and cultural insignificance. We were destined by our Creator to make a difference, to use our time and talents for the glory of God. Our calling is not just to get to heaven and to somehow keep from being stained by this evil world. No! Our calling is also to cultivate the earth, to serve our God and Creator by having dominion over His earth that He has placed us in, and to bring every area of life under the Lordship of His Son Jesus Christ.

We were destined by our Creator to make a difference, to use our time and talents for the glory of God.

The Sphere of This Mandate

To have dominion over the earth means that the Christian realizes that every area of life should be brought under the control and Lordship of Jesus Christ. The Dutch theologian, Abraham Kuyper, proclaimed that Christ was Lord over all spheres of life. Here is what he said: *"In the total expanse of human life there is not a single square inch of which the Christ, who alone is sovereign, does not declare, 'That is mine!'"*[6]

Again Kuyper writes:

> *The Son is not to be excluded from anything. You cannot point to any natural realm or star or comet or even descend into the depth of the earth, but it is related to Christ, not in some unimportant tangential way, but directly. There is no force in nature, no laws that control those forces that do not have their origin in that eternal Word. For this reason, it is totally false to restrict Christ to spiritual affairs and to assert that there is no point of contact between him and the natural sciences.*[7]

This work of dominion involves the family, the church, the state, the school, and the mind.

It is in the family that leaders are made. Leaders are not born; they are shaped and made by the families and godly influences around them. To have dominion over the earth, fathers need to teach and lead their children. This includes teaching our children the Word of God. Moses gave us these instructions in Deuteronomy 6:5-9:

> [5] *And thou shalt love the* LORD *thy God with all thine heart, and with all thy soul, and with all thy might.* [6] *And these words, which I command thee this day, shall be in thine heart:* [7] *And thou shalt teach diligently unto thy children, and shalt talk of them when thou sittest in thine house, and when thou walkest by the way, and when thou liest down, and when thou risest up.* [8] *And thou shalt bind them for a sign upon thine hand, and they shall be as frontlets between thine eyes.* [9] *And thou shalt write them upon the posts of thy house, and on thy gates.*

We should teach our children character qualities such as honesty, goodness, personal purity, the power of faith, assuming responsibility for one's actions, forgiveness, respect for authority, submission, patriotism, and serving others.

When I would take my son running when he was in middle school, I would discuss with him the various worldviews such as:

1. Christian Theism — the belief that God exists as Father, Son, and Holy Spirit.
2. Deism — the belief that an impersonal God created the world and then left it to run on its own without His aid or attention.
3. Nihilism — the belief that life is meaningless. A consistent nihilist would come to the conclusion that life is not worth living. Some who have held to this philosophy have committed suicide because of the despair that this position gave them.
4. Existentialism — the belief that since there is no god, one must discover the meaning and purpose for life in himself or by his own investigation as to what pleases him. This is a philosophy rooted in atheism.
5. Pantheism — the belief that everything in the universe is god. The word pantheism contains the prefix "pan" meaning "all" and the word "theism" meaning "god." Thus, everything is god or identified with god.
6. Naturalism — the belief that everything in the universe has arisen from natural and explainable causes. This is also a philosophy that is rooted in atheistic Darwinianism.
7. Communism — the belief that all property is owned by the state. This is the atheistic philosophy derived from the teachings of Karl Marx.

I wanted my son to understand early in life that there is a war of ideas being fought. When we take the time to teach our children these philosophies, we are helping them to be prepared for this culture war by knowing what they believe and why.

This work of dominion also involves the church. Today, for the most part, the church in America is a powerless, Christ-less, man-centered reflection of the humanistic culture in which she lives. The church needs conviction and passion in its mission. But sadly, this is lacking. This is not a time for sentimentalism or indifference. This is a time for conviction and character. We must be determined to reform the church in every area of its life and practice. Just ask most pastors, "What is your vision for the church?" "What is the driving force behind your ministry?" If they cannot say it is the glory of God, the person and work of Christ, the eschatology of victory, and the great truths that transformed the world during the Reformation, then the church is irrelevant to the culture. It will have little or no impact on the nations of the earth. It will not be able to implement the creation mandate.

Here are four areas that are absolutely crucial to the church of Jesus Christ:

1. If the eschatology of the church is defeatist and pessimistic, the church will be defeatist and retreat into Christian ghettoes of irrelevance. (Eschatology is the doctrine of last things.)
2. If the theology of the church is not God-centered, it will be a man-centered theology and will not affect the culture. At best, a man centered theology produces revivalism that is a temporary quick-fix and produces little lasting change or results.
3. If the worship of the church is entertainment-oriented and influenced by pop-culture, it will not be the source of life and reformation.
4. If the mission of the church is not driven by a passion for the glory of God, then the church will be powerless to affect the culture.

If it seems strange to challenge Christians to reform the church and have dominion over it, then consider the words of Dr. D. James Kennedy:

> *It may seem strange to talk about "Christianizing the church," but I believe this is certainly another sphere that needs to be brought under the lordship of Christ. I recognize that some people profess to believe in Christ but are not officially a part of the outward body of Christ. I do not think they are right in their attitude. The church is something that Jesus Christ created — it is His body. With all of*

the imperfections of the church — past and present — it is
still His bride. To Christianize the church, we have to make
sure we ourselves are Christians. We need to obey God's
first and last commands. And we need to be sure that we
don't abandon the instructions He Himself gave us.[8]

Christians do not control the state but should influence it.

This work of having dominion over the earth also involves the state. The Christian has the responsibility to proclaim to the state the laws of God. Christians should be involved in government — by voting, educating people, running for office, and exercising godly influence on society. Christians do not control the state but should influence it. What is the purpose of the government? Dr. D. James Kennedy made this comment:

> *According to the Scriptures, government is a necessary*
> *evil. It would not even exist were it not for the fall of man.*
> *It was the sin and rebellion of mankind that brought gov-*
> *ernment into existence in the first place. It was meant to*
> *restrain the evil tendencies and propensities in the hearts*
> *of men. Government was created by God to restrain ma-*
> *rauders both within and without. It was established to pro-*
> *tect citizens so they could live out their probation here on*
> *this earth in peace and safety and demonstrate whether*
> *they would submit to God and His law or whether they*
> *would rebel.*[9]

Christians have a responsibility to speak to the government and to the conscience of the nation, to spread the gospel of Christ, and to influence the nation in a direction of righteousness. The Scripture bluntly reminds us that *"Righteousness exalteth a nation but sin is a reproach to any people."* (Proverbs 14:34)

This work of exercising dominion over all the earth also involves the school. Christian parents should take an active role in shaping the curriculum and the goals of their local schools. Being involved with the school board, voicing opinions, and sharing concerns must be done on a regular basis with both teachers, administrators, and the school board itself. John Dunphy, in *The Humanist*, wrote:

> *The classroom must and will become an arena of conflict between the old and the new — the rotting corpse of Christianity, together with all its adjacent evils and misery, and the new faith of humanism, resplendent in it promise of a world in which the never-realized Christian ideal of "love thy neighbor" will be finally achieved.*[10]

The German reformer, Martin Luther, once wrote: "*I am much afraid that the schools will prove to be the great gates of hell unless they diligently labor in explaining the Holy Scriptures, engraving them in the hearts of the youth.*"[11]

No one can doubt that in the western world the battle for the culture is raging in the public school. Many concerned Christian parents have opted to home school or to send their children to private Christian schools or conservative academies. Even these people, who have opted for these alternatives to public education, must not surrender their right and Christian duty to seek to influence the public school system. Parents can have an impact on their local schools by being involved with the board of education, voicing concerns about curriculum, and voting for local officials that are consistent with Christian principles.

Finally, this work of having dominion involves the mind. The Apostle Paul wrote to the Corinthians and said, "*Casting down imaginations, and every high thing that exalteth itself against the knowledge of God, and bringing into captivity every thought to the obedience of Christ.*" (2 Corinthians 10:5) This means that we should bring every thought under the control of the Holy Spirit. Everything that we hear, we should evaluate and filter through the Word of God. If it is contrary to the Word, we reject it as false. Peter wrote in 1 Peter 1:13, "*Wherefore gird up the loins of your mind, be sober, and hope to the end for the grace that is to be brought unto you at the revelation of Jesus Christ.*" What does this mean? It means that we should surround our hearts and our minds with Scripture and allow the Scriptures to protect us and guide our lives.

The Optimism of This Mandate

There is a universal testimony in the Scriptures of both the Old and New Testaments that speaks of an optimistic future for the kingdom of God on earth. God's plan for history is summed up by the prophet Habakkuk, *"For the earth shall be filled with the knowledge of the glory of the Lord, as the waters cover the sea."* (Habakkuk 2:14) Because the promises of a greater and brighter future are so clear and so numerous, it is hard to understand why many today are so pessimistic in their view of what lies ahead for the people of God and for the church of Jesus Christ. Ideas have consequences. And when people embrace negative and pessimistic views of the future, sooner or later their negativity begins to show. In the paragraphs that follow, we will look at some of the many promises, parables of Jesus, and teachings of the Apostle Paul to demonstrate the optimism of the future of this Creation Mandate.

We have many promises from the Old Testament that God's kingdom will advance and be triumphant. Isaiah 2 and Micah 4 are very similar. These two prophets saw that in the last days the kingdom of God would grow and advance in the world, it would be exalted, and the nations (Gentiles) would flow into it. Here is the text of Isaiah 2:1-5:

> [1] *The word that Isaiah the son of Amoz saw concerning Judah and Jerusalem.* [2] *And it shall come to pass in the last days, that the mountain of the LORD's house shall be established in the top of the mountains, and shall be exalted above the hills; and all nations shall flow unto it.* [3] *And many people shall go and say, Come ye, and let us go up to the mountain of the LORD, to the house of the God of Jacob; and he will teach us of his ways, and we will walk in his paths: for out of Zion shall go forth the law, and the word of the LORD from Jerusalem.* [4] *And he shall judge among the nations, and shall rebuke many people:*

and they shall beat their swords into plowshares, and their
spears into pruninghooks: nation shall not lift up sword
against nation, neither shall they learn war any more. [5]
O house of Jacob, come ye, and let us walk in the light of
the LORD.

The prophet Isaiah foresaw a day when God's church would be exalted in the earth and all the nations would flow into it. That day has not yet come. With joyful and prayerful anticipation, we await the coming of that great day.

In the book of Habakkuk, we have another prophecy that should give us some understanding of the intentions of the Lord for His kingdom and people. Habakkuk 2:14 says, *"For the earth shall be filled with the knowledge of the glory of the Lord, as the waters cover the sea."* The prophet Habakkuk sees a day when the knowledge of God will spill into all the earth and cover the globe just as thoroughly as the waters cover the seas.

We also have the parables of Christ that teach the triumph of God's kingdom. For example, Mark 4:30-32 says,

[30] *And he said, Whereunto shall we liken the kingdom of*
God? Or with what comparison shall we compare it? [31]
It is like a grain of mustard seed, which, when it is sown in
the earth, is less than all the seeds that be in the earth: [32]
But when it is sown, it growth up, and becometh greater
than all herbs, land shooteth out great branches; so that
the fowls of the air may lodge under the shadow of it.

Jesus is showing us that notwithstanding the small insignificant beginning of the church, it will grow and eventually influence the entire world.

Next, we have the teaching of Paul in Romans 11 that the church will be triumphant. See Romans 11:15, 25-26. Paul sees a day coming when ethnic Israel will come to faith in Christ. The result of the ingathering of the Jews to the church will be a great revival that the Apostle Paul compares to a resurrection. In other words, the impact of the future conversion of the Jews will be dramatic in all the world. In Romans 11:15 Paul says, *"For if the* casting away of them [the Jews] be the reconciling of the world, what shall be the receiving of them be, but life from the dead?" In verses 25 and 26 Paul continues his line of reasoning, "[25] *For I would not, brethren, that ye should be ignorant of this mystery, lest ye should be wise in your own conceits; that blindness in part is happened to Israel, until the fullness of the Gentiles be come in. [26] And so all Israel shall be saved....*"

Finally, we have the prophecy of John that the kingdom of God will be triumphant. Revelation 11:15 says, "...*The kingdoms of this world are become the kingdoms of our Lord, and of his Christ; and he shall reign for ever and ever.*"

We must not be influenced by television or newspaper reports. Many people, when they hear about the promises of God in the Scriptures, will say, "I just don't see that happening in today's world." It is as if they think that the times are so much tougher than in days gone by and that God is no longer able to do great things today as He did then. The promises of God are not about what we think or what we see and hear. We must always believe that since God is on His throne,

> *We must always believe that since God is on His throne, nothing is impossible.*

nothing is impossible. Evangelist Del Fehsenfeld, Jr. used to say, "*As long as God is on His throne, revival is as possible as the sun rising tomorrow morning.*" One person recently said, "Isn't it great that there is so much evil in the world?" The person was asked, "What do you mean by that?" And he said, "Well, since there is so much evil in the world, it means that Jesus is going to come again soon." How incredible is that? We might as well stop rebuking sin and try to get people to sin all the more so it will hasten the return of Christ.

One way we fulfill the Creation Mandate is by obeying the Great Commission. In Matthew 28:19-20, Jesus said, "[19] *Go ye therefore, and teach all nations, baptizing them in the name of the Father, and of the Son, and of the Holy Ghost: [20] Teaching them to observe all things whatsoever I have commanded you: and, lo, I am with you always, even unto the end of the world."* The church needs to bring every area under the Lordship of Christ. God created man in His own image, gave man an assignment, and installed him in a great position to rule and take charge over His creation. Today, most Christian men have surrendered this great task to those who know the least about how to accomplish it. The Christian culture has, for the most part, retreated into ghettoes of irrelevance and has allowed the ungodly to rule the earth and set their own agendas, which are nearly always contrary to the will and laws of a sovereign God.

If Christians have a good understanding of the Creation Mandate, they will be a formidable foe in the great culture wars. The problem with so many professing believers today is that they have all but given up in the battle for the minds and hearts of their fellow men. In his book, *America Alone*, author and political columnist, Mark Steyn, astutely remarks, *"The object of war is not to destroy the enemy's tanks but to destroy his will."*[12] If Christians lose the will to fight and to continue in the battle for the souls of men, they will lose the ground gained from the sacrifices and victories of their forefathers in the faith. One of the greatest dangers facing the church today is the advance of militant Islam in the world. The worldview of the Muslim faith is one of victory and conquest. The Islamic worldview is fearless and has no thought of being defeated. The secular and pessimistic worldview of the West is no match for the Jihadists who believe they are destined to rule the world. No wonder, when Zacarias Moussaoui, the so-called "twentieth hijacker of 9/11" was sentenced to life in prison, he swaggered and scoffed at the judge and said, *"America, you lose."*[13] This terrorist was absolutely convinced that the cause he championed would eventually win. In order for the church to successfully compete in the world of such zealots, she herself must have a worldview that is based on the compelling dynamic power and authority of the Creation Mandate. Here is a list of things that we can do to take dominion over the earth.

1. Live a godly life. Put on the holiness of God. (See Colossians 3 for a list of things the Apostle Paul exhorts us to do!)

2. Be Christ-like, and be a light to the world. This means living a life that is consistent with the example and teachings of Christ.
3. Become a servant to others. Servant leadership is powerful. Ask, "How can I help?" "What can I do?" "What need can I meet?" This kind of spirit is contagious.
4. Die to self — i.e. turn the other cheek, go the extra mile, forgive others, be kind to your enemies, don't sow discord, be a peacemaker, etc.
5. Be a faithful witness — i.e. preach Christ. "Preach the gospel, and if necessary use words."
6. Disciple people with literature. Pass out books and use Christian literature to change the thoughts of those with whom you have influence.
7. Train your family for Christ. The family is the first church, the first government, and the first school for your children. Put the Lord first in your life and family.
8. Be a prayer warrior.
9. Preach the gospel of Jesus Christ and extend the kingdom of God to the ends of the earth.

The Creation Mandate gives us a purpose for living. It is a terrible tragedy that many people never discover the real purpose for their lives. This is just as true for believers as non-believers. Author Os Guinnes understood that all men have a yearning to discover their purpose in life. He also understood that a purpose for living comes from an understanding of God's call in our lives. Os Guinness writes: *"Nothing short of God's call can ground and fulfill the truest human desire for purpose."*[14]

The Creation Mandate is a clarion call from God to each of His children. It gives us our true purpose for living for Jesus.

How to Get Started

1. As we develop a Christian worldview, we must not forget that God has given us instructions — and all Christians must follow those instructions in their daily life and walk.

2. Study Genesis 1:26-28 and make sure that you understand clearly the instructions we have been given from God on how to live our lives in this present world.
3. Make a commitment to God to follow the instructions in the Creation Mandate so that you will not live a meaningless life.
4. Ask God in prayer to use you to be a "difference maker."
5. Encourage others to pray for the advancement of God's kingdom on earth. Invite people to your home to have a special time of prayer for this great goal of world evangelism and revival.

Thoughts for Consideration

- *"To talk about a Christian worldview is simply another way of saying that when we are redeemed, our entire outlook on life is re-centered on God and rebuilt on His revealed truth!"* Nancy Pearcy

- *"Creativity is the natural result of spirituality."* Erwin McManus

- *"He taught that the individual believer has a vocation to serve God in the world — in every sphere of human existence — lending a new dignity and meaning to ordinary work."* Alister McGrath on John Calvin

- *"For years, I thought my involvement in business was a second class endeavor — necessary to put bread on the table, but somehow less noble than the more sacred pursuit like being a minister or a missionary."* John Beckett

- *"Every occupation and calling in life is sacred if done for the glory of God."* Robert L. Dickie

- *"The creation mandate was precisely the requirement that man subdue the earth and exercise dominion over it. There is not one word of Scriptures to indicate or imply that this mandate was ever revoked.*" Rousas John Rushdoony

- "*Man is the captain of creation, and thus his job is to work with the world, organizing it and transforming it for God's glory.*" R. C. Sproul

- "*Christians are called to redeem entire cultures, not just individuals.*" Nancy Pearcey

- "*Ordinary Christians working in business, industry, politics, factory work, are the Church's front-line troops in her engagement with the world.*" Lesslie Newbigin

- "*God's absolute sovereignty...is what my mind seems to rest assured of, as much as of any thing that I see with my eyes.... The doctrine has very often appeared exceeding pleasant, bright, and sweet...It has often been my delight to approach God, and adore him as a sovereign God.*" Jonathan Edwards

Questions for Discussion

1. What is the Creation Mandate?

2. What does the word mandate mean?

3. What areas does this mandate involve?

4. How is it possible that the church often fails to have an impact on the culture around it?

5. Do you agree with me that Scripture gives us reason to hope for a better future?

6. List some of the ways that we can fulfill the Creation Mandate. Can you think of others, as well, that were not mentioned in this chapter?

2
Being a People of Destiny

"...and who knoweth whether thou art come to the kingdom for such a time as this?" Esther 4:14

"There is a destiny that shapes our ends, Rough-hew them how we will." Shakespeare in *Hamlet*, act 5, scene 2

One of the very first things necessary in developing a biblical world view is to realize that if we are Christians, we are people with a destiny. God has given His people a great purpose for their lives. In the book of Revelation we are told, *"Thou art worthy, O Lord, to receive glory and honour and power: for thou hast created all things, and for thy pleasure they were and are created."* Revelation 4:11

This verse has always been a blessing to my soul. It teaches me that I have been made by God to bring Him pleasure. I strive to live up to this great expectation. Some of my deepest sorrow is my awareness that I have not given my God and Savior the amount of glory and pleasure that He deserves.

As Christians we are to live for the glory of God. God has created each of us. We are uniquely designed to live on this planet. God's intention for our existence is that we would live to serve and honor Him. We are to live our lives so that people see Jesus Christ in all that we are and do. St. Francis of Assisi once said, *"Preach the gospel always, and if necessary use words."*

We may not know what special plans God has for our lives. But this much we do know — as we live for Christ our lives will touch, bless, and minister to all those with whom we come into

Preach the gospel always, and if necessary use words.

contact. Knowing that God has a plan for our lives gives us a sense that we are a people of destiny. God speaks to all of us through Jeremiah the prophet and says, *"For I know the plans I have for you, declares the Lord, plans to prosper you and not to harm you, plans to give you a hope and a future."* Jeremiah 29:11 NIV

God Has a Special Plan for Our Lives

In order for Christians to fulfill their destiny, they must see themselves as those for whose lives God has a special plan and mission. This idea that God has a plan or purpose for our lives is illustrated wonderfully for us in the book of Esther.

In the Old Testament Scriptures in the book of Esther there is an interesting story that gives us insight into the sovereignty of God over all of life. This story is set in the capital of the Persian Empire, early in the reign of King Ahasuerus (486-465 BC) who was the king of the Persians. The Persian Empire stretched from India to Ethiopia. During the reign of King Ahasuerus, there was a wicked attempt to exterminate the Jews. This wicked plan was thwarted by a heroic and beautiful Jewish woman named Esther. Esther was one of the many Jews that had been brought to the land of Persia as slaves after Jerusalem had fallen to the Babylonians. While growing up in Persia, Esther, because of her beauty, was selected to be the king's wife. Shortly thereafter Esther's Uncle Mordecai discovered an evil plan set up by a man named Haman. Mordecai came to his niece, who was now the queen, and pleaded with her to go to the king and reveal the nature of Haman's evil intentions. Esther was hesitant because she knew that it was not lawful to go into the king's presence without an invitation. To do this daring thing could mean death for her. But Mordecai insisted, and he told Esther that God would certainly deliver the Jewish people with or without her. *"But,"* he said, *"perhaps you have come to the kingdom for such a time as this!"* (See Esther 4:14.) One author made this comment on the story of Queen Esther:

*Mordecai not only realized the powerful position Esther
was in, but also challenged Esther to think in terms of
God's sovereign plan for her life. Could it be that all
the circumstances of the past — circumstances that had
resulted in her being queen — were planned by God just
for this vital occasion? I'm sure Esther thought about her
childhood and all that had happened to her. Then she
stepped out in faith to save her people.*[1]

Mordecai knew that the God of the Bible was a sovereign and
powerful God who could accomplish His will through the means
of anyone or anything He chose. Esther complied, and the plan
to have the Jews destroyed was overturned. Haman, the man
who had planned to exterminate the Jews, was eventually hung
on the very gallows he had designed for Mordecai. The deliver-
ance of the Jews from this scheme is still celebrated to this day in
Israel and among the Hebrews by the feast of Purim. Furthermore,
many archeological finds have been uncovered over the centuries
to verify the existence of these characters and the story that is
behind this passage.

The main point we need to see in the story of Esther is that
God raised her up for the time in which she lived. Esther's life was
not a meaningless existence in this world. I believe that each of us,
in a similar way, has significance and meaning as we realize that
we were born in this time, and that the living God of the universe
has a special purpose for each of our lives.

Your Life is a Special Gift from God

I urge each of you to realize that your life is a special gift from God.
You have been born in this hour, in this day, and in this time. This
is our moment in history. We can learn from the past, but we can't
change the past. Today is all we have. If we can be filled with faith
and confidence that God has a plan for our lives and has placed
us on this planet for this time, who knows what things we may accomplish. We should live so as to make every day count. Although
we can't change the past, we can have an impact on the future
by how we live each day right now. What Queen Esther's Uncle
Mordecai said to her is also a truth we should consider ourselves,

Although we can't change the past, we can have an impact on the future by how we live each day right now.

"*And who knoweth whether thou art come to the kingdom for such a time as this.*" Esther 4:14

In the study of the Bible, there is a doctrine that theologians have called "eschatology." Eschatology is the study of the last things. This doctrine is all about the events that will unfold at the end of time. There are those who have what we call an eschatology of defeat and pessimism. Then, there are those who have what we call an eschatology of victory and triumph. I happen to be one of those who believe that the God of the Bible is going to win in life. The God of the Bible will accomplish all of His eternal plans. All of the decrees of God will come to pass. Because of this view, I am greatly encouraged to live and act in such a way that reflects this view of coming victory. If we believe that we have a major purpose for life, and if we believe that God is going to use us in His overall plan on this earth, we will find ourselves greatly encouraged, despite the pressures, difficulties, and problems we may encounter in life. A person who believes he or she is a person of destiny is hard to be stopped. Show me a person with such a sense of his or her destiny, and I will show you a life ablaze with excitement, joy, peace, and confidence in spite of the times in which they live. It was Babe Ruth, a great American baseball star, who said, "*It is hard to beat a person who never gives up.*" And, I might add, it is hard to beat a person who believes he is destined to win! We may get knocked down again and again, but we keep getting back up!

One of the first real keys to success in life is connected to this view of confidence in God's plan for our lives. Do you see beyond the events of the present moment? Can you step back as it were, and take in the whole picture of what the Lord is doing in the world? To be fired up and charged with the sense of destiny will make an enormous difference in your life and the goals that you pursue. The Apostle Paul in the New Testament wrote, "*And we know that all things work together for good, to them that love*

God, to them that are called according to his purpose." Romans 8:28 We need to develop an attitude and a faith that enables us to see that we are alive right now for a great purpose. God has a plan for our lives. We are the tools in His hands that He will use to bring blessing and change to our world. The success of your business, your family, and your life is not just affecting you, but also all of those around you. It is true that no man is an island. My life is woven into the fabric of history, and everything I do or experience touches many others.

To have success in life, you need to have a purpose for living. What is your purpose in life? Do you know? Most people have no clue. One man put it very well when he said,

> *If you want to identify me, ask me not where I live, or what I like to eat, or how I comb my hair, but ask me what I think I am living for, in detail; and ask me what I think is keeping me from living fully the thing I want to live for. Between these two answers you can determine the identity of any person. The better answer he has, the more of a person he is.*[2]

You Are a Person of Destiny

It is very important that you see yourself as a person of destiny. You need to have, as I have said, an eschatology of victory. You need to see that your life has more to it than just the immediate gratification of your fleshly desires. If you can understand that your life, your business, and your success will be used by the God of the universe to touch many other lives, to advance His unseen and sovereign purposes, to mold your children, to shape your society, and to change and influence your culture, then you will be a flaming torch that will burn brightly in the night!

Christians today, for the most part, have lost this sense of divine destiny. This was not always the case. For much of the historic Christian church through the centuries, there has been a sense that the Bible taught that God's church would one day be victorious over the earth. Let me quote some verses that teach this wonderful and positive hope.

- *"All the ends of the world shall remember and turn unto the Lord: and all the kindreds of the nations shall worship before thee."* Psalm 22:27

- *"He shall have dominion also from sea to sea, and from the river unto the ends of the earth."* Psalm 72:8

- *"And blessed be his glorious name for ever: and let the whole earth be filled with his glory; Amen, and Amen."* Psalm 72:19

- *"And it shall come to pass in the last days, that the mountain of the Lord's house shall be established in the top of the mountains, and shall be exalted above the hills; and all nations shall flow unto it."* Isaiah 2:2

- *"They shall not hurt nor destroy in all my holy mountain: for the earth shall be full of the knowledge of the Lord, as the waters cover the sea."* Isaiah 11:9

- *"For the earth shall be filled with the knowledge of the glory of the Lord, as the waters cover the sea."* Habakkuk 2:14

- *"And I say unto you, That many shall come from the east and west, and shall sit down with Abraham, and Isaac, and Jacob, in the kingdom of heaven."* Matthew 8:11

- *"Then said he, Unto what is the kingdom of God like? And whereunto shall I resemble it? It is like a grain of mustard seed, which a man took, and cast into his garden; and it grew, and waxed a great tree; and the fowls of the air lodged in the branches of it."* Luke 13:18-19

- *"And so all Israel shall be saved: as it is written, There shall come out of Zion the Deliverer, and shall turn away ungodliness from Jacob."* Romans 11:26 (This chapter in Romans is predicting the future conversion of ethnic Israel. The ramifications of Paul's remarks are clearly outlined in Romans 11. The teaching Paul is giving us here is that with the future conversion of Israel will also come a worldwide revival that will be greater than anything that we have ever seen.)

This positive hope of a future revival was held by many Christian leaders throughout the centuries. Here are a few of the men who were inspired and motivated by an eschatology of victory: Jonathan Edwards, Matthew Henry, George Whitefield, Robert Murray McCheyne, John Owen, B. B. Warfield, John Murray, and R. C. Sproul. When the church had this positive worldview, it inspired many to take the gospel to the ends of the world. The British author, Ian Murray, wrote a marvelous book entitled "The Puritan Hope." This book shows how many of the major mission movements began as a result of this point of view. Men and women inspired by faith that God is on the throne and that He is planning on bringing the world under the dominion of the gospel of the Lord Jesus Christ went out and filled great portions of the earth with the good news of Christ. The labors of these men and women were greatly blessed with thousands of people coming to faith in Christ. Today, as a result of these early missionary efforts, millions around the world are now a part of the church of Jesus Christ. What inspired many of these people was their faith that God was sovereign and that he was going to shake the ends of the world with the gospel of Jesus Christ.

> *This positive hope of a future revival was held by many Christian leaders throughout the centuries.*

Today, in contrast to our forefathers, many Christians are very pessimistic about the future of the church. They have lost that faith in the power and purpose of God. Instead of being on fire for Christ, many Christian leaders are just telling us how bad things are and that there is little or nothing that can be done. The message of many is to be faithful in a world that is increasingly becoming anti-Christian. *"Perhaps,"* they say, *"we can save a few souls before the end comes."* This pessimistic view was not the view of many in the church throughout the ages. With the Christian church declining and losing its influence and vision, a strange new fire has come in among us. This is the fire of the false religion of radical Islam. Radical Islam is a religion that has stolen the Christian hope and confidence of God's purpose to bring the world under the influence of Christ and His Gospel. Here is a religion that does not have the true Scriptures, it does not know the glory of the precious gospel of Jesus Christ, and it does not have the power and influence of the Holy Spirit. And yet, this false religion is confident that it is destined to rule the world and to bring all nations to submit to Allah. We, as Christians, should be ashamed that people following a false god are more confident and zealous than we who have the true Scriptures and who follow the living and true God. One Islamic leader made this chilling statement: *"The governments of the world should know that Islam cannot be defeated. Islam will be victorious in all the countries of the world, and Islam and the teachings of the Koran will prevail all over the world."*[3]

O, how I long for all of my children and my children's children, and for all who read this book, to recover that precious faith that once inspired the Christian church to believe that our God is going to fill the earth with the glory of His Son Jesus Christ. Missionary statesman William Carey once said, *"Attempt great things for God, and expect great things from God."*

There are two poems that contrast the views of God's sovereignty over our destiny in life. One poem shows us the spirit of the world where a man defies the very rule and authority of God over his life. The other poem reveals the gracious way in which a believer submits to the hard providences in life with a sweet resignation to the will and eternal plan of a holy and sovereign God.

Invictus

Out of the night that covers me,
Black as the pit from pole to pole;
I thank whatever gods there be,
For my unconquerable soul.

In the fell clutch of circumstance,
I have not winced or cried aloud.
Under the bludgeonings of chance,
My head is bloodied, but unbowed.

Beyond this place of wrath and tears,
Looms but the horror of the shade.
And yet the menace of the years
Finds, and shall find me, unafraid.

It matters not how strait the gate,
How charged with punishments the scroll,
I am the master of my fate;
I am the captain of my soul.

William Ernest Henley

Now contrast this poem with the marvelous words written by Horatio G. Spafford and see the vast difference between the two men and their views of life and God.

It is Well with My Soul

When peace like a river attendeth my way,
When sorrows like sea-billows roll;
Whatever my lot, Thou hast taught me to say,
It is well, it is well with my soul!

Though Satan should buffet, though trials should come,
Let this blest assurance control,
That Christ hath regarded my helpless estate,
And hath shed His own blood for my soul.

My sin, O the bliss of this glorious thought!
My sin, not in part, but the whole,
Is nailed to His Cross, and I bear it no more;
Praise the Lord, praise the Lord, O my soul!

Horatio G. Spafford

What a contrast these two poems reveal. William Earnest Henley, in his poem, *"Invictus,"* reveals a heart that is angry, bitter, and filled with pride. Henley depicts the attitude of self-righteous defiance to God. How different is the poem by Horatio Spafford. Pastor Kirk Neely tells the wonderful story behind this poem.

> *Horatio Spafford was a Chicago businessman in the late nineteenth century. A senior partner in a prosperous law firm and devout elder in the Presbyterian church, Spafford and his wife, Anna, lived comfortably with their four young daughters. In 1871, when the Great Fire of Chicago reduced the city to ashes, it also destroyed Spafford's sizable investments.*
>
> *Two years later, the family planned a trip to Europe. At the last moment Spafford was detained by business. Anna and the girls went ahead, sailing on the ocean liner SS Ville de Havre. On November 21, 1873, the liner was accidentally rammed by a British vessel and sank within twelve minutes. Anna was rescued clinging to a floating board. The four children drowned. A fellow survivor recalled Anna saying, "God gave me four daughters. Now they have been taken from me. Someday I will understand why." Nine days after the shipwreck Anna landed in Cardiff, Wales, and cabled her husband, "Saved alone. What shall I do?"*
>
> *After receiving Anna's telegram, Spafford immediately left Chicago to bring his wife home. On the Atlantic crossing, the captain of his ship called Horatio to his cabin to tell him that they were passing over the spot where his four daughters had perished. Horatio wrote the words to the hymn "It Is Well With My Soul" as he passed over their watery grave.*[4]

What a difference between *"Invictus"* and *"It is Well with My Soul."* Spafford knew that he was a man with a destiny. Even the crushing sorrow from the death of his four daughters could not extinguish the optimistic flame that burned in his soul. Horatio Spafford knew that as a man with a destiny he was *"come to the*

kingdom for such a time as this."
A person driven by the conviction that his life has purpose will
be difficult to defeat.

I want all of you who know
the Lord to remember that you
are special. Your life has significance. God made you just as
you are. God has a plan for you
to fulfill. You are His children and the apple of His eye. God's plan
is for you to live your life with the confidence and joy that you are
alive right now to serve and honor God. None of us really knows
what great things we each might do for our Lord. This is your
moment in history. This is your time to shine for the high King of
heaven. Your life is a gift from God. May you each use it to make
a difference in the lives of all those around you.

J. Campbell White, the secretary of the Laymen's Missionary
Movement, once wrote,

> *Most men are not satisfied with the permanent output of
> their lives. Nothing can wholly satisfy the life of Christ
> within his followers except the adoption of Christ's pur-
> pose toward the world he came to redeem. Fame, plea-
> sure, and riches are but husks and ashes in contrast with
> the boundless and abiding joy of working with God for the
> fulfillment of his eternal plans. The men who are putting
> everything into Christ's undertaking are getting out of life
> its sweetest and most priceless rewards.*[5]

May we not forget that winning for God is not an option. Defeat,
in the long run, is not a possibility. We are on the winning side.
Victory is ours, and we must not forget that. We all enjoy thrilling
stories of bravery and courage. Perhaps we have all been stirred
by the true story of the Roman slave named Spartacus. Spartacus
led a revolt against imperial Rome. Defying all odds, he raised
an army of slaves that won impressive and astonishing victories
against Rome's mighty legions. But tragically, the story of Spartacus ends in profound sadness.

A person driven by the conviction that his life has purpose will be difficult to defeat.

> *When Marcus Licinius Crassus defeated the runaway slave Spartacus and his six thousand rebels, he crucified them at regular intervals along the highway leading to Spartacus's hometown. The general never issued the order to have the bodies or the crosses removed, so for years — perhaps decades — the macabre wooden memorials warned would-be revolutionaries, **this** could be you.*[6]

The grand cause of the gospel of Jesus Christ will not be defeated. Our victories will not be erased like the victories of Spartacus. It may appear at times that the church of Jesus Christ is doing poorly in this world. But remember the words of James Russell Lowell: *"Truth forever on the scaffold; wrong forever on the throne; yet that scaffold sways the future, and, behind the dim unknown, standeth God within the shadow, keeping watch above his own."*[7]

If we fail, as we all surely will, and if we find our best efforts have not made much of an impression on those to whom we have ministered, we must not be discouraged. Success is often built on a mountain of failed efforts and painful memories. But those who succeed in life are those who keep getting up when they have been knocked down. The great English Baptist preacher, C. H. Spurgeon, understood this and challenged his young ministerial students with these words:

Success is often built on a mountain of failed efforts and painful memories.

> *What is the use of regret unless we can rise by it to a better future? Sighs, which do not raise us higher, are an ill use of vital breath. Chasten yourselves, but be not discouraged. Gather up the arrows which aforetime fell wide of the mark, not to break them in passionate despair, but to send them (again) to the target with direct aim and a more concentrated force. Weave victories out of defeats. Learn success from failure, wisdom from blundering.*[8]

∽

How to Get Started

1. As we develop a biblical worldview for Christian living it must include this optimistic hope that we are a chosen people who have a date with destiny to make a difference in this world.
2. Ask yourself, "How much pleasure is God receiving from my life? Do I have a sense of purpose and destiny?"
3. Remind yourself that God is on the throne of the universe. God's eternal purposes are going to be accomplished.
4. Therefore, surrender yourself to God's will.
5. Pray that you might be used to help extend God's kingdom throughout the world. The place to begin is to see yourself as a person of destiny.

Thoughts for Consideration

- *"To give a man purpose, hope, and awareness that he is made in God's image, is to awaken that man to his destiny."* Robert L. Dickie

- *"Must one point out that from ancient times a decline in courage has been considered the first symptom of the end."* Aleksandr I. Solzhenitsyn

- *"Destiny is not a matter of chance, it is a matter of choice; it is not a thing to be waited for, it is a thing to be achieved."* William Jennings Bryan

- *"It is a mistake to look too far ahead. Only one link of the chain of destiny can be handled at a time."* Winston Churchill

- *"It is better to die for something than it is to live for nothing."* Bob Jones, Sr.

- *"Every life should have a purpose to which it can give the energies of its mind and the enthusiasms of its heart. That life without a purpose will be prey to the perverted ways waiting for the uncommitted life."* C. Neil Strait

- *"But seek ye first the kingdom of God, and his righteousness: and all these things shall be added unto you."* Matthew 6:33

- *"He hath shewed thee, O man, what is good; and what doth the Lord require of thee, but to do justly, and to love mercy, and to walk humbly with thy God."* Micah 6:8

- *"Great minds have purposes, little minds have wishes."* Washington Irving

- *"It's choice not chance that determines your destiny."* Jean Nidetch

- *"Out of our beliefs are born deeds; out of our deeds we form habits; out of habits grows our character; and on our character we build our destiny."* Henry Hancock

Questions for Discussion

1. What is the very first thing necessary to develop a Christian worldview?

2. How does the story of Queen Esther teach us that we have a special destiny ordained by God to fulfill?

3. Explain the significance of the contrast between the two poems, *Invictus* and *It is Well with My Soul*.

4. What does this verse mean to you: *"And who knoweth whether thou are come to the kingdom for such a time as this?"*

5. Can you explain the meaning of the word *eschatology*?

6. Explain how embracing an attitude of pessimism or optimism may shape the future destiny of a person's life.

3
Living for the Glory of God

"Whether therefore ye eat, or drink, or whatsoever ye do, do all to the glory of God." 1 Corinthians 10:31

"God made me fast, and when I run I feel His pleasure!" Eric Liddell, Scottish Gold Medal Winner in the Olympic Games[1]

Another great principle for all of us to learn, if we are to have a biblical worldview that leads us to success in life, is to realize that the most important thing in life is to live for the glory of God. In the Westminster Confession of Faith, the first question is this: *"What is the chief end of man?"* The answer is *"to glorify God and to enjoy Him forever!"*

Eric Liddell of Scotland was the fastest man alive in his day. He was a devout Presbyterian who felt called to take the gospel to the land of China. He would one day die in China as a martyr for the faith and the Lord that he so deeply loved. But he made this interesting remark once to a close friend. He said, *"God made me fast, and when I run I feel His pleasure!"* Here was this great athlete who wanted to go to China to serve his Lord, but he also knew that his running was a way to serve God. Eric Liddell knew that everything, if done for the Lord, was sacred and had spiritual meaning.

We must never forget that to live for the glory of God is not a sacrifice but a sacred privilege and true joy to those who know God in the gospel of Christ. J. Oswald Sanders was right on target when he said, *"Sacrifice is the ecstasy of giving the best we have to the One whom we love the most."*[2]

> *We must never forget that to live for the glory of God is not a sacrifice but a sacred privilege and true joy to those who know God in the gospel of Christ.*

David Livingston, the great missionary who gave his life in service to Jesus Christ his Lord and who was instrumental in opening up the continent of Africa to the gospel, also said,

For my part, I have never ceased to rejoice that God has appointed me to such an office. People talk of the sacrifice I made in spending so much of my life in Africa. Can that be called a sacrifice which is simply paid back as a small part of a great debt owing to our God, which we can never repay? Is that a sacrifice which brings its own blest reward in healthful activity, the consciousness of doing good, peace of mind, and a bright hope of a glorious destiny hereafter? Away with the word in such a view, and with such a thought! It is emphatically no sacrifice. Say rather it is a privilege. Anxiety, sickness, suffering, or danger, now and then...All these are nothing when compared with the glory which shall be revealed in and for us. I never made a sacrifice.[3]

To find success in our lives, we need to learn that whatever we do in life, as the Scriptures teach, we should do for the glory of the Lord. So whether we are working, playing, or spending time with our family, nothing is to be seen as worthless or insignificant. Everything we do has tremendous potential. We must learn the principle that everything is to be done for the glory of God. I have taught my children that their school work, their athletic competitions, their hobbies, and their interests in life are all very special. Do all of these things for God's glory. Be the best, and do the best you can at everything you put your hand to do. By teaching these things, we are instructing our children that all of life is sacred. We make a great mistake if we artificially divide life into sacred and secular. Some people think that unless they are called to full-time

Christian work then they are not really serving the Lord. This is not true. I would want all of you who read this to understand that God's calling for you is in every area of life and in everything that you do. Pastor and author Gordon MacDonald understood this. MacDonald writes:

> *Let us be frank: men and women have obeyed God's call and become martyrs. Others have undertaken unspeakably difficult and discouraging tasks and barely survived. Many more have lived the relatively common life between home and job. They hammer nails, sell widgets, create software, or fix things. But in the process they make a difference in the existence of the people around them. And they, too, are called.*[4]

The great English writer John Milton also once said, *"They also serve who only stand and wait."*[5] One of the greatest lessons we can all learn from this quote by Milton is that we are also serving God when we wait on Him in obedient adoration.

I sent an email to my son, Bob, who at the time was a Lieutenant in the U.S. Air Force, and asked him to send me some of the great quotes he had collected over the years. He sent me back an email that was better than any of the quotes I was looking for. This is what he sent me as he sat down to write back his note of response.

> *Below is a list of some of my favorite quotes. Each one of these are in my office either on the door, bulletin board, by my desk, or on the wall. I focus on them every day to help keep me on pace to finish my degree with a 4.0, to train harder than the day before, to work harder than any other Lieutenant on base, and to raise my family the best I can. It's a full life with lots of stress, but boy it sure is fun. I'm going to squeeze every last drop of life out of mine that I can so when I'm old and gray I won't be able to say, "Man, I could have done so much more, or I wish I had done that!"*

This note from my son reflects a desire and a commitment to excellence that must be taught and passed on to each generation that comes after us. These kinds of goals and qualities do not come naturally. We must learn them for ourselves and then teach them to our children so that they too can pattern their lives after the passion and example of excellence. We live in a world that is in love with mediocrity, that is content with mediocrity, and that basically produces mediocrity.

If you see your life and everything you do as being sacred, and as having purpose before God, you will be more inclined to strive for excellence in all that you do. This attitude makes our job, our work, and even our play sacred. It gives us the desire to do everything the best that we can for the honor and glory of the Lord whom we love and serve. Author Nancy Pearcey understood the importance of this when she wrote:

> *Probably most of us had not linked together the idea of Christian worldview with finding joy in life....It is only when we offer up everything we do in worship to God that we finally experience His power coursing through every fiber of our being. The God of the Bible is not only the God of the human spirit but also the God of nature and history. We serve Him not only in worship but also in obedience to the Cultural Mandate. If Christian churches are serious about discipleship, they must teach believers how to keep living for God after they walk out the church doors on Sunday.*[6]

We must instill into our children's heart a passion for excellence in all that they do.

We must instill into our children's hearts a passion for excellence in all that they do. Children learn discipline, hard work, and character at home. These great lessons must come from parents first, or they may never be learned at all. Author and public speaker James Hunter made this insightful comment:

Do we benefit our children by accepting mediocrity? Do
we help them by allowing them to get by doing the bare
minimum? Remember what Vince Lombardi said: "My
love will be relentless!" We should never talk about how
much we care for those we lead if we are avoiding the
hassle of confronting them with any gaps between the set
standards and their actual performance.[7]

God's purpose in life for all of us is to be the best parents, the best
partners, the best workers, the best citizens, and the best Christians that we can possibly be. By doing all things for the glory of
God, we are making these goals a reality.

If we would teach our children to be successful in life, and if
we would instill into their hearts at an early age a sense of purpose
for their lives, we must be sure to teach them the wisdom literature
of the Bible. I would especially urge each of you to teach your
children the Proverbs and to encourage them to read one chapter
of the Proverbs each day.

The "My Son" Passages in the Proverbs

There are a number of passages in the Proverbs that are referred
to as "My Son" passages. These verses will instill a sense of spiritual purpose in the lives of our youth.

- "[1] *My son, if thou wilt receive my words, and hide*
  my commandments with thee; [2] So that thou incline
  thine ear unto wisdom, and apply thine heart to un-
  derstanding; [3] Yea, if thou criest after knowledge,
  and liftest up thy voice for understanding; [4] If thou
  seekest her as silver, and searchest for her as for hid
  treasures; [5] Then shalt thou understand the fear of
  the Lord, and find the knowledge of God." Proverbs
  2:1-5

- "[1] *My Son, forget not my law; but let thine heart*
  keep my commandments: [2] For length of days, and
  long life, and peace, shall they add to thee. [3] Let
  not mercy and truth forsake thee: bind them about thy

neck; write them upon the table of thine heart: [4] *So shalt thou find favour and good understanding in the sight of God and man.*" Proverbs 3:1-4

- "[11] *My son, despise not the chastening of the Lord; neither be weary of his correction:* [12] *For whom the Lord loveth he correcteth; even as a father the son in whom he delighteth.*" Proverbs 3:11-12

- "[21] *My son, let not them* [God's commandments] *depart from thine eyes: keep sound wisdom and discretion:* [22] *So shall they be life unto thy soul, and grace to thy neck.* [23] *Then shalt thou walk in the way safely, and thy foot shall not stumble.*" Proverbs 3:21-23

- "[10] *Hear, O my son, and receive my sayings; and they years of thy life shall be many.* [11] *I have taught thee in the way of wisdom; I have led thee in right paths.* [12] *When thou goest, thy steps shall not be straitened; and when thou runnest, thou shalt not stumble.*" Proverbs 4:10-12

- "[20] *My son, attend to my words; incline thine ear unto my sayings.* [21] *Let them not depart from thine eyes; keep them in the midst of thine heart.* [22] *For they are life unto those that find them, and health to all their flesh.*" Proverbs 4:20-22

- "[1] *My son, attend unto my wisdom, and bow thine ear to my understanding:* [2] *That thou mayest regard discretion, and that thy lips may keep knowledge.*" Proverbs 5:1-2

- "[1] *My son, if thou be surety* [guarantee] *for thy friend, if thou hast stricken thy hand* [made a pledge] *with a stranger,* [2] *Thou art snared with the words of thy mouth, thou art taken with the words of thy mouth.*

[3] *Do this now, my son, and deliver thyself, when thou art come into the hand of thy friend; go, humble thyself, and make sure thy friend.*" Proverbs 6:1-3

- "[20] *My son, keep thy father's commandment, and forsake not the law of thy mother; [21] Bind them continually upon thine heart, and tie them abut thy neck. [22] When thou goest, it shall lead thee; when thou sleepest, it shall keep thee; and when thou awakest, it shall talk with thee. [23] For the commandment is a lamp; and the law is light; and reproofs of instruction are the way of life: [24] To keep thee from the evil woman, from the flattery of the tongue of a strange woman. [25] Lust not after her beauty in thine heart; neither let her take thee with her eyelids.*" Proverbs 6:20-25

- "[1] *My son, keep my words, and lay up my commandments with thee. [2] Keep my commandments, and live; and my law as the apple of thine eye. [3] Bind them upon thy fingers, write them upon the table of thine heart. [4] Say unto wisdom, Thou art my sister; and call understanding thy kinswoman; [5] That they may keep thee from the strange woman, from the stranger which flattereth with her words.*" Proverbs 7:1-5

These "*My Son*" passages remind us that we have been created (designed) by God and that as created beings we have a great need to have God direct, control, and guide our lives. Learning to submit to God in every area of life and to live for His glory is something that most men are hesitant to do. It is part of our sinful and fallen human nature to want to be independent and live apart from God. Author Jim Berg in his wonderful book *Changed into His Image* understood this and wrote:

> *Man can make a space shuttle, build a house, manufacture an automobile, and construct a superhighway; but since*

none of these items are self-created, none of them are self-sustaining. They are dependent upon the one who made them. The space shuttle and the automobile have to be refueled and serviced. The house and the highway have to be repaired. Creation inherently demands dependency. Man can acknowledge this about everything he makes for himself in this world, but he rebels against the thought that somehow he is dependent upon his own Creator. Yet everything around us demonstrates that "a river cannot rise higher than its source." Subordination and dependence are inherent for everything that is made by someone else. God reminds us in Psalm 100:3, "It is he that hath made us, and not we ourselves." The fact of man's creation has enormous implications for the creature. The governing principle here is if you need somebody to make you, you need somebody to maintain you. Man must face his dependency, repent of his proud attempts to make life work his own way, and submit to the ways of his Creator.[8]

The British author, C. S. Lewis, said something very similar in his book *Mere Christianity*:

God made us: invented us as a man invents an engine. A car is made to run on gasoline, and it would not run properly on anything else. Now God designed the human machine to run on Himself. He Himself is the fuel our spirits were designed to burn, or the food our spirits were designed to feed on. There is no other. That is why it is just no good asking God to make us happy in our own way without bothering about religion. God cannot give us a happiness and peace apart from Himself, because it is not there. There is no such thing.[9]

To live for the glory of God means that we must be committed to doing everything in life, great or small, to the best of our ability. God's glory demands that we strive for excellence and aim to please Jesus in all things. The Apostle Paul said, "*And whatsoever ye do, do it heartily, as to the Lord, and not unto men."* Colossians 3:23 Some make the mistake of only putting their best efforts in the big things or the great tasks that have been handed to them. This is a tragic mistake and a misunderstanding of what it means to live for God's glory. We must strive to do our best in every task. Spurgeon wrote:

To live for the glory of God means that we must be committed to doing everything in life, great or small, to the best of our ability.

> *Do not think of waiting until you can do some great thing for God; do little things, and then the Master will bid you go up higher....If one wishes to be a steward in God's house, he must first be prepared to serve as a scullion in the kitchen, and be content to wash out the pots and clean the boots. Remember our Lord's rule, "Whosoever exalteth himself shall be abased; and he that humbleth himself shall be exalted."*[10]

Have you discovered your purpose for life? If you are a Christian, it involves living for the glory of God. The hour in which we live is full of pressing dangers and challenges. The enemies rising up against the Christian faith are many. Whatever else you do in life, my desire and prayer for all of you is to consecrate your life to the great cause of glorifying God and defending His truth and church. To take our stand with those in the Lord's army will mean we need to read, to study, to pray, and to think. An ignorant Christian church will be powerless to resist the destructive ideas and philosophies that are pressing the church on every side. Perhaps there has never been a more important time when the Lord's people need to be serious students and deep thinkers. In a Newsweek article, *"Thinking: A Neglected Art,"* a writer said,

> *Intelligence is just as much a part of human nature as sociability. It would certainly be unnatural for a person to allow his mind to die of neglect...if we are to survive as a*

free people, we will have to take some course of action as soon as possible, because regardless of what some advertisers have led us to believe, this country does not run on oil. It runs on ideas.[11]

It is time to think. It is time for us to teach our children how to think. If we would have a biblical worldview that would propel us on to success in life, then we must discover once again this great principle of living for the glory of God. It is important to think about this and understand how we should apply it to every area of our lives.

How to Get Started

1. Make sure that everything you do in life is being done for the glory of God.
2. Be committed to excellence in everything you do.
3. Reject the spirit of mediocrity that rules this present age.
4. Study the *"My Son"* passages of Proverbs and learn these lessons well.
5. Write out your purpose for life or missions statement. Make sure it includes the idea of living for the glory of God.

Thoughts for Consideration

- *"The chief end of man is to glorify God and to enjoy Him forever."* Westminster Catechism

- *"You have formed us for Yourself, and our hearts are restless till they find rest in Thee."* Saint Augustine

- *"Shut out every other consideration and keep yourself before God for this one thing only — 'My utmost for His Highest' I am determined to be absolutely and entirely for Him and Him alone."* Oswald Chambers

- *"This is, indeed, the proper business of the whole life, in which men should daily exercise themselves, to consider the infinite goodness, justice, power and wisdom of God, in this magnificent theatre of God."* John Calvin

- *"In commanding us to glorify him, God is inviting us to enjoy him."* C. S. Lewis

- *"All who are ignorant of the purpose for which they live are fools and madmen."* John Calvin

- *"Spiritual life depends on the purpose we cherish."* C. H. Spurgeon

- *"God made us to be worshippers. That was the purpose of God in bringing us into the world."* A. W. Tozer

- *"The man without purpose is like a ship without a rudder."* Thomas Carlyle

- *"Be such a man, and live such a life, that if every man were such as you, and every life a life like yours, this earth would be God's paradise."* Phillips Brooks

- *God made us for himself; that is the first and last thing that can be said about human existence and whatever more we are is but commentary."* A. W. Tozer

Questions for Discussion

1. What does it mean to live for the glory of God?

2. How can we, by developing a Christian worldview of life, make a difference in the lives of others?

3. Why should we never be content to settle for mediocrity?

4. How can parents use the "My Son" passages in Proverbs to prepare their children for success?

5. In a summary statement, what is every man's purpose for living?

4
Fearing the Lord

"The fear of the Lord is the beginning of knowledge: but fools despise wisdom and instruction." Proverbs 1:7

"Coram Deo" — Latin phrase meaning *"living in the presence of God."*

∽

O ne of the most important aspects of developing a biblical worldview that will lead to success is to live in the fear of God. This is not a slavish fear where we cringe and cower before God. Rather, the fear of God is reverence and profound awe filled with wonder at His presence. It is the fear of God and the knowledge that we live in His continual presence that prevents us from living in sin. In the Scriptures, we read that Abraham was the friend of God, and that Enoch walked with God. I believe this meant that these men practiced the presence of God in their lives. Sin in our lives can distract us from doing and being the people we would want to be. Imagine the headaches, the problems, the scorn, and the shame people would have avoided had they been disciplined in their private and moral lives! Leaders must be able to have the courage and character to point to their lives and say, "Don't merely do as I say, but also do as I do." The Apostle Paul could write to his readers on numerous occasions and say to them, *"Brethren, be followers together of me, and mark them which walk so as ye have us for an ensample."* Philippians 3:17

Pastor David D. Ireland defined the fear of the Lord in this fashion:

The fear of the Lord speaks of reverence, honor, and esteem that God is to receive freely from His creation. Fear in this context does not suggest a cowering posture. A healthy fear of the Lord cherishes God's leadership, will, preferred lifestyle, and full oversight of our lives....Someone who fears the Lord demonstrates a desire for knowledge, a hatred for evil, and an appreciation for wisdom.[1]

> ## *To be successful as leaders or as parents, we must live lives above reproach.*

To be successful as leaders or as parents, we must live lives above reproach: that is, without shame. Can we say to our families and associates, "Follow my example: be like me!" This should be the goal of all who lead others. When you are tempted to compromise your principles and in ethical areas of your life, stop for a moment and consider the consequences any lapse of character will have on those you love the most. Think of how hurt your family and friends will be if you are caught cheating, lying, stealing, or doing other such things. Whatever a person may gain by dishonesty or by impurity of life — is it worth the shame, reproach, disappointment, and pain that we create when we fail in our moral and spiritual lives? Author Pat Williams tells this story:

> *In California, a banker sat down over coffee with one of his managers and said, "You're going to find out soon enough, so I want you to hear it from me. The bank examiners are closing in on me, so I've hired an attorney and I'm going to turn myself in. That's right, I embezzled half a million dollars." The manager was stunned. "You," he said, "Embezzlement? You're the last person I would have suspected." "I'm looking at prison time and complete financial ruin," said the banker. "But that's the least of it. Now comes the hard part. I have to go home and tell my wife and two daughters what I've done."[2]*

The Fear of the Lord Will Keep Us from Sin

The fear of the Lord will keep us from sin and the shame that often follows it. An old American evangelist, D. L. Moody, once said, *"Sin will keep you from God's Word or God's Word will keep you from sin."* The way to develop the fear of the Lord in our lives is by reading the Bible daily and applying its principles in our lives.

Legendary basketball coach, John Wooden of UCLA, whose teams won a record ten national championships, was once asked about his secret of a long and happy life. He replied, *"There is no pillow so soft as a clear conscience."*[3]

All people, young or old, when deciding on what values and principles to guide their lives,

> *There is no pillow so soft as a clear conscience.*

would be wise to make sure they add the fear of the Lord to their list of virtues. The fear of God will fill your life with a profound peace that nothing else can ever replace. Over the years as a pastor, I have counseled many people that have been tormented by past sins and failures. These dear people live in the shadow land of guilt and shame. Some are tormented on a daily basis with the fear that their past and secret lives may some day catch up with them. Rather than fear the past, why not fear God and enjoy the peace that this will bring to your life?

The fear of the Lord is not an unpleasant burden for the true Christian. As Scottish theologian P. T. Forsyth once said, *"The first duty of every soul is not to find its freedom, but to choose its master."*[4] When a Christian chooses Christ as his master, he has not only made a wise choice, but he has also made a choice that will lead to tremendous joy in his life. In the book of Nehemiah, we are told by Nehemiah himself that, *"The joy of the Lord is your strength."* Nehemiah 8:10 Never forget that true and lasting joy comes from the fear of God. As one man has said so well,

> *Human accomplishment, even remarkable human accomplishment, cannot ultimately deliver joy to the human heart. There may be a fleeting sensation that feels like joy, but it is a cheap substitute for the real thing and may even*

become an idol set up in place of the Lord, who enabled us to complete the project…ultimately joy grows out of being right with God.[5]

The Fear of the Lord Leads Us to Please the Lord

The fear of the Lord means that we desire to please the Lord in all that we do. Author Ken Collier coined an expression that he has used over the years to teach his children the importance of obedience. The phrase is a little poetic rhyme: *"Just two choices on the shelf, pleasing God or pleasing self."*[6] When loved ones or friends are behaving badly, we need to ask them what Ken Collier asks his children, "At this moment are you pleasing God or are you pleasing self?" Those who fear the Lord train themselves to ask this question, and they force themselves to be brutally honest about the answer and response that they give. Fearing God means to be devoted to pleasing Him above all others.

We should never forget that sin leaves a terrible legacy and brings hurtful and lasting consequences. F. B. Meyer, a preacher and author, once said,

> *This is the bitterest of all — to know that suffering need not have been; that it has resulted from indiscretion and inconsistency; that it is the harvest of one's own sowing; that the vulture which feeds on the vitals is a nestling of one's own rearing. Ah me! This is pain! There is an inevitable Nemesis in life. The laws of the heart and home, of the soul and human life, cannot be violated with impunity. Sin may be forgiven; the fire of penalty might be changed into the fire of trial: the love of God may seem nearer and dearer than ever and yet there is the awful pressure of pain; the trembling heart; the failing of eyes and pining of soul; the harp on the willows; the refusal of the lip to sing the Lord's song.*[7]

The Fear of the Lord Prepares Us for Judgment

If we truly feared the Lord we would all take more seriously the thought that we have an appointment with God at the end of life.

The apostle writes in Hebrews 9:27, *"It is appointed to men once to die and after that the judgment."* I am trying to live my life with that divine appointment in mind. Because I fear God and know that He will call me into His presence to give an account of my life, I strive to take a daily accounting of all that I do. If we do not crucify our lusts and passions in this life, we will find that the life to come will be filled with everlasting shame. This is no trifling matter. Every Christian who pursues a biblical worldview would be wise to cry out to God that the fear of the Lord would be planted deep into their hearts. Philip Henry, the father of the great English commentator, Matthew Henry, was thirty years old when he wrote in his diary, *"So old and older than Alexander when he conquered the great world; but I have not subdued the little world of myself."*[8]

The fear of the Lord will drive us to mortify our flesh and to prepare for the divine appointment when we will give account of our life and our time to the Creator who gave us life and breath. The English evangelist and preacher, George Whitefield (1714-1770) was a man who was driven with a holy passion to fear God and walk in His ways. Before he retired for bed each night, he searched his soul with these probing questions that he had written in his journal:

- *Have I been fervent in prayer?*
- *Have I after or before every deliberate conversation and action, considered how it might tend to God's glory?*
- *Have I after any pleasure, immediately given thanks?*
- *Have I planned business for the day?*
- *Have I been meek, cheerful, affable in everything I said and did?*
- *Have I been proud, vain, unchaste, or enviable of others?*
- *Have I thought or spoken unkindly to anyone?*
- *Have I confessed all sins?*[8]

It is the fear of God that enables one to live for God's glory and to be mindful of keeping our flesh under the influence of the Holy

Spirit. My observations in life have been that when a life is lived carelessly and sinfully, it has always been a sign that the fear of God has been absent.

Be Accountable to Someone

Because we fear God and know that we must one day stand before His presence to give an account of our sins, we should do everything we can in our power to break the power and the grip that sin has on our lives. One of the most effective ways to do that is to have someone as an accountability partner. When a husband, wife, friend, or mentor holds us accountable, it has positive and lasting effects on our outward behavior. The benefits of accountability have been stated like this:

> Behavioral sciences in recent years have expounded the simple truth that "behavior that is observed changes." People who are accountable by their own choice to a group of friends, to a therapy group, to a psychiatrist or a pastoral counselor, to a study group or prayer group, are people who are serious about changing their behavior, and they are finding that change is possible.
>
> Studies done in factories have proven that both quality and quantity of work increases when the employees know that they are being observed. If only God knows what I am doing, since I know He won't tell, I tend to make all kinds of excuses for myself. But if I must report to another or a group of others, I begin to monitor my behavior. If someone is keeping an eye on me, my behavior improves.[10]

Men of intemperate minds never can be free; their passions forge their fetters.

There is very little preaching on the fear of God in the church today. This is a lost topic in the evangelical world. Perhaps many pastors don't understand the implications of this great truth. The fear of God is not something that should frighten people. This truth is what should set our hearts free from the bondage and tyranny of indwelling sin. Edmund Burke understood that an undisciplined life given over to the flesh is a life of slavery and not freedom. Burke wrote, *"Men of intemperate minds never can be free; their passions forge their fetters."*[11]

How to Get Started

1. Pursue with all your strength a desire to fear the Lord. Fearing God is an essential aspect of holy living and is necessary in developing a Christian worldview.
2. Practice the presence of God. This means you realize that God is always near and that there is nothing hidden from Him.
3. Choose your master. Jesus is Lord. Surrender every area of your life to the Lordship of Christ.
4. Pray to the Lord for a tender conscience, knowing that one day you must give an account to God for all that you say and do.
5. Ask a close friend or associate to hold you accountable to a holy life.
6. Declare war on all sins in your life that have held you in spiritual bondage.

Thoughts for Consideration

- *"It is when we face ourselves and face Christ, that we are lost in wonder, love, and praise. We need to rediscover the almost lost discipline of self-examination and then a re-awakened sense of sin will beget a re-awakened sense of wonder."* Andrew Murray

- *"He who does not fear God has need to fear everything else."* Anonymous

- *"Nothing is more powerful to overcome temptation than the fear of God."* John Calvin

- *"The fear of God is the beginning of wisdom, and they that lack the beginning have neither the middle nor the end."* John Bunyan

- *"It is only the fear of God that can deliver us from the fear of man."* John Witherspoon

- *"The fear of God promotes spiritual joy; it is the morning star that ushers in the sunlight of comfort."* Thomas Watson

- *"The fear of God is the soul of godliness."* John Murray

- *"The learning of the Christian man ought to begin with the fear of God."* Thomas Cranmer

- *"He who knows what it is to enjoy God will dread his loss. He who has seen his face will fear to see his back."* Richard Alleine

- *"Christ can never be known without a sense of awe and fear accompanying the knowledge...No one who knows him intimately can ever be flippant in his presence."* A. W. Tozer

- *"The more we lose sight of the otherness of God, the more shallow our worship will be."* Alwyn Pritchard

Questions for Discussion

1. What is the biblical meaning of the fear of the Lord?

2. According to P. T. Forsyth, what is the first duty of the soul?

3. Why does the fear of the Lord lead to true and lasting joy in life?

4. How can the fear of the Lord help us to prepare for death?

5. What are some of the signs or evidences of the fear of the Lord in a person's life?

5
Loving the Word of God

"Thy words were found, and I did eat them; and thy word was unto me the joy and rejoicing of mine heart: for I am called by thy name, O Lord of hosts." Jeremiah 15:16

"God's Word will keep you from sin or sin will keep you from God's Word." D. L. Moody

I f we are going to live for Jesus Christ and to develop a biblical worldview it is essential that we have a deep love and reverence for the Word of God. Without a daily intake of the Bible as food for our soul, it will be impossible to really grow spiritually or to become a man or a woman of God. Jesus reminded His disciples of the importance of living each day by feasting on the Scriptures. He said, *"It is written, Man shall not live by bread alone, but by every word that proceedeth out of the mouth of God."* Matthew 4:4 Peter also encouraged his readers to have a daily intake of the Word of God. In 1 Peter 2:2 he said, *"As newborn babes, desire the sincere milk of the word, that ye may grow thereby."* The Apostle Paul spoke of the Word of God with these moving statements: *"All scripture is given by inspiration of God, and is profitable for doctrine, for reproof, for correction, for instruction in righteousness: That the man of God may be perfect, thoroughly furnished unto all good works."* 2 Timothy 3:16-17 The word "inspiration" in this verse means "God-breathed." The great scholar and Christian minister Benjamin Warfield had this to say about the inspiration of the Scriptures:

...by a special, supranatural, extraordinary influence of the Holy Ghost, the sacred writers have been guided in their writing in such a way, as while their humanity was not superseded, it was yet so dominated that their words became at the same time the words of God, and thus, in every case and all alike, absolutely infallible.[1]

The Importance of the Word of God

I once came across this statement on the Word of God that has been a blessing to me over the years. I read this often and have, in fact, committed it to memory. This statement shows us how precious and important the Word of God should be in all of our lives.

The Bible reveals the mind of God, the need of man, the way of salvation, the doom of sinners, and the happiness of believers. Its doctrines are holy, its precepts are binding, its histories are true, and its decisions are immutable. Read the Bible to be wise, believe the Bible to be safe, and practice the Bible to be holy. The Bible contains light to direct you, food to support you, and comfort to cheer you. The Bible is the traveler's map, the pilgrim's staff, the pilot's compass, the soldier's sword, and the Christian's charter. In the Bible Paradise is restored, Heaven is opened, and the gates of hell are closed. Christ is its grand subject, our good the design, and the glory of God its end.

> ***Read the Bible to be wise, believe the Bible to be safe, and practice the Bible to be holy.***

The Bible should fill the memory, rule the heart, and guide the feet. Read it slowly, frequently, and prayerfully. It is a mine of wealth, a paradise of glory, and a river of pleasure. It is given you in life, will be opened in judgment, and remembered forever. It involves the highest responsibility, will reward the greatest labor, and will condemn all who trifle with its sacred contents.[2]

The importance of the Bible in our lives is also testified by R. C. Chapman, a man whom Baptist minister, Charles Spurgeon, called "the saintliest man he ever knew." Chapman wrote:

> *The book of God is a store of manna for God's pilgrim children...The great cause of neglecting the Scriptures is not want of time, but want of heart, some idol taking the place of Christ. Satan has been marvelously wise to entice away God's people from Scripture. A child of God who neglects the Scriptures cannot make it his business to please the Lord of Glory; cannot make Him Lord of the conscience; ruler of the heart; the joy, portion, and treasure of the soul...If the Bible be used aright by anyone, it will be to him the most pleasant book in the world.*[3]

One of the great missionaries in the nineteenth century was Hudson Taylor who went to China to take the gospel of Christ to those who had never heard of Jesus. The Word of God was an integral part of his life that helped sustain him during his long and fruitful ministry in China. Hudson Taylor's son revealed how important the Word of God was for his father.

> *It was not easy for Mr. Taylor, in his changeful life, to make time for prayer and Bible study, but he knew that it was vital. Well do the writers remember traveling with him month after month in northern China, by cart and wheelbarrow with the poorest of inns at night. Often with only one large room for coolies and travelers alike, they would screen off a corner for their father and another for themselves, with curtains of some sort; and then, after sleep at last had brought a measure of quiet, they would hear a match struck and see the flicker of candlelight which told that Mr. Taylor, however weary, was pouring over the little bible in two volumes always at hand. From two to four a.m. was the time he usually gave to prayer; the time he could be most sure of being undisturbed to wait upon God.*[4]

The great English evangelist, John Wesley, made this statement about the importance of the Bible: *"I am a creature of a day. I am a spirit come from God, and returning to God. I want to know one thing the way to heaven. God himself has condescended to teach me the way. He has written it down in a book. Oh, give me that book!"*[5]

The Most Important Bible Readings that Should be Known to All

The Bible is a wonderful book. But many people, who are unfamiliar with its contents, have no clue where to begin to study or to read when they pick it up. Let me give you what I consider the most important readings in the Scriptures that everyone should know and be familiar with. Here is my irreducible minimum of Bible readings and topics.

1. The Creation Mandate — Genesis 1:26-28

> [26] *And God said, Let us make man in our image, after our likeness: and let them have dominion over the fish of the sea, and over the fowl of the air, and over the cattle, and over all the earth, and over every creeping thing that creepeth upon the earth. [27] So God created man in his own image, in the image of God created he him; male and female created he them. [28] And God blessed them, and God said unto them, Be fruitful, and multiply, and replenish the earth, and subdue it: and have dominion over the fish of the sea, and over the fowl of the air, and over every living thing that moveth upon the earth.*

2. The Fall of Man — Genesis 3:1-17

> [1] *Now the serpent was more subtil than any beast of the field which the* LORD *God had made. And he said unto the woman, Yea, hath God said, Ye shall not eat of every tree of the garden? [2] And the woman said unto the serpent, We may eat of the fruit of the trees of the garden: [3] But*

of the fruit of the tree which is in the midst of the garden, God hath said, Ye shall not eat of it, neither shall ye touch it, lest ye die. [4] And the serpent said unto the woman, Ye shall not surely die: [5] For God doth know that in the day ye eat thereof, then your eyes shall be opened, and ye shall be as gods, knowing good and evil. [6] And when the woman saw that the tree was good for food, and that it was pleasant to the eyes, and a tree to be desired to make one wise, she took of the fruit thereof, and did eat, and gave also unto her husband with her; and he did eat. [7] And the eyes of them both were opened, and they knew that they were naked; and they sewed fig leaves together, and made themselves aprons. [8] And they heard the voice of the LORD God walking in the garden in the cool of the day: and Adam and his wife hid themselves from the presence of the LORD God amongst the trees of the garden. [9] And the LORD God called unto Adam, and said unto him, Where art thou? [10] And he said, I heard thy voice in the garden, and I was afraid, because I was naked; and I hid myself. [11] And he said, Who told thee that thou wast naked? Hast thou eaten of the tree, whereof I commanded thee that thou shouldest not eat? [12] And the man said, The woman whom thou gavest to be with me, she gave me of the tree, and I did eat. [13] And the LORD God said unto the woman, What is this that thou hast done? And the woman said, The serpent beguiled me, and I did eat. [14] And the LORD God said unto the serpent, Because thou hast done this, thou art cursed above all cattle, and above every beast of the field; upon thy belly shalt thou go, and dust shalt thou eat all the days of thy life: [15] And I will put enmity between thee and the woman, and between thy seed and her seed; it shall bruise thy head, and thou shalt bruise his heel. [16] Unto the woman he said, I will greatly multiply thy sorrow and thy conception; in sorrow thou shalt bring forth children; and thy desire shall be to thy husband, and he shall rule over thee. [17] And unto Adam he said, Because thou hast hearkened unto the voice of thy wife, and hast eaten of the tree, of which I commanded thee, saying, Thou shalt not eat of it: cursed is the ground for thy sake; in sorrow shalt thou eat of it all the days of thy life;

3. The Ten Commandments — Exodus 20:1-17

[1] *And God spake all these words, saying, [2] I am the* Lord *thy God, which have brought thee out of the land of Egypt, out of the house of bondage. [3] Thou shalt have no other gods before me. [4] Thou shalt not make unto thee any graven image, or any likeness of any thing that is in heaven above, or that is in the earth beneath, or that is in the water under the earth. [5] Thou shalt not bow down thyself to them, nor serve them: for I the* Lord *thy God am a jealous God, visiting the iniquity of the fathers upon the children unto the third and fourth generation of them that hate me; [6] And shewing mercy unto thousands of them that love me, and keep my commandments. [7] Thou shalt not take the name of the* Lord *thy God in vain; for the* Lord *will not hold him guiltless that taketh his name in vain. [8] Remember the sabbath day, to keep it holy. [9] Six days shalt thou labor, and do all thy work: [10] But the seventh day is the sabbath of the* Lord *thy God: in it thou shalt not do any work, thou, nor thy son, nor thy daughter, thy manservant, nor thy maidservant, nor thy cattle, nor thy stranger that is within thy gates: [11] For in six days the* Lord *made heaven and earth, the sea, and all that in them is, and rested the seventh day: wherefore the* Lord *blessed the sabbath day, and hallowed it. [12] Honor thy father and thy mother: that thy days may be long upon the land which the* Lord *thy God giveth thee. [13] Thou shalt not kill. [14] Thou shalt not commit adultery. [15] Thou shalt not steal. [16] Thou shalt not bear false witness against thy neighbor. [17] Thou shalt not covet thy neighbor's house, thou shalt not covet thy neighbor's wife, nor his manservant, nor his maidservant, nor his ox, nor his ass, nor any thing that is thy neighbor's.*

4. The Birth of Christ — Matthew 1:18-25

[18] *Now the birth of Jesus Christ was on this wise: When as his mother Mary was espoused to Joseph, before they came together, she was found with child of the Holy Ghost. [19] Then Joseph her husband, being a just man, and not willing to make her a publick example, was minded to put her away privily. [20] But while he thought on these things, behold, the angel of the LORD appeared unto him in a dream, saying, Joseph, thou son of David, fear not to take unto thee Mary thy wife: for that which is conceived in her is of the Holy Ghost. [21] And she shall bring forth a son, and thou shalt call his name JESUS: for he shall save his people from their sins. [22] Now all this was done, that it might be fulfilled which was spoken of the Lord by the prophet, saying, [23] Behold, a virgin shall be with child, and shall bring forth a son, and they shall call his name Emmanuel, which being interpreted is, God with us. [24] Then Joseph being raised from sleep did as the angel of the Lord had bidden him, and took unto him his wife: [25] And knew her not till she had brought forth her firstborn son: and he called his name JESUS.*

5. The Crucifixion of Christ — John 19:16-24

[16] *Then delivered he him therefore unto them to be crucified. And they took Jesus, and led him away. [17] And he bearing his cross went forth into a place called the place of a skull, which is called in the Hebrew Golgotha: [18] Where they crucified him, and two other with him, on either side one, and Jesus in the midst. [19] And Pilate wrote a title, and put it on the cross. And the writing was JESUS OF NAZARETH THE KING OF THE JEWS. [20] This title then read many of the Jews: for the place where Jesus was crucified was nigh to the city: and it was written in Hebrew, and Greek, and Latin. [21] Then said the chief priests of the Jews to Pilate, Write not, The King of the Jews; but that he said, I am King of the Jews. [22] Pilate*

answered, What I have written I have written. [23] Then the soldiers, when they had crucified Jesus, took his garments, and made four parts, to every soldier a part; and also his coat: now the coat was without seam, woven from the top throughout. [24] They said therefore among themselves, Let us not rend it, but cast lots for it, whose it shall be: that the scripture might be fulfilled, which saith, They parted my raiment among them, and for my vesture they did cast lots. These things therefore the soldiers did.

6. The Resurrection of Christ — Luke 24:1-10

[1] Now upon the first day of the week, very early in the morning, they came unto the sepulchre, bringing the spices which they had prepared, and certain others with them. [2] And they found the stone rolled away from the sepulchre. [3] And they entered in, and found not the body of the Lord Jesus. [4] And it came to pass, as they were much perplexed thereabout, behold, two men stood by them in shining garments: [5] And as they were afraid, and bowed down their faces to the earth, they said unto them, Why seek ye the living among the dead? [6] He is not here, but is risen: remember how he spake unto you when he was yet in Galilee,[7] Saying, The Son of man must be delivered into the hands of sinful men, and be crucified, and the third day rise again [8] And they remembered his words, [9] And returned from the sepulchre, and told all these things unto the eleven, and to all the rest. [10] It was Mary Magdalene and Joanna, and Mary the mother of James, and other women that were with them, which told these things unto the apostles.

7. The Love of God — John 3:16

For God so loved the world, that he gave his only begotten Son, that whosoever believeth in him should not perish, but have everlasting life.

8. The Wrath of God — Romans 1:18-20

[18] *For the wrath of God is revealed from heaven against all ungodliness and unrighteousness of men, who hold the truth in unrighteousness; [19] Because that which may be known of God is manifest in them; for God hath shewed it unto them. [20] For the invisible things of him from the creation of the world are clearly seen, being understood by the things that are made, even his eternal power and Godhead; so that they are without excuse:*

9. The Beatitudes — Matthew 5:3-12

[3] *And seeing the multitudes, he went up into a mountain: and when he was set, his disciples came unto him: [2] And he opened his mouth, and taught them, saying, [3] Blessed are the poor in spirit: for theirs is the kingdom of heaven. [4] Blessed are they that mourn: for they shall be comforted. [5] Blessed are the meek: for they shall inherit the earth. [6] Blessed are they which do hunger and thirst after righteousness: for they shall be filled. [7] Blessed are the merciful: for they shall obtain mercy. [8] Blessed are the pure in heart: for they shall see God. [9] Blessed are the peacemakers: for they shall be called the children of God. [10] Blessed are they which are persecuted for righteousness' sake: for theirs is the kingdom of heaven. [11] Blessed are ye, when men shall revile you, and persecute you, and shall say all manner of evil against you falsely, for my sake. [12] Rejoice, and be exceeding glad: for great is your reward in heaven: for so persecuted they the prophets which were before you.*

10. The Nature of True Christian Love — 1 Corinthians 13

[1] *Though I speak with the tongues of men and of angels, and have not charity, I am become as sounding brass, or a tinkling cymbal. [2] And though I have the gift of prophecy, and understand all mysteries, and all knowledge; and*

though I have all faith, so that I could remove mountains, and have not charity, I am nothing. [3] And though I bestow all my goods to feed the poor, and though I give my body to be burned, and have not charity, it profiteth me nothing. [4] Charity suffereth long, and is kind; charity envieth not; charity vaunteth not itself, is not puffed up, [5] Doth not behave itself unseemly, seeketh not her own, is not easily provoked, thinketh no evil; [6] Rejoiceth not in iniquity, but rejoiceth in the truth; [7] Beareth all things, believeth all things, hopeth all things, endureth all things. [8] Charity never faileth: but whether there be prophecies, they shall fail; whether there be tongues, they shall cease; whether there be knowledge, it shall vanish away. [9] For we know in part, and we prophesy in part. [10] But when that which is perfect is come, then that which is in part shall be done away. [11] When I was a child, I spake as a child, I understood as a child, I thought as a child: but when I became a man, I put away childish things. [12] For now we see through a glass, darkly; but then face to face: now I know in part; but then shall I know even as also I am known. [13] And now abideth faith, hope, charity, these three; but the greatest of these is charity.

11. The Lord's Prayer — Matthew 6:9-13

[9] After this manner therefore pray ye: Our Father which art in heaven, Hallowed be thy name. [10] Thy kingdom come, Thy will be done in earth, as it is in heaven. [11] Give us this day our daily bread. [12] And forgive us our debts, as we forgive our debtors. [13] And lead us not into temptation, but deliver us from evil: For thine is the kingdom, and the power, and the glory, for ever. Amen.

12. The Apostle's Creed (not Scripture but a concise summary of the primary teachings of the Christian faith)

I believe in God the Father Almighty, maker of heaven and earth; And in Jesus Christ His only Son, our Lord;

who was conceived by the Holy Spirit, born of the Virgin
Mary, suffered under Pontius Pilate, was crucified, dead
and buried; He descended into hades; the third day He
rose again from the dead; He ascended into heaven, and
sitteth on the right hand of God, the Father Almighty; from
thence He shall come to judge the quick and the dead. I
believe in the Holy Spirit, the holy Christian church, the
communion of saints, the forgiveness of sins, the resurrection of the body, and the life everlasting. Amen.

13. The New Heaven and the New Earth — Revelation 21:1-5

[1] *And I saw a new heaven and a new earth: for the first
heaven and the first earth were passed away; and there
was no more sea. [2] And I John saw the holy city, new
Jerusalem, coming down from God out of heaven, prepared as a bride adorned for her husband. [3] And I heard
a great voice out of heaven saying, Behold, the tabernacle
of God is with men, and he will dwell with them, and they
shall be his people, and God himself shall be with them,
and be their God. [4] And God shall wipe away all tears
from their eyes; and there shall be no more death, neither
sorrow, nor crying, neither shall there be any more pain:
for the former things are passed away. [5] And he that sat
upon the throne said, Behold, I make all things new. And
he said unto me, Write: for these words are true and faithful.*

Master these texts. Know the contents of these passages and readings. This would be a great place to begin reading the Bible. But
having learned these passages, here has been my plan of Bible
reading over the years.

1. I try to read five chapters of the Psalms and one chapter of
    Proverbs every day. By doing this, I go through the Psalms
    and Proverbs once a month. These two books are a part of the
    wisdom literature of the Old Testament. Wisdom and devotion
    to God are greatly increased by this little plan.

2. I am always reading one of the four gospels, Matthew, Mark, Luke, and John. These gospels are a recording of the life of Jesus Christ our Lord. I feel one should never have his or her eyes off the life and teachings of our Lord and Savior Jesus Christ.

3. I believe a new Christian should read the gospel of John as the first book. When I became a Christian, I read John's gospel first and then went back and read through the entire New Testament.

4. When January rolls around, it would be good for every person to begin to read the Bible through from cover to cover. If everyone did this each year, their knowledge of the Bible would be greatly increased. To do this, one should read five chapters a day from the Old Testament and three chapters from the New Testament.

5. When I pour over my Bible in my morning devotions I am like the man in Proverbs searching for silver and hidden treasures. *"If thou seekest her as silver, and searchest for her as for hid treasures; then shalt thou understand the fear of the Lord, and find the knowledge of God."* Proverbs 2:4-5 I mark key words that I need to define and explore their deeper meaning. I pause to meditate on certain phrases or thoughts that speak to my soul. I pray over the text and plead with God to form these commandments and teachings in my daily walk and life. I search the Scriptures like a man searching for precious gold and silver. This is the way all of us must read and study the Word of God.

The great English Baptist minister, C. H. Spurgeon, challenged his young students who were preparing for ministry to study and grow intellectually by reading the Scriptures and reading widely in many areas of thought. Spurgeon spurred them on with these comments:

> *We must, I say, make every effort to acquire information, especially of a Biblical kind. We must not confine ourselves to one topic of study, or we shall not exercise our whole mental manhood. God made the world for man, and He*

made man with a mind intended to occupy and use all the world; he is the tenant, and nature is for a while his house; why should he shut himself out of any of its rooms[6]

On another occasion, Spurgeon made this comment about John Bunyan, the great English preacher who wrote *Pilgrims's Progress*: "*Prick him anywhere; and you will find that his blood is Bibline, the very essence of the Bible flows from him. He cannot speak without quoting a text, for his soul is full of the Word of God.*"[7]

There is simply no excuse for any of us not to read the Bible every day. It is our daily bread. The Bible is food for our souls. To go without the Bible on a daily basis is like going without food and water. To neglect to eat or drink would kill us physically. So too, to neglect the Word of God is to eventually shrivel up and die spiritually. I read a story recently that moved my heart and made me realize how fortunate I was to be able to read my Bible every day. Listen to what this author has to say about reading the Scriptures daily:

The Bible is food for our souls.

In his book *The Wonders of the Word of God*, evangelist Robert L. Sumner tells about a man who was severely injured in a terrible explosion. The man's face was badly disfigured and he lost his eyesight as well as both hands. He had recently become a new Christian, and one of his greatest disappointments was that he could no longer read the Bible. Then he heard about a lady in England who read Braille with her lips. Hoping to do the same, he sent for some books of the Bible in Braille. Much to his dismay, however, he discovered that the explosion had also destroyed the nerve endings in his lips. But one day, as he brought one of the Braille pages to his lips, his tongue happened to touch a few of the raised characters and he could feel them. In a flash he thought, *I can read the Bible using my tongue*. At the time Robert Sumner wrote his book, the man had read through the entire Bible four times.[8]

My father-in-law, an old southern evangelist, Dr. Del Fehsenfeld, used to say:

> "Read the Bible through.
> Pray the Bible in.
> Live the Bible out.
> Pass the Bible on.
> And you'll not have any trouble standing on your feet."

That the Bible will have a powerful impact on our Christian lives and transform us by its amazing message is a fact that none can deny. I suggest that there can be no Christian living without having the Bible as a fundamental part of one's worldview. Dr. D. James Kennedy records the impact that the Bible had on a man who was a professed and arrogant atheist.

> Henry Stanley said that in the 1880's, when he entered the interior of Africa, he was the most swaggering atheist in the world. In the depths of the jungles of central Africa he came upon David Livingston — a man so mild, so meek, and yet so firm and so definite in his purpose and desire to proclaim the gospel. Stanley lived in that man's tent for months and listened to Livingston read from his little Bible day by day. As a result, the most swaggering atheist in the world was transformed by the gospel of Jesus Christ and was brought to the Savior.[9]

There is a poem about the Bible that I have written on the inside cover of my personal Bible that I use when I preach. This poem encourages, inspires, and challenges me.

The Bible

> Though the cover is worn, and pages are torn,
> And places bear traces of tears,
> Yet more precious than gold, is this book worn and old,
> That can shatter and scatter my fears.

When I prayerfully look, in this precious old book,
As my eyes scan the pages I see,
Many tokens of love from the Father above,
Who is nearest and dearest to me.
This old book is my guide, 'tis a friend by my side,
It will lighten and brighten my way.
And each promise I find soothes and gladdens my mind.
As I read it and heed it today.

How to Get Started

1. Begin to read your Bible every day.
2. Have a specific place and time set aside in your schedule to be alone with God to study the Scripture.
3. I would suggest that you purchase Matthew Henry's Commentary on the Bible (the single volume that is abridged) and keep it with you when you study the Bible.
4. Make sure you are attending a Bible believing church where the gospel is preached. The Scripture admonishes us, *"Not forsaking the assembling or ourselves together, as the manner of some is...."* Hebrews 10:25

Thoughts for Consideration

- *"Never let good books take the place of the Bible. Drink from the well, not from the streams that flow from the well."* Amy Carmichael

- *"The Bible, the whole Bible, and nothing but the Bible is the religion of Christ's church."* C. H. Spurgeon

- *"A partially inspired Bible is little better than no Bible at all."* J. C. Ryle

- *"As we go to the cradle only in order to find the baby, so we go to the Scriptures only to find Christ."* Martin Luther

- *"The Bible is a letter God has sent to us; prayer is a letter we send to him."* Matthew Henry

- *"He who has the Holy Spirit in his heart and the Scriptures in his hands has all he needs."* Alexander MacLaren

- *"We believe that the most scientific view, the most up-to-date and rationalistic conception, will find its fullest satisfaction in taking the Bible story literally."* Winston Churchill

- *"Nothing has affected the rise and fall of civilization, the character of cultures, the structure of governments, and the lives of the inhabitants of this planet as profoundly as the words of the Bible."* Charles Colson

- *"The Bible is alive, it speaks to me; it has feet, it runs after me; it has hands, it lays hold on me."* Martin Luther

- *"All things desirable to men are contained in the Bible."* Abraham Lincoln

- *"It is impossible to rightly govern the world without God and the Bible."* George Washington

Questions for Discussion

1. How can reading the Bible keep us from sin?

2. Why is the Bible the most important book ever written?

3. What are some of the most important passages in the Bible that we should know?

4. What is your plan for reading and studying the Bible?

5. What is the central message in the Bible?

6. What is your favorite passage in the Bible?

6
Walking with God

"And Enoch walked with God; and he was not; for God took Him." Genesis 5:24

"It is such a small step from close communion with God on earth to perfect communion with God in Heaven."[1] C. H. Spurgeon

I will never forget when I was a teenager and a new Christian, I went to the first Baptist Church of Pontiac, Michigan to hear pastor Robert Shelton. Pastor Shelton spoke on the text of Genesis 5:24. I will always consider that message one of the highlights of my Christian life. My pastor ignited within me, by the power of the Holy Spirit, an intense desire to know the true and living God. He stirred my soul to think of the joys, the possibilities, and the wonder of walking with God through the days and the years of my life. The intense longing that that message created in my heart to walk with God has never left me. Through these many years, since that day, I have had one great passion in my life. I want to be a man of God that walks with the Lord on a daily basis.

Commenting on Genesis 5:24, C. H. Spurgeon shared these thoughts:

> *Enoch walked with God 400 years; what a long walk that was! What a splendid journey through life! Why should not you begin, dear Christian brother, today, if you have not begun, and walk with God through the few years which remain? Oh to get up above yon mists which dim the valley! Oh to climb the mountain's top which laughs in the*

sunlight! Oh to get away from the heavy atmosphere of worldliness and doubt, of fear, of care, of fretfulness; to soar away from the worldlings who are always earth-hunting, digging into its mines and prying after its treasures, and to get up there where God dwells in the innermost circle of heavenly seclusion; where none can live but men who have been quickened from among the dead; where none can walk but men who are crucified with Christ, and who live only in him. Oh to get up there! where no more question concerning our security can molest us; where no carking care can disturb because all is cast upon the Lord, and rests wholly with him. Oh to live in such an entireness of confidence and childlike faith that we will have nothing to do with anything now except with serving him and showing forth the gratitude we owe to him who has done so much for us. Christ has called you to fellowship with himself, and he is not in the grave now. He is risen! rise you! He is ascended! ascend with him and learn what this meaneth, "He hath raised us up together and made us sit together in heavenly places in Christ Jesus."[2]

To walk with God means to be in fellowship with Him. Those who walk with God are people who sincerely desire to know God and fellowship with Him in their inner lives. It is easy to go through life faking it and being pretenders. How repulsive it is to meet hypocritical self-servers and how refreshing to meet sincere servants of the living God. Someone has astutely remarked,

Both in history and in life it is a phenomenon by no means rare to meet with comparatively unlettered people who seem to have struck profound spiritual depths…while there are many highly educated people of whom one feels that they are performing clever antics with their minds to cover a gaping hollowness that lies within.[3]

Those who walk with God have learned the secret of having quiet times with Him in personal devotion. There can be no growth in grace, no development of soul or spiritual progress made if we do not spend much time alone with God. Those who truly know the Lord find that the most satisfying moments of their lives are during their private devotions with Christ. Walking with God means spending time with Him in personal and private devotion. In his autobiography Elton Trueblood writes:

> *Those who walk with God have learned the secret of having quiet times with Him in personal devotion.*

> A public man, though he is necessarily available at many times, must learn to hide. If he is always available, he is not worth enough when he is available. I once wrote a chapter in the Cincinnati Union Station, but that was itself a form of hiding because nobody knew who the man with the writing pad was. Consequently nobody approached me during five wonderful hours until the departure of the next train to Richmond. We must use the time which we have because even at best there is never enough.[4]

Walking with God means you have a passion to learn more about this great God who loves you and who saved you. God is inexhaustible. Even after a lifetime spent in communing with Him there will still be so much that we will never fully grasp or understand. But the joy of searching, learning, and growing is worth every effort made to study to know this wonderful King who rules our world and our lives. One author summed it up nicely with this comment:

> Your appetite for learning will motivate you to keep seeking the Lord. Walking with the Lord is about learning more about Him…His ways…His will…and His plan for the world. You will never tire of the knowledge you will gain about the Lord. It is inexhaustible and unfathomable. But it is worth searching out.[5]

Walking with God means to become more like Him as we grow in our faith. One way to evaluate our growth in grace is to consider how Christ-like we are becoming. To do this we simply need to look at the fruit of the Spirit described in Galatians 5:22-23. In that text the apostle Paul says, *"But the fruit of the Spirit is love, joy, peace, longsuffering, gentleness, goodness, faith, meekness, temperance: against such there is no law."* Commenting on these fruits of the Spirit author Jim Berg writes:

> *Being Christlike…means acquiring His communicable attributes — those generally known as the 'fruit of the Spirit.' Galatians 5:22-23 lists several facets of the Spirit's fruit. It lists the following:*
>
> - *Love — genuine self-sacrifice for the good of others*
> - *Joy — a feeling of great pleasure and delight in who God is and what He has provided*
> - *Peace — a sense of well-being; rest; tranquility; contentment*
> - *Longsuffering — stability under pressure; self-control under provocation from people*
> - *Gentleness — kindness toward others; reasonableness; flexibility*
> - *Goodness — benevolent thoughts and actions toward others; generosity*
> - *Faith — faithfulness; reliability*
> - *Meekness — willingness to be governed; submissive attitude toward authority and circumstances*
> - *Temperance — self-control, especially of one's passions*[6]

Walking with God involves cultivating an intimacy with Him that satisfies the soul as nothing else can do. An American pilot shot down over North Vietnam and held prisoner shares with us the importance and benefits that an intimate walk with God can provide in the dark times of life.

*During those longer periods of enforced reflection it be-
came so much easier to separate the important from the
trivial, the worthwhile from the waste. For example, in the
past, I usually worked or played hard on Sundays and had
no time for church. For years Phyllis [his wife] had encouraged me to join the family at church. She never nagged
or scolded — she just kept hoping. But I was too busy,
too preoccupied, to spend one or two short hours a week
thinking about the really important things.*

*Now the sights and sounds and smells of death were
all around me. My hunger for spiritual food soon outdid
my hunger for a steak. Now I wanted to know about that
part of me that will never die. Now I wanted to talk about
God and Christ and the church. But in Heartbreak (the
name POWs gave their prison camp) solitary confinement,
there was no pastor, no Sunday-school teacher, no Bible,
no hymnbook, no community of believers to guide and
sustain me. I had completely neglected the spiritual di-
mension of my life. It took prison to show me how empty
life is without God.*[7]

Walking with God means loving those principles that the Scriptures teach us about spiritual life. This means obeying the commands of the Apostle Paul to:

1. Be filled with the Spirit — this is based on Ephesians 5:18
   that says, "*And be not drunk with wine, wherein is excess, but
   be filled with the Spirit.*" This is a command expressed in the
   present tense of the verb. It means literally "Be continually
   being filled with the Spirit of God." How do we do this? I try
   to begin each day by praying that God will fill me with His
   Holy Spirit. When we became Christians we were indwelled
   by God's Spirit. In seeking to be filled with the Spirit we are
   not asking to get more of the Spirit for He already is indwelling us. What we are asking is that the Holy Spirit might have
   more of us. I not only pray this way at the beginning of each
   day; I pray this many times a day and before every special
   occasion that might arise where I need a fresh outpouring of

God's Spirit in my life. British author Stuart Olyott explains in his commentary on Ephesians what it means to be filled with the Holy Spirit,

> ...how do we get filled? Verse 18 [Ephesians 5:18] makes everything clear. How does a person get drunk with wine? He drinks and drinks and drinks again, until what he has drunk takes control. The same principle applies in the spiritual realm. We must drink spiritual things until we are under the Spirit's influence...being constantly filled with the Spirit is a matter of constantly drinking. We are to go to Christ and drink of Him. We do this in prayer, listening to biblical preaching, studying God's Word for ourselves, engaging in Christian fellowship, meeting around the Lord's table, and in every form of spiritual and devotional exercise.[8]

2. Bear the fruit of the Spirit in our lives — this means that as we are filled with the Spirit of God the fruits of the Spirit that are listed in Galatians 5:22-23 will be manifested in our everyday living. There are nine fruits that the Apostle Paul mentions: love, joy, peace, longsuffering, gentleness, goodness, faith, meekness, and temperance. When we are filled with the Holy Spirit these fruits will be visible in our daily actions and responses to people and situations. When I find that I am not behaving well I can always trace it back to the fact that I am not filled with the Spirit and as a result I am not walking in the influence of the Spirit's presence in my life.

3. Put to death the works of the flesh — this idea of putting to death the works of the flesh is found in the teachings of the Apostle Paul. Paul tells the people at Colosse to mortify the flesh. The word "mortify" is from a Greek word that means "to put to death." In Colossians 3:5 the apostle says, "*Mortify therefore your members which are upon the earth, fornication, uncleanness, inordinate affection, evil concupiscence, and covetousness, which is idolatry.*" The word "members" refers to our various body parts. The Apostle Paul is not saying that

we should literally kill or cut off our hands, feet, or head. This is a figure of speech called metonymy where our various limbs or body parts are used to represent the various actions that we use with them. What we are being told to do in this passage of Colossians 3:5 is to put to death the behaviors, attitudes, and actions that we commit with our body, mind, and soul. This is a serious command. The apostle knows that if we do not wage war on the activities that he has listed in Colossians 3:5 such as fornication (immoral behavior), uncleanness (dirty and filthy way of thinking and living), inordinate affection (sinful and evil passions), evil concupiscence (evil desires and tendencies burning out of control), and covetousness (the unlawful desire of the material or property of others), we will be destroyed and damned by these activities. The Christian is one who is putting these things to death in his or her life. If we fail to do this we will be destroyed by these sins and they will eventually lead our souls to death and judgment before a holy God.

Over the years there have been a number of people that I have observed that taught me by their example much about walking with God. My first pastor, Robert Shulton, under whose ministry I sat in Pontiac, Michigan, was one such man. My father-in-law, Dr. Del Fehsenfeld, and my brother-in-law, Del Fehsenfeld, Jr. also stirred my heart. My spiritual mentors, Pastor Bill Tipton, Vernon Higham, and Edgar Andrews have also fueled my desire to walk with God.

In the same way, I have found that reading the biographies of the great heroes of the faith have filled my heart with the passionate desire to walk with the Lord. Biographies on such men as George Whitefield, C. H. Spurgeon, John G. Paton, Robert Murray McCheyne, Martyn Lloyd-Jones, and Jim Eliot are treasures of inspiration to feast upon.

The importance of walking with God should be self evident. How thrilling it is to go through life while developing a personal and intimate friendship with the Son of God, the Lord Jesus Christ. How precious are those times that are spent in His presence, learning at His feet, and listening to the voice of His Word. What joy and peace belong to the one who walks with God! There is nothing in life that can compare to the joy of walking with the Lord. The Psalmist cried out in Psalm 42:1-2, "*As the hart* [deer] *panteth after the water brooks, so panteth my soul after thee, O God. My soul thirsteth for God, for the living God...*" All those who walk with God have known this intense longing of the soul to know and fellowship with God. God is our delight. God becomes the greatest joy of our lives. When God is your friend, the passion of your life, and the supreme goal of your future, you will know the complete satisfaction that only He can give. The British author, C. S. Lewis, once wrote: "*We are half-hearted creatures, fooling around with drink and sex and ambition when infinite joy is offered us, like an ignorant child who wants to go on making mud pies in a slum because he cannot imagine what is meant by the offer of a holiday at the sea.*"[9]

> *When God is your friend, the passion of your life, and the supreme goal of your future, you will know the complete satisfaction that only He can give.*

When developing a biblical worldview, make sure that your heart is fixed on this great principle of learning early in life the joys and the privileges of walking with God. Christian living means that Christians must learn how to walk with God. When we walk with God, we are showing others by our own example what it means to be a follower of Christ. By our example, witness, and prayers, we can bring others to a saving knowledge of Jesus Christ. A famous Scottish Christian, Sir Harry Lauder, was sharing an incident that he witnessed one night at the hotel where he was staying with friends. This story is an illustration of what walking with God should accomplish in the lives of those around us.

> *I was sitting in the gloamin', an' a man passed the window. He was the lamplighter. He pushed his pole into the lamp and lighted it. Then he went to another and another. Now I couldn't see him. But I knew where he was by the lights as they broke out down the street, until he had left a beautiful*

avenue of light. Ye're a' lamplighter. They'll know where ye've been by the lights ye have lit.[10]

All those who walk with God will be like this lamplighter. They will be instruments in the hands of God to light up the lives of those who live in spiritual darkness.

The prophet Micah gives us this scriptural advice on walking with God, *"He hath shewed thee, O man, what is good; and what doth the Lord require of thee, but to do justly, and to love mercy, and to walk humbly with thy God."* Micah 6:8 This passage in Micah has been called the Micah Mandate. In this text the Lord reveals what He expects of those who walk with Him. God would have us practice righteousness in our daily living. Righteousness is simply doing the things that are right and commanded of us in His Word. God would also have us be merciful in all dealings with our fellow man. And finally, the Lord would have us walk every day of our lives in humble obedience and joyful worship before His presence.

To walk with God involves humility. Christian author Bob Russell relates this note from history on the importance of humility in the Christian life:

> *In the chapel of the Nativity in Bethlehem, the entrance is so low that everyone has to stoop to get in, but if you stand back from the doorway, you can see the outline of an old door that was much larger. It is said that in the Middle Ages, the knights would come to the chapel seeking the priest's blessing before they went on their crusades. Often a knight would proudly ride right through the door and expect to receive a blessing without even dismounting from his horse. The priests finally blocked up the old doorway and made the entrance so small that no one could come seeking God's blessing without getting off his horse and bowing low when he came into the presence of God. God opposes the proud but gives grace to the humble.*[11]

Walking with God in Christian humility is not easy. It cuts against the flow of our fallen human nature that always craves attention, self-advancement, and praise from others. Learning the secret of walking humbly with God in lowly service to others is a much-needed lesson for all to learn. Leonard Bernstein, a great symphony conductor, was once asked by a friend what was the most difficult instrument to play. It is said that he replied by saying, "*Second fiddle.*"

There is a joy found in walking with God and developing a personal relationship with Him. The people in the world who are not Christians know nothing of this great joy. Lewis Sperry Chafer, the founder of Dallas Theological Seminary, commented on the emptiness that even many Christians have: "*Much of our Christian life is nothing more than a cheap anesthetic to deaden the pain of an empty life.*"[12]

> *Much of our Christian life is nothing more than a cheap anesthetic to deaden the pain of an empty life.*

A. W. Tozer said something very similar: "*May not the inadequacy of much of our spiritual experience be traced back to our habit of skipping through the corridor of the kingdom like children in the marketplace, always chattering about everything, but learning the true value of nothing.*"[13]

When I was a young man growing up and learning the joys of walking with God, I read a little book by a wonderful man of God named Oswald J. Smith. In this book he had written a poem entitled, *I Walked Alone With Jesus.*

> "*I walked alone with Jesus*
> *in a fellowship divine,*
> *Never more can earth allure me,*
> *for I am His and He is mine.*
>
> *In my failure sin and sorrow,*
> *Broken hearted crushed and torn.*
> *I have felt His presence near me,*
> *He has all my burdens born.*

In the darkness, in the shadows,
with the Savior I have trod,
Sweet indeed have been the blessings,
since I walked alone with God.

On the mountain I have seen Him,
Christ my Comforter and Friend
And the glory of His presence
Will be with me to the end.

I have seen Him, I have known Him,
And He deigns to walk with me;
And the glory of His presence will
be mine eternally.

Oh, the glory of His presence,
Oh, the beauty of His face,
I am His and His forever,
He has saved me by His grace."

Oswald J. Smith

As we walk with God in life, we will be used by the Lord to reach many others with the wonderful message of Jesus Christ. This is what life is all about. We should be passionate about making a difference in the lives of others. If we are negligent in our walk and witness, we may one day in eternity feel the sorrow and the shame of having missed so many opportunities to serve, help, and witness to others. This poem entitled *You Forgot My Soul* by an unknown author hauntingly reminds us of the importance of walking with God.

You Forgot My Soul

You lived next door to me for years;
We shared our dreams, our joys and tears.
A friend to me you were indeed,
A friend who helped me when in need.

My faith in you was strong and sure.
We had such trust as should endure.
No "words" between us could impose;
Our friends were like — and so, our foes.

What sadness, then, my friend, to find
That, after all, you weren't so kind;
The day my life on earth did end,
I found you weren't a faithful friend.

For all those years we spent on earth,
You never talked of second birth.
You never spoke of my lost soul
And of the Christ Who'd make me whole.

I'm lost today eternally
And tell you now my earnest plea.
You cannot do a thing for me —
No words today my bonds will free.

But — do not err, my friend, again —
Do all you can for souls of men.
Plead now with them quite earnestly,
Lest they be cast in hell with me.

Author Unknown

Those who walk with God will by their daily life, example, and words share with others the precious gospel of Jesus Christ. It is impossible to truly walk with God and continually fail to tell others about their need of Jesus Christ.

How to Get Started

1. Remember there is no greater adventure in life, and certainly nothing more thrilling than walking with God every day.

2. Every Christian should make a commitment to walk with God.
3. This means developing an intimacy with Him. This comes as we pray and seek His face. God spoke through the Prophet Jeremiah and said, *"And ye shall seek me and find me when ye search for me with all your heart."* Jeremiah 29:13
4. Commit your life to humility and purity, and pray to be conformed to the image of Christ.
5. Ask God to help you love what He loves and hate what He hates.
6. Begin every day by asking the Lord to fill you with His Holy Spirit.

Thoughts for Consideration

• *"If we love Christ our devotion will not remain a secret."* Anonymous

• *"True love for Christ will mean hatred of sin."* John Benton

• *"The church has no greater need today than to fall in love with Jesus all over again."* Vance Havner

• *"I would hate my own soul if I did not find it loving God."* Augustine

• *"Love to God is the essence of all virtue."* Augustus H. Strong

• *"It does not take great men to do great things; it only takes consecrated men."* Phillips Brooks

• *"He is no fool who gives up what he cannot keep, to gain the things that he cannot lose."* Jim Elliot

• *"When I really enjoy God, I feel my desires of Him more insatiable and my thirstings after holiness more unquenchable."* David Brainerd

• *"Apathy toward God is the result of being passionate toward something or someone else."* Jim Berg

• *"Nothing in life can compare with the thrill of knowing God and knowing he knows you."* Charles E. Jones

Questions for Discussion

1. What does it mean to walk with God?

2. What is necessary to walk with God on a daily basis?

3. Why is it important to walk with God in our youth?

4. How does having a specific time of private Bible study every day help us to walk with God?

5. List, in your own words, some of the benefits we gain if we walk with God.

6. As you evaluate your present spiritual condition — are you walking with God?

Part II: The Practical Aspects of Christian Living

7
Using Our Time Wisely

"Redeeming the time, because the days are evil." Ephesians 5:16

"The heights by great men reached and kept
Were not attained by sudden flight,
But they, while their companions slept,
Were toiling upward in the night."[1]

Henry Wadsworth Longfellow

There are few things that are as valuable as the time that the Lord has given to us. Time is precious because it is a gift from God. How we use our time tells us a great deal about ourselves. In developing a biblical worldview for Christian living, we need to be sure that it includes a biblical understanding of the gift of time.

The proper use and management of time is one thing that all great Christians and leaders have in common. No leader who has ever achieved success was handed that success on a platter. Great leaders and successful people become great by the performance of unseen habits, duties, and practices that they perform every day while others are sleeping. The Russian author

Great leaders and successful people become great by the performance of unseen habits, duties, and practices that they perform every day while others are sleeping.

Dostoevsky, when writing to his brother, made this confession about his misuse of the gift of time:

> *When I look back at my past and think how much time I wasted on nothing, how much time has been lost in futilities, errors, laziness, incapacity to live; how little I appreciated it, how many times I sinned against my heart and soul — then my heart bleeds. Life is a gift. Life is happiness, every minute can be an eternity of happiness! Si la jeunesse savait! [If youth only knew].[2]*

Time Management is a Stewardship before God

Time is a stewardship of which we must give an account to the Lord one day. There is no escaping this. We must all stand before our Creator and give an account for how we used the precious time that was given to us at birth. J. Oswald Sanders in his book, *Paul the Leader*, gives us these rules for the wise use of our time:

1. Set priorities and have a definite schedule.
2. Avoid time wasters, be they people or activities.
3. Don't waste time tinkering around.

These three rules by J. Oswald Sanders, if followed carefully, will help us to avoid becoming procrastinators. A procrastinator is someone who is always putting off present duty. The simple but wise advice, "Do it now!" will ensure that we don't fall victim to the curse of procrastination. The missionary David Livingston is an amazing example of how a person can harness their time and make it count.

> *David Livingston used to work in a cotton mill in his native Dumbarton from six in the morning until eight at night. He commenced work when he was ten. He could surely have been excused if he pleaded that he had no time for study. But so purposefully did he utilize his "leisure" hours that he mastered Latin and could read Horace and Virgil with*

ease before he was sixteen. By the time he was twenty-seven, he had battled his way through a medical course, as well as a course in theology.[3]

Time Management Takes Discipline

To manage our time wisely takes discipline. A disciplined life will be a fruitful and successful life. If we are developing a Christian worldview with the goal of knowing success in our lives then being people who are disciplined in our use of time is absolutely essential. Bible scholar William Barclay made this sobering observation of the undisciplined life of Samuel Taylor Coleridge:

A disciplined life will be a fruitful and successful life.

Coleridge is the supreme tragedy of indiscipline. Never did so great a mind produce so little. He left Cambridge University to join the army; he left the army because he could not rub down a horse; he returned to Oxford and left without a degree. He began a paper called The Watchman *which lived for ten numbers and then died. It has been said of him: "he lost himself in visions of work to be done, that always remained to be done. Coleridge had every poetic gift but one — the gift of sustained and concentrated effort." In his head and in his mind he had all kinds of books, as he said, himself, "completed save for transcription. I am on the even," he says, "of sending to the press two octavo volumes." But the books were never composed outside Coleridge's mind, because he would not face the discipline of sitting down to write them out. No one ever reached any eminence, and no one having reached it ever maintained it, without discipline.*[4]

In seeking to plan our time to the best advantage, it may be helpful to bear the following suggestions in mind:

1. Everyone has been entrusted with the same amount of time.
2. God's plan leaves sufficient time for the fulfillment of all His will for each day.
3. The Lord expects of us daily only what is reasonable and achievable.
4. When we select our priorities carefully, they should not conflict with our obvious duties.
5. The conflicts and pressures we experience usually arise as we confuse human desires or pressures — either our own or those of someone else — with the duties God expects us to fulfill.
6. Time is too valuable to be spent on secondary matters when primary matters are screaming for attention.
7. "I didn't have time" is usually the unconscious confession of someone who is making a wrong choice of priorities.[5]

Time Management Takes Wisdom

I have tried to instill into my children and those who come to my church the wise use of time. It takes a great deal of wisdom and courage to not be robbed of our time. We need to set priorities, and we need to make sure that we do not allow things that are not important or essential to our calling to rob us of our time. We need to avoid those things that waste our time. We need to avoid those individuals who would waste our time. Time is too valuable to waste on nonessentials. There is nothing wrong with taking time for disciplined relaxation or rest, but we must be careful of wasting huge chunks of our days doing nothing of value.

Here are some practical observations about time that we need to remember:

1. We need to use our time wisely because by doing so, we are, in fact, preparing for eternity where we will give an account to the Lord for the time He allowed us in life.
2. Because time is short, and it is a gift from God, it is extremely valuable.
3. Because the remaining time we have on earth is uncertain, we should use it wisely. We may have many years left, or we may have few. Let us use it wisely, one day at a time.

4. We must never forget that lost time cannot be regained. *"Only one life, 'twill soon be past, Only what's done for Christ will last!"*
5. We must remember how easily time can be squandered and lost. How easy it is to lose time, to have it stolen from us by time-robbers and time-wasters. Once lost, time is gone forever. We cannot buy it back! On his death bed, French infidel Voltaire said to his doctor, *"I will give you half of what I am worth if you will give me six months' life."* Similarly, another skeptic from England said when he was dying, *"If I had the whole world, I would give it to live one day."*[6]
6. Finally, we should not forget the great value of time as it is regarded in heaven. There, we will all be grateful for the time we spent for the Lord, and we will be remorseful for the time that we wasted on earth.

Time Management Leads to Success

Someone once said that *"When the time to perform has arrived, the time to prepare has past."* I don't know who said this, but it is very wise and very true. Use your time wisely. If you have worked hard and have made all sacrifices necessary for your preparation, then when the time comes to perform, you will have the confidence you need to get the job done.

> *When the time to perform has arrived, the time to prepare has past.*

Let us not forget that to be successful in life as a parent, athlete, worker, husband, or wife, takes a great deal of planning and time. Time is what life is made of. Let's not waste it! Learn the secret that time is a gift from God. One great secret in life is to realize that your time, if used wisely, can be invested to impact future generations. *"Philosopher William James affirmed that the great use of one's life is to spend it for something that will outlast it, for the value of life is computed not by its duration but by its donation. Not how long we live, but how fully and how well."*[7]

For those who are seeking to develop a Christian worldview let me suggest some things that should be a part of the routine of your daily life and walk with God. Make sure that you have time for:

1. Daily personal devotions — begin and end each day with the Lord. The great Baptist preacher C. H. Spurgeon once said, *"When thou liest down in the evening look to Him, and when thou risest up in the morning look to Him."*
2. Daily family devotions.
3. Daily prayer.
4. Attending the services of the church where you worship. A good rule of thumb should be when the doors are open and services are being held you should be there unless providentially hindered.
5. Your wife or husband.
6. Your children.

Gordon MacDonald who wrote an immensely practical book *Ordering Your Private World*, said this about the need to be conscious of using time wisely in life: *"Fred Mitchell, a leader in world missions, used to keep a motto on his desk that read, 'Beware of the Barrenness of a Busy life."*[8] Speaking of busy people MacDonald also said,

> [Busy people] *rarely think they have accomplished enough, they seize every available minute to attend more meetings, to study more material, to initiate more projects. They operate on the precept that a reputation for busyness is a sign of success and personal importance. Thus they attempt to impress people with the fullness of their schedule. They may even express a high level of self-pity, bemoaning the "trap" of responsibility they claim to be in, wishing aloud that there was some possible release from all that they have to live with. But just try to suggest a way out!*
>
> *The truth is that the very worst thing that could happen to them would be if someone provided them with a way out. They really wouldn't know what to do with themselves if there were suddenly less to do. Busyness for the driven person becomes a habit, a way of life and thought.*

They find it enjoyable to complain and gather pity, and they would probably not want it any different. But tell a driven person that, and you'll make him angry.[9]

Time Management is Essential to Christian Living

Knowing how to use our time wisely is one of the secrets of Christian living. Developing a Christian worldview must include the wise management of one's time. This was understood by one author who made these comments on laziness and what the Bible teaches about the slothful man:

> *While Christians should maintain a healthy balance between work and rest, we should not be lazy. The Book of Proverbs is filled with condemnation for the lazy or slothful person. According to Proverbs, the lazy person will...*
>
> a. *be poor (Proverbs 10:4)*
> b. *irritate those around him (Proverbs 10:26)*
> c. *serve someone else (Proverbs 12:24)*
> d. *never be satisfied (Proverbs 13:4)*
> e. *have difficult obstacles to overcome (Proverbs 15:19)*
> f. *be paranoid of unrealistic danger (Proverbs 22:13)*
>
> *When we are lazy, we bring disgrace to ourselves and are a poor reflection of the character of God. When we work hard, we honor God.*[10]

Rest Time is Not Wasted Time

Let it be understood that taking time to rest and replenish your strength and health is not wasted time. An old saying goes that *"sometimes we may do more by doing less."* Pastor David Ireland tells a story that clearly illustrates this point:

> *One day a man challenged another to an all-day wood-chopping contest. The challenger worked very hard, stop-*

ping only for a brief lunch break. The other man had a leisurely lunch and took several breaks during the day. At the end of the day, the challenger was surprised and annoyed to find that the other fellow had chopped substantially more wood than he had. "I don't get it," he said. "Every time I checked, you were taking a rest, yet you chopped more wood than I did." "But you didn't notice," said the winning woodsman, "that when I sat down to rest, I was sharpening my ax."[11]

In building a Christian worldview for the purpose of seeking success in one's life, don't make the mistake of thinking that being busy is the equivalent of being successful. MacDonald has it right. Often busy people are living barren and meaningless lives. Know how to use your time wisely for it is a gift from God, and once spent can never be brought back again.

How to Get Started

1. Remember that time wasted can never be retrieved.
2. Remember that the judgment is approaching fast. We will give account of our time to God.
3. Make a list of your priorities. Make sure they are things that please the Lord and then pursue them with all your heart.
4. Eliminate any time-wasters that keep you from pursuing your priorities.

Thoughts for Consideration

- *"Never complain about the time: it only wastes more time and keeps you from using the time you have to the best advantage."* Warren Wiersbe

- *"The world is full of disorganized people who have lost control of their time."* Gordon MacDonald

- *"We must use the time which we have because even at best there is never enough."* Elton Trueblood

- *"Wasting time is just as serious as breaking any of the Ten Commandments. The Lord allotted us a certain amount of time on earth and wasting it is being ungrateful and selfish, not only to the God above, but to our fellow citizens."* Bob Feller

- *"How you spend your time is more important than how you spend your money. Money mistakes can be corrected, but time is gone forever."* David B. Norris

- *"Suspect each moment, for it is a thief, tiptoeing away with more than it brings."* John Updike

- *"Kill time and you murder opportunity."* Anonymous

- *"Right now counts forever."* R. C. Sproul

- *"Time is not a commodity that can be stored for future use. It must be invested hour by hour, or else it is gone for ever."* Thomas Edison

- *"The year is made up of minutes. Let these be watched as having been dedicated to God. It is in the sanctification of the small that the hallowing of the large is secure."* G. Campbell Morgan

- *"What is past cannot be recalled; what is future cannot be insured."* Stephen Charnock

Questions for Discussion

1. Why is time precious to each person?

2. What is the one thing that all great leaders and men have in common?

3. How does the life of Samuel Taylor Coleridge depict a misuse of time?

4. As you evaluate your life as it is right now, would you say that you are busy and cluttered or organized and disciplined?

5. List some of the steps you can take to avoid wasting time.

6. How well do you manage your time?

8
Developing a Biblical View of Wealth

"Lay not up for yourselves treasures upon earth, where moth and rust doth corrupt, and where thieves break through and steal: But lay up for yourselves treasures in heaven, where neither moth nor rust doth corrupt, and where thieves do not break through nor steal: For where your treasure is, there will your heart be also." Matthew 6:19-21

"Make all you can, save all you can, give all you can."[1] John Wesley, on the subject of money

Nothing seems to be more troubling to Christians than the subjects of money and success. A Christian worldview needs to take into account the proper use and possible misuse of money. There seems to be a strange view circulating among Christians these days that to be successful or to be wealthy is somehow contrary to true Christian spirituality. I think Dr. R. C. Sproul said it rightly when he wrote,

> *Because there's a lot of affluence in our culture, there tends to be a lot of guilt about the enjoyment of prosperity. If you read the Old Testament for ten minutes, you'll see that the Jewish people did not perceive prosperity as a crime. God was constantly promising the blessing of material well-being to people as a consequence of obedience. The issue for Jesus is, Where's the heart? Our priority is to be the seeking of the kingdom and His righteousness. If, in the seeking of the kingdom, God is pleased to bless you*

with abundance and prosperity, don't feel guilty about it,
but thank him for it and use it responsibly.[2]

We need to understand that there is nothing wrong with Christians striving for success and greater material gain in the world in which they live. As a matter of fact, it is most inconsistent with Christian principles to conclude that somehow if we are poor, and if we are mediocre, that that is somehow more pleasing to the Lord. Having said this, however, we need to be alert to the dangers that wealth and material prosperity can have over us. Here are a number of thoughts from some Christian thinkers who have understood the inherent dangers of wealth and prosperity. All those who live in America, whatever their income, live far above most of the people of the world. Most people in the Western world would be wise if they too would consider these cautious warnings. J. C. Ryle, the English bishop of the nineteenth century, warned,

Is it for nothing that the Lord Jesus spoke the parable of the rich fool and blamed him because he was not "rich towards God" (Luke 12:21)? Is it for nothing that in the parable of the sower he mentions the "deceitfulness of riches" as one reason why the seed of the Word bears no fruit (Matt. 13:22)? Is it for nothing that he says, "Make to yourselves friends of the mammon of unrighteousness" (Luke 16:9)? Is it for nothing that he says, "When thou makest a dinner or a supper, call not thy friends, not thy brethren, neither thy kinsmen, nor thy rich neighbors; lest they also bid thee again, and a recompense be made thee. But when thou makest a feast, call the poor, the maimed, the lame, the blind: and thou shalt be blessed; for they cannot recompense thee; for thou shalt be recompensed at the resurrection of the just" (Luke 14:12-14)? Is it for nothing that he says, "Sell that ye have and give alms; provide yourselves bags which wax not old, a treasure in the heavens that faileth not, where no thief approacheth, neither moth corrupteth" (Luke 12:33)? Is it for nothing that he says, "It is more blessed to give than to receive" (Acts 20:35)?[3]

A. W. Tozer, a Christian writer and pastor and one of the great leaders of the evangelical movement in the twentieth century, made a similar observation concerning the dangers of wealth in a chapter of his book entitled, *"The Blessedness of Possessing Nothing."* Tozer said,

> *...before the Lord God made man upon the earth he first prepared for him by creating a world of useful things for his sustenance and delight...Sin has introduced complications and has made those very gifts of God a potential source of ruin to the soul.*[4]

Elizabeth Eliot spoke of the dangers of covetousness when she challenged her readers to live with contentment. Her comments are insightful and compelling:

> *Thanksgiving requires the recognition of the Source. It implies contentment with what is given, not complaint about what is not given. It excludes covetousness. The goodness and love of God choose the gifts, and we say thank you, acknowledging the Thought Behind as well as the thing itself. Covetousness involves suspicion about the goodness and love of God, and even his justice. He has not given me what he gave somebody else. He doesn't notice my need. He doesn't love me as much as he loves him. He isn't fair. Faith looks up with open hands. "You are giving me this, Lord? Thank you. It is good and acceptable and perfect."*[5]

James Montgomery Boice who wrote a wonderful book on Christian discipleship also gave similar warnings concerning the abuse of wealth and the seductive nature of riches.

> *Possessions are dangerous because we tend to serve them rather than God, which means that things become an idol and our service to them becomes idolatry...earthly treasure is perishable. Frequently it fails to last even in this life. It certainly will not go with us into heaven. So what are*

Possessions are dangerous because we tend to serve them rather than God, which means that things become an idol and our service to them becomes idolatry...

we to use it for? The answer is that we are to use possessions to do good so that those good deeds will themselves produce treasures for us — not on earth, but in heaven, "where moth and rust do not destroy, and where thieves do not break in and steal" (Matthew 6:20)...I put the matter as clearly as I know how. The money you spend on yourself (which is necessary up to a point) will not produce treasure in heaven. It will be gone with the spending, and its benefits will perish when you do. But money you spend on others (which should be a rising percentage of your income, as God prospers you) — That treasure will last forever. It will be translated into eternal treasures to be presented to you at the Lord's coming.[6]

If Christians are not careful, they may make a god out of their possessions and the wealth that the Lord has blessed them with. We must not forget that true happiness does not come from hoarding our wealth, or even by acquiring more wealth. True happiness comes when we can joyfully invest our wealth into the lives of others and the cause of God's kingdom on earth. The Apostle Paul reminded us that Jesus once taught His disciples that *"It is more blessed to give than to receive,"* Acts 20:35 Pastor John Kitchen makes a powerful point about the dangers of greed and covetousness when he wrote:

Erwin Lutzer [Pastor of Moody Memorial Church in Chicago, Illinois] *recounts a legend from the land of India...One day a beggar caught sight of a wealthy rajah approaching him in a glorious chariot. Seizing his opportunity, the beggar took up his position at the side of the road with his bowl of rice extended. He was astonished, however, when the rajah stopped and, instead of making a contribution, demanded some of his rice!*

Anger welled up within the beggar. Begrudgingly he placed one grain of rice in the rajah's hand.

"More!" was the demand from the rajah. An additional grain was placed in the wealthy man's hand.

"More please!" was the repeated request. Vexed beyond words, the beggar placed one additional grain in the man's hand and stormed away.

As the chariot rattled down the road, the beggar looked down into his rice bowl and saw something glimmering in the sun. It was a grain of gold! As he searched his bowl, he found two more just like it.

The lesson, says, Lutzer, is simple: "For every grain of rice, a grain of gold." And he adds, "If we clutch our bowl of rice, we shall lose our reward. If we are faithful and give God each grain, He gives us gold in return."[7]

As we develop a Christian worldview to guide and pattern our lives after, we need to realize that we must be careful stewards of the wealth and resources that the Lord has given to us. It is pleasing to the Lord for us to be financially free from debt, to be able to give joyfully to the cause of God and truth, and to be able to use our wealth for the advancement of God's kingdom on earth. In the book of Acts we read this wonderful statement, *"I have showed you all things, how that so laboring ye ought to support the weak, and to remember the words of the Lord Jesus, how he said, It is more blessed to give than to receive."* Acts 20:35 By hard work, and by trusting the Lord for an increase in our wealth, we are in turn able to give joyfully to the causes and ministries he may lay on our hearts.

There are some dangers, however, that we must be aware of. These things should be carefully avoided, if at all possible. As you strive for success in your life, vocation, and business, beware of the pitfalls and dangers that are always lurking in the shadows of life.

1. Beware of those who would teach you that poverty is a sign of
    being spiritual. This cannot be supported by Scripture.
2. Beware of those who would teach you that wealth is a sign of
    being spiritual. This too cannot be supported by Scripture.
3. Beware of those so-called Christian leaders who would fleece
    the sheep instead of feed them. Never trust a Christian leader
    who says to you, "God told me to tell you to give to me or to
    this cause, and if you do, you will have success." Men like this
    are charlatans who are only interested in stealing your money.
    There are basic biblical principles that we should all follow in
    regards to giving. Beyond that, we should be very wary of
    those who come with schemes to tell us how and where to
    give our money.
4. Beware of those who would put you on a guilt trip if you
    are successful, if you live in a nice home, or if you have nice
    things. We believe what has been termed, "The Priesthood of
    the Believer." This is a the principle of the Reformation that
    teaches us that we each must give an account to the Lord for
    our time, possessions, and money. No other person has the
    right to judge us (apart from the principles of Scripture) and
    to use guilt to manipulate us as to how we spend our money.
    For example, someone may criticize you for the car you drive
    or the home in which you live. It may be said, "You could live
    in a more modest home and give more money to the Lord."
    There is no end to that kind of guilt manipulation. No matter
    how small our home or how modest our car, there is always
    something smaller or less expensive we could buy. We could
    say to these self-righteous critics, "Why don't you go out and
    live in a tent? Then you could give the money you saved to
    the Lord's work!"
5. Beware of those who seek to manipulate God's people with
    the so-called health-and-wealth gospel. They teach that it is
    always God's will for you to be wealthy and healthy. This
    too is false. These false teachers will again use false guilt to
    manipulate you by teaching that if you are not successful,
    wealthy, and healthy, it is a matter of a lack of faith on your
    part. We should strive for success. We should do our best in all

things. But in the end, we are bound to submit to the sovereignty of God in these matters. God Himself determines the parameters, boundaries, and extent of our success and influence. We are to do our best for the glory of God and then leave the results in the hands of an all-wise and gracious God who does all things well on our behalf. Some of the greatest

> *We are to do our best for the glory of God and then leave the results in the hands of an all-wise and gracious God who does all things well on our behalf.*

Christians in the history of the church have been those who had enormous wealth, or those who also knew great poverty. Would we judge suffering Christians in countries where they are persecuted as lacking in faith? Neither should we judge those in other places who have voluntarily made themselves poor for the kingdom's sake if they felt led of the Lord to do so. (I'm thinking of those who have chosen to live meager and humble lives in Christian service so that others would not judge them as being covetous. Paul was an example of a man who made this kind of sacrifice, when he would not take help from others at times lest he be criticized for taking advantage of the people he ministered to.)

Biblical Principles to Follow for Financial Success

We should always remember that wealth, success, and striving to improve our place in life is not wrong or sinful. Beware of those who would take advantage of you in these areas. There are some biblical principles, however, that we should be aware of in the area of money and success. Let me list a few of them.

1. Strive for success, but leave the results in the hands of the Lord.
2. Remember money is not evil; it is the love of money that is evil.

3. Be sure to check out your motive for wanting greater wealth and success in life. Is it for the glory of God? Or is it for your own personal lust and desires?
4. In the Scriptures we are taught to give to the Lord's work. In the Old Testament, the tithe was ten percent of all that we made. Anything beyond that is simply voluntary. God does bless us if we are generous with our giving, but beware of those who use guilt manipulation to promise things the Scriptures do not promise when it comes to giving. I would caution you to be wary of those ministries that are always focused on money and are always telling you to give to them so you might be blessed in a greater way.
5. Practice delayed gratification. Pay off all your debts before you make other purchases.
6. Don't spend more than you make. Set up a budget and stick to it.
7. If you use credit cards, pay them off each month and avoid paying interest on them.
8. Avoid the temptation of hoarding and coveting. Let your greatest joy be in giving and ministering to others. "…*Remember the words of the Lord Jesus, how he said, It is more blessed to give than to receive.*" Acts 20:35

The Importance of Tithing

In developing a biblical worldview for success, we need to remember that the Christian is taught in the Word of God to tithe to the Lord's work. Failure to tithe is not only a sin, but also a sign of rebellion and ingratitude for all that the Lord has given us. Studies have shown that over ninety-five percent of the Christian church does not tithe. These studies are not saying that Christians don't give. They are saying they don't tithe. To tithe is to give a tenth back to the Lord in accordance with the teachings of

> *Failure to tithe is not only a sin, but also a sign of rebellion and ingratitude for all that the Lord has given us.*

the Bible. Many Christians give but don't tithe. As a matter of fact, if most Christians tithed, there would be little shortage in the church for missions and for other projects that God has called His people to engage in. The charge that Christians are materialistic in America is a serious challenge. Most people think that if Christians in America have wealth, that is a sign of being materialistic. Nothing could be farther from the truth. It is not having wealth that is a sin. It is not tithing that wealth that is a sin. I have consistently challenged those who make money to not forget that the tithe is the Lord's. If we do not tithe on all of our income, we are sinning and robbing God.

Concerning the subject of tithing, there have been differences of opinions on some points. For the sake of clarity, let me make a few brief observations that I trust will help us in this matter. If we are to have a Christian worldview that will shape our lives and lead us on into success, then these principles on giving and tithing should be observed.

- We are to tithe on our gross income, not just on net income.
- We are not obligated to tithe on the taxable income. (This means that after we consider what will be removed for taxes, we should tithe on all else that we have made.)
- If we have failed to tithe on the past income, we should clear our consciences with God by paying that back just as we would expect any thief to make restitution for his theft.
- Remember that tithing is one sure way to tell where our hearts are in relationship to our God.
- As our yearly income comes in, we cannot escape the duty to tithe by putting money in tax sheltered annuities, off shore accounts, or other such places and think that we only need to tithe on what we are living on. This practice would be considered theft to the Lord.

The importance of tithing has been stated by the late author and Christian theologian A. W. Pink:

> *There are few subjects on which the Lord's own people are more astray than on the subject of giving. They profess*

to take the Bible as their one rule of faith and practice, and yet in the matter of Christian finance, the vast majority have utterly ignored its plain teachings and have tried every substitute the carnal mind could devise; therefore it is no wonder that the majority of Christian enterprises in the world today are handicapped and crippled through the lack of funds. Is our giving to be regulated by sentiment and impulse, or by principle and conscience?[8]

There are those who claim that because we are no longer under the Old Testament law, we are not obligated to give a tenth back to the Lord. This is just a clever way of trying to exclude our obligations to give to the Lord's work. The Christian author and church leader, J. Oswald Sanders, made this convicting comment on the subject of giving and tithing:

Judaism was an expensive religion, and as a devout Jew who fulfilled the whole law, our Lord was meticulous in fulfilling it financial obligations. What would He pay into the Temple treasury from what He earned as a carpenter? A Jew was first required to give one-tenth to God. Then at harvest time, the farmer must give the first-fruits to God, and that consisted of one-sixth of his increase. Then every three years a second tenth was given for the poor — social security tax. In addition were the special offerings of cleansing and consecration. That means that his total contributions to religion were nearer a fifth of his income than a tenth — and that does not include voluntary support to the local synagogue…So here we have our answer to how much of His income Jesus gave to God.

If we object by saying that the Jews were under law and we Christians are under grace, and that for us the law of the tithe had been abrogated, another question arises. Will a Christian who is experiencing intimacy with his Lord wish to take advantage of grace so that he can give less to God's work than the less privileged Jew who knew nothing of Calvary's sacrifice and the inestimable blessings it has brought?...Jesus gave tithes and offerings. Is the servant greater than his Lord?[9]

Every Christian should seek to answer these questions from J. Oswald Sanders with humility and honesty.

Similarly, author Larry Burkett writes,

Those who give less than a tenth of their income limit what God can do for them according to His own word. "Will a man rob God? Yet you are robbing Me! But you say, 'How have we robbed Thee?' In tithes and offerings." (Malachi 3:8) Lest we somehow believe that this principle applies only to the Old Covenant, Paul amplifies it for us: "Now this I say, he who sows sparingly shall also reap sparingly; and he that sows bountifully shall also reap bountifully." (2 Corinthians 9:6) A lack of giving is an external material indicator that spiritual changes need to be made.[10]

For the child of God who has been purchased from the slave markets of sin by the precious blood of Jesus, giving back to the Lord should be a joy and pleasure. The Apostle Paul reminds us in 2 Corinthians 9:6-7,

> *But this I say, He which soweth sparingly shall reap also sparingly; and he which soweth bountifully shall reap also bountifully. Every man according as he purposeth in his heart, so let him give; not grudgingly, or of necessity: for God loveth a cheerful giver.*

> *For the child of God who has been purchased from the slave markets of sin by the precious blood of Jesus, giving back to the Lord should be a joy and pleasure.*

We give cheerfully and joyfully if we remember the following principles about our giving and tithing:

1. Giving will be a delight if we never forget that we are giving to our Lord. (We all love to give gifts to those we love! How much more so to give to the God who has saved us and called us out of darkness into His marvelous light?)
2. Giving will be a delight if we see it as an act of worship and obedience to our Lord.
3. Giving will be a delight if we realize that by our giving we are privileged to serve the Lord and further His kingdom on earth.
4. Giving will be a delight if we remember that by our giving we are laying up treasures in heaven that will be revealed in the day of judgment.
5. Giving will be a delight when we realize that Jesus Himself taught us that it is more blessed to give than to receive. Acts 20:35, "...*remember the words of the Lord Jesus, how he said, It is more blessed to give than to receive.*"

The great English bishop J. C. Ryle made this plea to all Christians in his book *Walking With God*:

> *We should always be thinking of how we can do most good with our money in our short lives. Could we not spend less on ourselves and more on others? Remember that spiritually we were like Lazarus. We lay sick, helpless and starving at heaven's gate till Jesus came to relieve us. He went about doing good, and died on the cross to save us. Let us be like him in doing good to others.*[11]

Two Major Dangers

I would leave this point by warning you to be alert for two major dangers: first, those who are jealous of your success and use false guilt to manipulate you, and second, those who want to take advantage of your success by using false principles and promises of success to rob you of what God has given to you. There is nothing wrong with striving for success if it is sanctified and done for the glory of God. Remember, Abraham lived in a big tent! As we are blessed and prosper, we are accountable to the Lord to use what

He has graciously given to us for His glory and the advancement of His kingdom on the earth.

Money cannot buy happiness, success, or true purpose in life.

Money cannot buy happiness, success, or true purpose in life. Money, if received by our fulfillment of the Creation Mandate, will give us choices, opportunities, and blessings. But money can also prove to be a deadly curse if not used for the glory of God. Money often changes those around us and makes us the target of scams, theft, and unscrupulous associations. This was pointed out so well by Bob Russell in his book *Money, a Users Manual.* Russell wrote of a man who won the lottery and it had a deadly impact on his life and family that was simply tragic.

> On September 1, 1996, the Chicago Tribune carried an article with the following headline: "Luck Ran Out Quickly for Lottery Millionaire." "Buddy Post may be the unluckiest lucky man alive. In 1988, Buddy Post won more than sixteen million dollars in the Pennsylvania Lottery, but since then his life has been anything but lucky.
>
> In 1992, Post was forced to give one-third of his winnings to his former landlord, Ann Karpik, who said that she shared the lottery ticket with Post. He had trouble keeping up with the legal fees since he was blocked from receiving access to the winnings during the court battle. Neither could he afford the bills he incurred for the bar, used car lot, and the other failed business ventures he and his siblings began after his jackpot win."
>
> In 1993, "Post's brother, Jeffrey, was convicted of plotting to kill Buddy and his wife, Constance...as part of a scheme to gain access to the lottery money," the article revealed.
>
> By 1994, Post had filed for bankruptcy. His wife had filed for divorce. He was $500,000 in debt, not counting taxes and legal fees. He was trying to auction off the remaining lottery payments to pay his attorney's fees, home

mortgage, and other debts — and rid himself of the "Lottery albatross."

"Money didn't change me," Post said, "It changed people around me that I knew, that I thought cared a little bit about me. But they only cared about the money."

When he was asked what he was going to do next, Post said, "I'm just going to stay at home and mind my P's and Q's. Money draws flies."[12]

John Bunyan, the author of the timeless Christian classic, *Pilgrim's Progress*, wrote in poetic verse this quaint saying:

"There was a man,
Some called him mad;
The more he gave,
The more he had."

How to Get Started

1. Remember that the Creation Mandate includes the biblical instruction and command to be productive and to accumulate wealth. Use your wealth to have influence for Christ in the world.
2. Pray that God will give you a proper view of money and wealth.
3. Begin to tithe your wealth regularly.
4. If you struggle with covetousness, repent and ask God to help you to have a biblical perspective on wealth.

Thoughts for Consideration

• *"Money does not commend us to God."* Erwin W. Lutzer

- "Happiness is not in the mere possession of money; it lies in the joy of achievement, in the thrill of creative effort." Franklin Roosevelt

- "Never work just for money or for power. They won't save your soul or help you sleep at night." Marian Wright Edelman

- "Money never made a man happy yet, nor will it. There is nothing in its nature to produce happiness. The more a man has, the more he wants. Instead of its filling a vacuum, it makes one." Ben Franklin

- "Economy is half the battle of life; it is not so hard to earn money as to spend it well." C. H. Spurgeon

- "If you want to feel rich, just count the things you have that money can't buy." Old proverb

- "If you work just for money, you'll never make it, but if you love what you're doing and you always put the customer first, success will be yours." Ray Kroc

- "He that goes a borrowing goes a sorrowing." Ben Franklin

- "When money speaks, the truth is silent." Anonymous

- "Money is never more wisely used than in forwarding the cause of God." George Barlow

- "Few things test a person's spirituality more accurately than the way he uses money." John Blanchard

- "It is possible to love money without having it, and it is possible to have it without loving it." J.C. Ryle

∽

Questions for Discussion

1. Should a Christian feel guilty if he or she is prosperous and has been greatly blessed by God with wealth and success?

2. What did the Apostle Paul mean when he said the "Love of money was the root of all evil?"

3. What can you learn from the comments of Elizabeth Eliot on covetousness and contentment?

4. Why are possessions dangerous? (See the quote by James Montgomery Boice.)

5. According to Jesus, what is one of the most blessed things to do in life?

6. What is the proper meaning of tithing?

9
Nurturing a Biblical Self-image

"And God said, Let us make man in our image, after our likeness: and let them have dominion over the fish of the sea, and over the fowl of the air, and over the cattle, and over all the earth, and over every creeping thing that creepeth upon the earth." Genesis 1:26

"Man was created in God's image to be God's vicegerent over that realm under God. The image of God involves knowledge, righteousness, and holiness, and dominion over the earth and its creatures."[1] Rousas John Rushdooney

Developing a biblical self-image is an essential aspect of a Christian worldview. This is especially true for young people. Many teenagers go through their early years with great pain and difficulty because of the unkindness and cutting remarks made by other young people. Having a biblical worldview that includes a proper self-image will protect them from much of this pain.

Self-image has been a term that defines the opinion and value we place on ourselves. This attitude often originates from the comments and attitudes that our parents, friends, husbands or wives, employees, or children project towards us.

We all know how devastating a poor self-image can be when unkind words are hurled at us, or when thoughtless comments spear our hearts. The old saying goes, *"Sticks and stones may break my bones but names can never hurt me."* This is not a true and accurate statement. Words have an overwhelming impact on our daily lives, and they do indeed hurt to the very core of our souls. Words have a powerful impact on each of our lives for good or evil. It is important for each of us to listen to the voice of God rather than the voice of some unkind critic or enemy. St. Francis of Assisi once prayed, *"God grant me the serenity to accept the things I cannot change; the courage to change the things that I can; and the wisdom to know the difference."*

We must not let our days, years, and lives be spoiled by the sarcastic and sore comments made by thoughtless people. At the end of the day — learn this lesson well — the only opinion that matters about you is God's.

The Critic Doesn't Count!

One of the great quotes that I have found to be an inspiration to me has been one made by President Theodore Roosevelt. Concerning attitudes, criticism, and unkind and judgmental remarks he said:

> *It is not the critic who counts: not the man who points out how the strong man stumbled or where the doer of deeds could have done them better. The credit belongs to the man who is actually in the arena; whose face is marred by dust and sweat and blood; who strives valiantly; who errs, and comes short again and again, because there is no effort without error and shortcoming; who does actually try to do the deed; who knows the great enthusiasm, the great devotion, and spends himself in a worthy cause; who, at the worst, if he fails, at least fails while daring greatly.*
>
> *Far better it is to dare mighty things, to win glorious triumphs even though checkered by failure, than to rank with those poor spirits who neither enjoy nor suffer much because they live in the gray twilight that knows neither victory nor defeat.*[2]

I have tried to teach my children and my congregation that it is rarely wise to respond to your critics. Critics are plentiful. And trying to chase down rumors to defend oneself is often a futile experience and a great waste of time and resources. One author put it this way from an account in history:

C. H. Spurgeon, the renowned English preacher, came to a disagreement with the equally well-known Joseph Parker. It was largely a private matter, but Parker made it public by publishing an open letter to his colleague in the newspaper. The press had a heyday with the public charges leveled by one pastor against another. Spurgeon's response? Silence. He never made any mention of the matter in public. He just let it go and got on with his work.[3]

In developing a biblical worldview we must come to a point in our lives where we realize that we are just sinners saved by God's grace. Having a humble opinion of ourselves will save us from the spirit of resentment and bitterness. These attitudes often arise in our hearts when our pride is hurt by the criticisms and unkind comments of others. A. W. Tozer understood that the way to avoid bitterness and resentment is to die to self and to be humble. Tozer states:

> *Having a humble opinion of ourselves will save us from the spirit of resentment and bitterness.*

As long as you set yourself up as a little god to which you must be loyal there will be those who will delight to offer affront to your idol. How then can you hope to have inward peace? The heart's fierce effort to protect itself from every slight, to shield its touchy honor from bad opinion of friend and enemy, will never let the mind have rest. Continue this fight through the years and the burden will become intolerable. Yet the sons of earth are carrying this burden continually, challenging every word spoken against them, cringing under every criticism, smarting under each fancied slight, tossing sleepless if another is preferred before them.[4]

Let us each remember how important our words are to those around us. The words and speech that we use daily can either build others up or tear them down. Our words can either heal or kill. We should make a decision early in our lives to be people who encourage, edify, and build up others and inspire joy, confidence, and love in them.

The Scriptures admonish us concerning our speech. Here are a few verses that point this out:

- *"There is that speaketh like the piercings of a sword: but the tongue of the wise is health."* Proverbs 12:18
- *"Heaviness in the heart of man maketh it stoop: but a good word maketh it glad."* Proverbs 12:25
- *"Pleasant words are as an honeycomb, sweet to the soul, and health to the bones."* Proverbs 16:24
- *"A word fitly spoken is like apples of gold in pictures of silver."* Proverbs 25:11
- *"Let no corrupt communication proceed out of our mouth, but that which is good to the use of edifying, that it may minister grace unto the hearers."* Ephesians 4:29

We have, in many cases today, lost the art of healing people with kind words, compliments, and edifying speech. I believe it is a sign of Christ-likeness when people stop thinking of themselves, and find joy in praising, encouraging, edifying, and complimenting others. And if you are given praise or a compliment, accept it with thankful humility. *"Accept each compliment as you would a present, words wrapped up in a box with a bow on top. Say thank you and you'll receive more; reject the praise and you'll soon receive none."*[5]

Learn the Importance of Giving Praise

One of the ways we can enable others to have a healthy self-image is to give praise and recognition to them when it is fitting and due. We should never hold back on giving compliments and praise if it is sincere and deserved. When we pour out praise on our wives, husbands, children, or those working with or for us, we are giving them a precious gift. Praise will encourage and inspire them to be their best. Someone once said of recognition, *"Babies cry for it and grown men die for it."* Let's be generous in pouring out this precious gift to those that we can encourage.

Steps to Developing a Biblical Self-image

Do you struggle with your opinion of yourself? Many Christians are tormented by feelings of inferiority, failure, and rejection. These people limp through life in a living hell of self-imposed torment. Instead of seeing themselves as God sees them, they have either listened to the cruel words of others or the whisperings of the devil. Pastor Erwin Lutzer of Moody Memorial Church in Chicago, Illinois gives some very practical and helpful advice on this subject:

> *People reject themselves for many reasons: physical appearance, lack of ability and intelligence, or because of the failures of the past. Others...have warped views of themselves because of their family background. Thank God, this can be changed! The Scriptures provide the information necessary to be at peace with ourselves and be free from the bondage of self-deception.*
>
> *Our opinion of ourselves is formed largely by the attitude of others toward us. If, as children, we are ridiculed for our physical appearance or our lack of ability, we may develop deep-seated inferiority and the belief that we are doomed to be a failure.*
>
> *Children are often unintentionally cruel in pointing out one another's physical idiosyncrasies. If a child is too fat, too skinny, too tall, or too short, he can become so self-conscious that he loses his self-respect and esteem. Sometimes the emotional scars are so deep that the person may never develop self-confidence again.*[6]

In order to develop a biblical self-image there are a number of steps that we can take:

• Remember that we were each made by God and everything about us was determined by His wise and sovereign plan.

- Remember that God never makes mistakes!
- Remember that if we do not accept God's authority over us, we may never come to a place of peace in our hearts concerning who we are and what our gifts and abilities are.
- Remember, therefore, to thank God for everything in your life.
- Remember that the inward qualities of character are much more important than outward beauty or physical appearance.

Remember that God never makes mistakes!

What Does the Scripture Teach about Man?

It is very important for each of us to have a biblical view of man if we are to know and have success with the Lord. This idea of self-image simply means that we realize what the Scriptures teach about all men. There are three main principles to remember:

1. Man was made in the image of God. This means that man has certain characteristics and qualities that distinguish him from the rest of creation. Man has spiritual, intellectual, and moral capabilities. In other words, only man can be holy, moral, immoral, have communion with the Almighty, feel guilt, and know God in an intimate way. This also teaches us that all men regardless of their race are special and have value before God. It was this knowledge that has helped the church through the ages treat men in a humane and civil way, because we knew that all men were made in God's image, not just some men.

2. Man lost the glory of that image by the fall in the Garden of Eden. As a result of that spiritual fall, man is guilty before a holy God and has no power to return to the Lord or restore that fallen image. Man is therefore under a curse, and as such, he needs the grace of God in order to come back into fellowship with the living God. The Apostle Paul understood that man was fallen and wrote about it in the book of Romans. Here is Paul's view of mankind as found in Romans 3:10-18:

[10] *As it is written, There is none righteous, no, not one:* [11] *There is none that understandeth, there is none that seeketh after God.* [12] *They are all gone out of the way, they are together become unprofitable; there is none that doeth good, no, not one.* [13] *Their throat is an open sepulchre; with their tongues they have used deceit; the poison of asps is under their lips:* [14] *Whose mouth is full of cursing and bitterness:* [15] *Their feet are swift to shed blood:* [16] *Destruction and misery are in their ways:* [17] *And the way of peace have they not known:* [18] *There is no fear of God before their eyes.*

3. Man has a way back to God. The way back is through God's plan of restoring His image upon us. We call this the plan of salvation, or justification by faith alone. The greatest question in life is this: "**How can I, a sinner, be accepted by a Holy God**?" The answer is found in the Christian Scriptures of the New Testament. In Romans 5:1 we read, "*Having been justified by faith we have peace with God through our Lord Jesus Christ.*" We are described in the Bible as being fallen and sinful. We need a righteousness greater than our own. We could never keep the Law of Moses sufficiently enough to please God. So God sent his Son, the Lord Jesus Christ, who kept the law on our behalf. By His life and death, we can be restored to the image of God. We have the righteousness of Jesus imputed and credited to our account. By this action, we are given a righteousness greater than our own. This is the doctrine of justification by faith alone.

The importance of justification by faith alone cannot be emphasized enough. Without this truth, we have no Christian faith. By understanding the doctrine of justification by faith alone, we have peace with God and ourselves. A person who has such inner peace and awareness that he or she is accepted with God is a person who can be very powerful in their private and public life. There is something about the person whose joy, faith, enthusiasm, and life impacts all of those who come in contact with him or her. People who are at peace with God and themselves are a happy, joyful, and contagious people. These people are filled with the praise of God, and they love to be a blessing to all those around them.

Here are some verses that demonstrate the special peace and joy that we have in the forgiveness of God:

- "[8] *The Lord is merciful and gracious, slow to anger, and plenteous in mercy. [9] He will not always chide; neither will He keep His anger for ever. [10] He hath not dealt with us after our sins; nor rewarded us according to our iniquities. [11] For as the heaven is high above the earth, so great is His mercy toward them that fear Him. [12] As far as the east is from the west, so far hath He removed our transgressions from us. [13] Like as a father pitieth his children, so the Lord pitieth them that fear him. [14] For He knoweth our frame; He remembereth that we are dust.*" Psalm 103:8-14

- "*Therefore having been justified by faith, we have peace with God through our Lord Jesus Christ.*" Romans 5:1

- "*There is therefore now no condemnation to them which are in Christ Jesus, who walk not after the flesh, but after the Spirit.*" Romans 8:1

- "*And their sins and iniquities will I remember no more.*" Hebrews 10:17

- "[5] *And beside this, giving all diligence, add to your faith virtue; and to virtue knowledge; [6] And to knowledge temperance; and to temperance patience; and to patience godliness; [7] And to godliness brotherly kindness; and to brotherly kindness charity. [8] For if these things be in you, and abound, they make you that ye shall neither be barren nor unfruitful in the knowledge of our Lord Jesus Christ. [9] But he that lacketh these things is blind, and cannot see afar off, and hath forgotten that he was purged from his old sins.*" 2 Peter 1:5-9

These verses stirred my soul as a young Christian. I find these verses on God's love and forgiveness still ravishing my heart today! Meditate on these gracious promises and they will bless your life as well.

The Power of a Biblical Self-image

The idea of having a biblical self-image is of great importance in Christian living. When people are at peace with themselves and understand that they have peace with God, they will be people who are strategically placed to impact those around them. The opposite is also true. When people do not have a biblical self-image, they are driven to find meaning and purpose for their lives in other things. Many times these other things may be very harmful and unhealthy for society at large. An article from the Australian Commission for the Future made this telling comment:

> when a society fails to imbue people's lives with a sense of worth [self-image] and meaning, then they must attempt to find these qualities as individuals...Robbed of a broader meaning to our lives, we appear to have entered an era of mass obsession, usually with ourselves: our appearance, our health and fitness, our work, our sex lives, our children's development, our personal development.[7]

Only a biblical self-image can prevent us from falling into this trap.

How to Get Started

1. Every Christian should remember that they have been created and made in the image of God. Everything about you is a gift from God.
2. Remember God chose you and sent His Son Jesus Christ to die for you on the cross. You are His special treasure.
3. Thank God for the gift of life.

4. Thank God for your family, your friends, and for how He made you. (Give praise to the Lord for everything about your life: appearance, race, and all physical features.)

Thoughts for Consideration

- *"We must accept ourselves, for if we are not at peace with ourselves, we cannot be at peace with others or with God."* Erwin W. Lutzer

- *"To escape criticism — do nothing, say nothing, be nothing."* Elbert Hubbard

- *"Never fear criticism. If the critic is right, he has helped you. If he is wrong, you can help him. Either way, somebody gets helped."* A. W. Tozer

- *"Never kick a skunk. You may manufacture a worse problem then you started with."* Anonymous

- *"Grant me prudently to avoid him that flatters me, and to endure patiently him that contradicts me."* Thomas à Kempis

- *"The more we ponder the offense, the more we defend ourselves; and the more we defend ourselves, the more anxious we are to prove we are right. Then, when we least expect it, we launch our attack — and wish we had kept our mouth shut."* Warren Wiersbe

- *"Never be afraid to test yourself by your critic's words."* John Blanchard

- *"I have seldom ever heard a criticism about myself that didn't indeed contain a kernel of useful truth."* Gordon MacDonald

- "*Any fool can criticize, condemn and complain — and usually does.*" Dale Carnegie

- "*Sensitivity about self — is not this one of the greatest curses in life? It is a result of the Fall. We spend the whole of our life watching ourselves.*" D. Martyn Lloyd-Jones

Questions for Discussion

1. What does the term "self-image" refer to?

2. Why don't critics count?

3. Explain the power of words to give life or bring death.

4. What steps can a person take to create a biblical image of himself or herself?

5. What does the Bible teach about the nature and character of man?

6. How does the teaching on forgiveness help us in our view of ourselves?

10
Being a True Friend

"A friend loveth at all times, and a brother is born for adversity."
Proverbs 17:17

"Those friends thou hast, and their adoption tried, Grapple them unto thy soul with hoops of steel." Shakespeare in Hamlet, act one, scene three, Polonius to Laertes

∞

A biblical worldview must also include the concept of friendship. Jesus was called "the friend of sinners." To be a true friend to others is to be like Christ. How sad it is to see that the gift of friendship is so often neglected. If you pass through life and have three or four true friends, you are indeed a fortunate person. A true friend is hard to come by in this selfish and sinful world.

> *To be a true friend to others is to be like Christ.*

To be successful in life, it is essential that we understand the importance of being a friend. Let me share some of the special qualities that I believe are a part of being a good friend.

Being a Friend Who Loves

A friend is someone who loves, as the Scripture teaches us, *"at all times."* Friendship is not to be taken lightly. When one has a good friend, there is a bond of love that ties heart to heart. When the bond of friendship ties two people together, nothing should ever be allowed to unravel the tie that binds your hearts together.

A good friend must love at all times even in times of sickness, sorrow, trials, and tragedies. Those who only love when there is a personal benefit for them have not known the true meaning of friendship. Some of the most painful memories I have had in my life and ministry were to watch people, whom I thought were friends, leave the church or drop our friendship when tough times came upon us. We should all be reminded that Jesus loves us at all times. He has promised in His Word that He will never leave nor forsake us. Christians should seek to follow the Lord's example in friendship. Never forget the benefit of pouring your love out on your friends. Love poured out will return to you with many more blessings besides. Dr. Karl Menninger once said, *"Love cures people — both the ones who give it and the ones who receive it."*[1]

Being a Friend Who Listens

A true friend is also someone who is a good listener. Most people today are starving for a friend who will do nothing more than listen. To listen is to care. To be a good listener is to be a person who is demonstrating the true quality of Christian love. If we can just learn this one thing, what a difference it will make in our lives. A good listener is a rare treasure today. Florence Littauer, in her book, *It Takes So Little to be Above Average,* had this to say about the quality of listening:

> *Once people think we understand or at least want to understand, they will pour out their problems and all we have to do is listen. We don't have to be brilliant or even have a three-step solution. We only have to listen. No one listens to anyone any more; they're all too busy, so if we just listen we become a devoted friend. Everywhere I go, on planes, in lines, in the ladies room, I find people who give me their buckets of burdens. I don't have to make up case histories, I only have to listen. They can sense that I care and they talk. Sometimes a stranger after pouring out a whole life upon me will suddenly say, "I don't know why I told you all this." She had to tell it to someone, and I was there.*

My dear friend Frances Thomas in Dallas has been coping with cancer for many years. When I asked her how people could be of help to her she replied:

The key to the whole thing is to LISTEN. Some days we want to talk about it and some days we don't, so be sensitive. Francis, who says her aim in life is "to be attuned to what God wants me to do for Him," says her "greatest asset is the love of godly friends."

Be available to listen. Long-term patients especially need to have someone sit beside them. Dr. MacDonald says they don't fear death so much as they fear being alone.

Sometimes our greatest ministry to one in bereavement or one waiting through a loved one's surgery is to just be there and be sensitive. The poet John Milton said, "They also serve who only stand and wait."[2]

Dietrich Bonhoeffer, a German pastor who was martyred during World War II, said that listening to others was the first step to genuine Christian service to others. Bonhoeffer writes:

The first service that one owes to others in the fellowship consists in listening to them. Just as love to God begins with listening to his Word, so the beginning of love for the brethren is learning to listen to them. It is God's love for us that he not only gives us his word but also lends us his ear. So it is his work that we do for our brother when we learn to listen to him. Christians, especially ministers, so often think they must always contribute something when they are in the company of others, that this is the one service they have to render. They forget that that listening can be a greater service than speaking.[3]

James Montgomery Boice expresses the reasons that listening is so important in our world today:

The reason that listening is so important is not always that people have a great deal to say but rather that they are desperate to have someone listen to them. Our world is characterized by a great cacophony of voices. People are shouting at us everywhere. They are shouting in commercials, in books and magazines, in signs by the roadside, at home, at work, at play. Everywhere we go someone is trying to get some message across to us. No one is listening to what we have to say. Everyone is too busy talking.[4]

Whatever else we may share about friendship, it is important to know that a true friend is a good listener. Over the years, I have often observed that there are few people who really understand the art of being a good listener. This is why true friendship is a rare quality today. A biblical worldview is enhanced when it includes the development of friendship.

...a true friend is a good listener.

Being a Friend Who Comforts

A good friend is also a person who is a comforter. Just as people are desperate to have someone to listen to them, many people also are desperate to be comforted in a world that is often dark, lonely, and difficult. The Scriptures exhort us to comfort one another. *"Comfort ye, comfort ye my people, saith your God."* Isaiah 40:1 A friend is someone who knows how to cheer a person's spirits. A friend can sense when we are lonely, discouraged, and despondent, and will seek to lift us out of those feelings of despair and loneliness. How special it is to have such a friend in times like this. To be successful in life, we must pursue the art of comforting those who are spiritually down and emotionally distraught. In the Psalms, David seems to have often been in need of comfort. In Psalm 69:20 David relates his own painful and disappointing experience of seeking for a friend to be a comfort to him in his time of need. David writes, *"Reproach hath broken my heart; and I am full of heaviness: and I looked for some to take pity, but there was none; and for comforters, but I found none."* We can all identify with the pain and bitter frustration that David felt. How special it is to have a friend who can understand our sorrows and comfort us in our times of grief and loneliness. Never forget the mutual benefit of having friends who minister to us just as we minister to them. Good friends stir our hearts, and fill us with joy and purpose. Good friends make us better people. English minister Charles Simeon was once entertaining some of his close friends and he said to them, *"I love to view all my Christian friends as fuel. Having gathered you all together at my hearth, I warm myself at your fire, and find my Christian love burns and glows."*[5]

As we go through life developing the gift of friendship we will need to remember that there will be times when we are called upon to comfort our friends in times of grief when their loved ones have passed away. Here is a letter that I read that was an important reminder to me of how to comfort my friends when passing through times of grief:

> *Of the many personal visits and cards and letters my mother received at the time of my father's death, she says, "I was particularly comforted by those that recalled a special memory of how my husband's life influenced theirs. It was wonderful to hear for the first time stories about things he had done years ago."*[6]

Author Florence Littauer also quotes a pastor's wife who virtually said the same thing:

> *My husband, after fifty years in the ministry (forty-three as pastor on one church) died suddenly last fall. I received hundreds of cards, letters, expressing sympathy. I soon saw that most fell into one of two categories. One was the "devotional thought" with Scripture — pointing to the joys of heaven, etc. The second which I found much more comforting were the "I-will-miss-him-too" expressions which included some humorous story or some generous act involving my husband. They mostly ended with "I'm so glad I knew him." Certainly, I'll remember this when I try to comfort others.*[7]

Being a Friend Who is Loyal

It also needs to be said that a true friend is a person who is loyal. I count loyalty as one of the most important aspects of any relationship including friendship. Loyalty is a quality that is missing in many relationships today. Think for a moment how devastating it is when loyalty is missing from a marriage, from a business partnership, or from those whom we serve. Loyalty can fill our hearts with great comfort and peace. Loyalty can inspire us to go on, for we know we are not alone. Loyalty makes us brave in the face of dangers, for we know that there are others walking in step with us towards our dreams and goals. Never forget that a good friend is also a loyal supporter in all things.

If you have a few really true and faithful friends, you are blessed indeed.

Friendship is a rare gift in life. If you have a few really true and faithful friends, you are blessed indeed. As we travel through life, we need to develop the art of friendship. Choose your friends wisely. Shakespeare wrote in *The Life of King Henry V* these words that have become so famous and so often quoted: *"We few, we happy few, we band of brothers."*

Who are your friends? Can you name them? Are they more than just one or two special people? Your husband or wife should be one of your choicest friends. The sad reality for many Christians is the sorrow of going through life with superficial relationships devoid of true and lasting friendship. For all of my readers, I would ask you to think of those that you would put in this category of the few, the happy few, the band of brothers or sisters that enrich your life and fill you with joy and gladness. Who has the joy of your time? Who has the privilege of your presence? Who has the opportunity to share your thoughts and secrets? With whom are you willing to live, and for whom are you willing to die? Who knows you better than most others? Who is willing to give and not just take from you? Whom do you miss when they are absent? Whom do you long to see? These people that come to mind are *the few, the happy few, the band of brothers.*

True friends will not only inspire us to walk with God, but they will also hold us to higher standards in our daily lives. Just as the Scripture tells us that *"Iron sharpeneth iron,"* so too, a good friend will stir us on to greater heights of being like Christ. I remember many years ago a friend of mine asked me what I really wanted in life. This was not a difficult question for me. I had decided very early in life that I wanted to be a man of God. I have found over the years that true friends will inspire me in this quest to be like Christ. My Christian friends light the fires of my passion to walk with God. The man who is my spiritual father in the faith is one such friend. I never spend time with him that I do not come away a better Christian. In fact, I consider it a waste of time if I leave a friend and have not been stirred to be a better man, father, husband, or Christian. And it is also true that I desire to have that impact on those with whom I spend time. After having spent time with our friends — have they been edified, encouraged, challenged, filled with hope, and made to hunger to be better people because they have been in our presence? Far too often our conversations are filled with empty, silly, and worldly chatter. Yes, true friends will hold us to a higher standard. I read a wonderful story that illustrates this point:

> *Stanley Jones wrote of a moment when he penned a response to a letter from a harsh critic. Irritated by the letter, Jones gave vent to his feelings of hurt and defensiveness. He determined that he would be honest, to the point, respectful. But before he mailed his response, he offered his friends a chance to read it and to offer judgment.*
>
> *When the unsent letter was returned to him, he saw that one of his [friends]…had written across the top "not sufficiently redemptive." Wise man that Jones was, he destroyed the letter. His friends had held him to a higher standard.*[8]

Charles Hadden Spurgeon made a similar comment about the importance of choosing the right friends to be your lifelong associates and companions.

The mountain of life must be scaled; crevasses, chasms, precipices, must be encountered. Almost without exception we must be roped together in this mountaineering: let the wise man accept only as his partners those who will pursue the ways of faith and virtue, for with these only will he reach the summit.[9]

Gordon MacDonald in his book, *A Resilient Life*, lists a series of questions that we can ask which will reveal who our friends really are:

- Who coaches you?
- Who stretches your mind?
- Who listens to and encourages your dreams?
- Who protects you? (A true friend will not listen to slander, or make misrepresentations about you.)
- Who shares your tears?
- Who rebukes you?
- Who seeks God with you?

No worldview is complete if we do not develop true Christian friends who can share the joys and sorrows of life with us.

A Christian worldview that inspires us to live for Christ must include this sacred subject of friendship. Remember, a friend is a person who: loves, listens, comforts, and is loyal.

How to Get Started
1. Make a list of your friends.
2. Begin today to be one who loves, listens, comforts, and is loyal to his or her friends.
3. Ask your closest friend how you can improve your friendship.
4. The greatest friend a Christian has is Jesus Christ the friend of sinners. Study the life of Jesus to learn how to be a better

friend.
5. Sit down and take a long look at your life. What kind of friend are you to those you say you love? Would your friends agree with your conclusion?

Thoughts for Consideration

* *"The reason why we have two ears and only one mouth is that we may listen the more and talk the less."* Zeno of Citium, who lived 300 years before Christ

* *"One of the toughest things for people to do is become vulnerable with one another."* David D. Ireland

* *"Friendship is one soul abiding in two bodies."* Aristotle

* *"The self-centered person cannot keep friends even when he makes them; his selfish sensitiveness is always in the way, like a diseased nerve ready to be irritated."* Hugh Black

* *"A friend loveth at all times, and a brother is born for adversity."* Proverbs 17:17

* *"When men face the world together, and are ready to stand shoulder to shoulder, the sense of comradeship makes each strong. This help may not often be called into play, but just to know that it is there if needed is a good comfort — to know that if one falls the other will lift him up."* Hugh Black

* *"The true art of friendship is hidden in the word choice; whom you choose to bring in or not to bring into your life. Choose your friends wisely."* Robert L. Dickie

* *"It takes a great soul to be a true friend. One must forgive much, forget much, forebear much."* Anna Robertson Brown

- *"When once the relationship of being the friends of Jesus is understood, we shall be called upon to exhibit to everyone we meet the love He has shown us."* Oswald Chambers

- *"A true friend never gets in your way unless you happen to be going down."* Arnold H. Glasow

Questions for Discussion

1. What are four main ingredients of friendship?

2. Why is listening essential to developing and maintaining friendships?

3. What benefits does friendship add to a life to help make it successful?

4. What part does "choice" play in forming true friendships?

5. List those whom you would call true friends.

6. Who is your closest friend?

7. How does being a friend make you like Christ?

11
Understanding the Biblical Purpose of Sex and Marriage

"And the Lord God said, It is not good that man should be alone; I will make him an help meet for him." Genesis 2:18

"Sex is a wonderful gift from God, but it makes a terrible idol, brutal and unyielding in the misery it inflicts." Randy Alcorn

O ne thing necessary for all of us to have a biblical worldview is to understand that our sexual drives are not sinful. God has made us to enjoy the sexual relationship with our wives or husbands within the context of marriage.

A worldview that does not take into account the powerful and motivating drive that is found in all men and women would be missing one of the main ingredients of human nature. Here is a comment regarding the Christian view of sexuality.

> *One thing the world seems pretty certain about: Christianity is a killjoy, anti-sex religion. But this is a lie. Nothing in the Bible says that sex is wrong. The Bible does hold the view that sex is such a mysterious and powerful thing that it ought to be subject to certain boundaries — like marriage. The Bible views the body as something important — something to be taken care of and used in God's service, not used as a sexual toy.*[1]

One of the great battles in Christian living is to live a life of sexual purity.

One of the great battles in Christian living is to live a life of sexual purity. The Christian today must battle not only his or her own inner nature, which is bad enough, but must also contend with the constant bombardment of sexual images from the internet, television, movies, and music. It is not enough to just say no to the sexual perversions that are assaulting each of us every day; we need to understand that there is a cultural war being waged on this front. Nancy Pearcey understood this fact of the cultural battle being waged today in the worldview of many who are non-Christian. Pearcey stated:

> When Madonna was asked in a recent interview why she had published her raunchy book *Sex* back in 1992, she responded, "I thought I was doing a service to mankind, being revolutionary, liberating women."
>
> This attitude explains why it is so difficult to stop the sexualizing of our culture. Sexual liberation is not just a matter of sensual gratification or titillation: It is a complete ideology, with all the elements of a worldview. To stand against it, we cannot simply express moral disapproval or say, "That's wrong." We have to remember that morality is always derivative — it stems from one's worldview. In order to be effective, we have to engage the underlying worldview.[2]

We need to make a number of observations about sex as we understand what the Bible says about this subject.

- Sex and marriage were designed by God for pleasure and intimacy.
- Sex and marriage were designed by God for companionship and fellowship.
- Sex and marriage were designed by God for comfort and encouragement.

- Sex and marriage were designed by God to fulfill the Creation Mandate.

In the Proverbs, Solomon gives us a number of somber warnings that all men need to give heed to concerning the dangers of abusing the precious gift of sex that God has given to us. Although sex is a special gift from God, it is also a gift that can be abused if used improperly or engaged in outside of marriage. These passages in Proverbs warn us of the abuse of this wonderful gift from God.

- "[16] *To deliver thee from the strange woman, even from the stranger which flattereth with her words; [17] Which forsaketh the guide of her youth, and forgetteth the covenant of her God. [18] For her house inclineth unto death, and her paths unto the dead. [19] None that go unto her return again, neither take they hold of the paths of life."* Proverbs 2:16-19

- "[1] *My son, attend unto my wisdom, and bow thine ear to my understanding: [2] That thou mayest regard discretion, and that thy lips may keep knowledge. [3] For the lips of a strange woman drop as an honeycomb, and her mouth is smoother than oil: [4] But her end is bitter as wormwood, sharp as a two-edged sword. [5] Her feet go down to death; her steps take hold on hell. [6] Lest thou shouldest ponder the path of life, her ways are moveable, that thou canst not know them. [7] Hear me now therefore, O ye children, and depart not from the words of my mouth. [8] Remove thy way far from her, and come not nigh the door of her house: [9] Lest thou give thine honor unto others, and thy years unto the cruel: [10] Lest strangers be filled with thy wealth; and thy labors be in the house of a stranger; [11] And thou mourn at the last, when thy flesh and thy body are consumed, [12] And say, How have I hated instruction, and my heart despised reproof; [13] And have not obeyed the voice of my teachers, nor inclined mine ear to them that instructed me! [14] I was almost in all evil in the midst of the congregation and assembly. [15] Drink waters out of thine own cistern, and running waters out of thine own well. [16] Let thy fountains be dispersed abroad, and rivers of waters in the streets. [17] Let them be only thine own, and not strangers' with thee. [18] Let thy fountain be blessed: and rejoice with the wife of thy youth. [19] Let her be as the loving hind and pleasant roe; let her breasts satisfy thee at all times; and be thou ravished always with her love. [20] And why wilt thou, my son, be ravished with a strange woman, and embrace the bosom of a stranger? [21] For the ways of man are before the eyes of the LORD, and he pondereth all his goings. [22] His own iniquities shall take the wicked himself, and he shall be holden with the cords of his sins. [23] He shall die without instruction; and in the greatness of his folly he shall go astray."* Proverbs 5

- *"[23] For the commandment is a lamp; and the law is light; and reproofs of instruction are the way of life: [24] To keep thee from the evil woman, from the flattery of the tongue of a strange woman. [25] Lust not after her beauty in thine heart; neither let her take thee with her eyelids. [26] For by means of a whorish woman a man is brought to a piece of bread: and the adultress will hunt for the precious life. [27] Can a man take fire in his bosom, and his clothes not be burned? [28] Can one go upon hot coals, and his feet not be burned? [29] So he that goeth in to his neighbor's wife; whosoever toucheth her shall not be innocent."* Proverbs 6:23-29

- *"[32] But whoso committeth adultery with a woman lacketh understanding: he that doeth it destroyeth his own soul. [33] A wound and dishonor shall he get; and his reproach shall not be wiped away."* Proverbs 6:32-33

- "[1] *My son, keep my words, and lay up my commandments with thee. [2] Keep my commandments, and live; and my law as the apple of thine eye. [3] Bind them upon thy fingers, write them upon the table of thine heart. [4] Say unto wisdom, Thou art my sister; and call understanding thy kinswoman: [5] That they may keep thee from the strange woman, from the stranger which flattereth with her words. [6] For at the window of my house I looked through my casement, [7] And beheld among the simple ones, I discerned among the youths, a young man void of understanding, [8] Passing through the street near her corner; and he went the way to her house, [9] In the twilight, in the evening, in the black and dark night: [10] And, behold, there met him a woman with the attire of an harlot, and subtil of heart. [11] (She is loud and stubborn; her feet abide not in her house: [12] Now is she without, now in the streets, and lieth in wait at every corner.) [13] So she caught him, and kissed him, and with an impudent face said unto him, [14] I have peace offerings with me; this day have I payed my vows. [15] Therefore came I forth to meet thee, diligently to seek thy face, and I have found thee. [16] I have decked my bed with coverings of tapestry, with carved works, with fine linen of Egypt. [17] I have perfumed my bed with myrrh, aloes, and cinnamon. [18] Come, let us take our fill of love until the morning: let us solace ourselves with loves. [19] For the goodman is not at home, he is gone a long journey: [20] He hath taken a bag of money with him, and will come home at the day appointed. [21] With her much fair speech she caused him to yield, with the flattering of her lips she forced him [22] He goeth after her straightway, as an ox goeth to the slaughter, or as a fool to the correction of the stocks; [23] Till a dart strike through his liver; as a bird hasteth to the snare, and knoweth not that it is for his life. [24] Hearken unto me now therefore, O ye children, and attend to the words of my mouth.*

[25] *Let not thine heart decline to her ways, go not astray in her paths. [26] For she hath cast down many wounded: yea, many strong men have been slain by her. [27] Her house is the way to hell, going down to the chambers of death."* Proverbs 7

• "[13] *A foolish woman is clamorous: she is simple, and knoweth nothing. [14] For she sitteth at the door of her house, on a seat in the high places of the city, [15] To call passengers who go right on their ways: [16] Whoso is simple, let him turn in hither: and as for him that wanteth understanding, she saith to him, [17] Stolen waters are sweet, and bread eaten in secret is pleasant. [18] But he knoweth not that the dead are there; and that her guests are in the depths of hell."* Proverbs 9:13-18

• "[27] *For a whore is a deep ditch; and a strange woman is a narrow pit. [28] She also lieth in wait as for a prey, and increaseth the transgressors among men."* Proverbs 23:27-28

The dangers and consequences of failing to keep the marriage covenant pure are detailed by British author Sharon James in her devotional book *Gentle Rain on Tender Grass*. James writes:

The breaking of the marriage bond was regarded with such horror that it carried the death penalty in the Old Testament. In the New Testament, we are told that adulterers will not enter heaven (Rev. 21:8). Certainly there is full forgiveness in Christ whenever a sinner repents. But we are warned in the strongest terms throughout Scripture that we are to flee temptation. Giving way to lust can destroy lives. The book of Proverbs compares playing with sexual temptation to playing with fire. The godly young man Joseph fled rather than risk succumbing to the advances

Giving way to lust can destroy lives.

of his employer's wife (Gen. 39:12). Jesus tells us that we are in danger of hell itself if we fall into lust, and it is preferable to cut off one's own hand or tear out an eye (Matt. 5:27-30). He confirms that it is not only actual sexual infidelity that constitutes adultery. Desiring anyone other than one's spouse, looking with lust at another woman — all such things are adultery. Paul warns that if we fall into sexual immorality, we sin against our own bodies, but also against the Lord (1 Cor. 6:18-20). God's design is for the husband and wife to enjoy their sexual relationship (Song of Songs; 1 Cor. 7:3-5). Sexual activity of any kind outside of marriage is forbidden (the biblical term for this is "fornication"). Single believers are to abstain from sexual relationships. Their devotion is to be focused exclusively on the Lord. (1 Cor. 7:32-34)[3]

How to Overcome Temptations of the Flesh

Every Christian should be aware of the power and enticement of the lust of the flesh. When a man sees an attractive woman, it is in the nature of his fallen flesh to be tempted. Again, listen to the warning of the wise man in Proverbs 23:33: *"Thine eyes shall behold strange women, and thine heart shall utter perverse things."*

The wise man in Proverbs is warning all young men not to be confused or surprised by the power of the flesh. Men are aroused in their feelings by sight, whereas women are aroused by touch and tender words. So when a man finds himself tempted by the sight of an attractive woman, he must apply the Scripture to his heart to control his thoughts and any lust that might be aroused by these feelings. There are a number of things that can be done to help him overcome the temptations to lustful thoughts. Here are some of them.

1. Begin with repentance. Don't let ungodly thoughts come into your heart or mind without taking them to the Lord in repentance. This means confessing these lustful thoughts as being ungodly and unpleasing to the Lord.
2. You should make every effort to resist thoughts that come to you and tempt you to lust and uncleanness. In Daniel 1:8, we

see that when Daniel was given a command that he could not obey with a clear conscience, that he *"purposed in his heart that he would not defile himself with the King's meat..."* To resist sin means that we should purpose in our hearts to be committed to doing what is right.

3. When we are tempted with lustful thoughts, we should remember the terrible consequences of sin. Remember what happened to Saul, David, Absalom, Judas, and others who sinned and faced the awful consequences of their choices. Among other things, because of sin Saul lost his throne, David lost his testimony, Absalom lost his life, and Judas lost his soul.

> *When we are tempted with lustful thoughts, we should remember the terrible consequences of sin.*

4. We should also depend on the power of the Holy Spirit. Christians should seek the filling of the Holy Spirit on their lives. And we should determine not to grieve the Spirit. With utter dependence upon Him we should seek to walk in the Spirit in our daily life.

5. Another thing we can do is to put on the Christian armor that is mentioned by the Apostle Paul in Ephesians 6:11-17.

6. We should crucify the works, deeds, and activities of the flesh as Paul mentions in Colossians 3:1-9. To crucify the flesh means to put it to death.

7. Prayer is yet another step in dealing with lustful thoughts that come into our minds and tempt us to sin. Jesus said in Matthew 26:41, *"Watch and pray, that ye enter not into temptation: the spirit indeed is willing, but the flesh is weak."* We should know ourselves. We must be aware of our weaknesses and by what means or avenues that sin may travel into our lives to tempt us and to lead us away from our love and walk with God.

8. Every true believer, when tempted, should fill his heart and mind with the Word of God. As one great servant of God once

said, "God's Word will keep you from sin, or sin will keep you from God's Word."

9. We can practice the presence of Christ. We should never forget that God is everywhere and He observes our every action. Proverbs 15:3 tells us, *"The eyes of the Lord are in every place, beholding the evil and the good."*

If we do these things when we are tempted with impure thoughts, it will help us overcome the seductive power of temptation. It is not easy in this sinful and fallen world to live pure lives. But with the right attitude and a plan before us of how to tackle these temptations, we can live lives that are pure and pleasing to the Lord. Sex and marriage were also designed by God for companionship and fellowship. In the book of Ephesians 5:22-33, the Apostle Paul gives us the foundation of a biblical marriage.

[22] *Wives, submit yourselves unto your own husbands, as unto the Lord. [23] For the husband is the head of the wife, even as Christ is the head of the church: and he is the saviour of the body. [24] Therefore as the church is subject unto Christ, so let the wives be to their own husbands in every thing. [25] Husbands, love your wives, even as Christ also loved the church, and gave himself for it; [26] That he might sanctify and cleanse it with the washing of water by the word, [27] That he might present it to himself a glorious church, not having spot, or wrinkle, or any such thing; but that it should be holy and without blemish. [28] So ought men to love their wives as their own bodies. He that loveth his wife loveth himself. [29] For no man ever yet hated his own flesh; but nourisheth and cherisheth it, even as the Lord the church: [30] For we are members of his body, of his flesh, and of his bones. [31] For this cause shall a man leave his father and mother, and shall be joined unto his wife, and they two shall be one flesh. [32] This is a great mystery: but I speak concerning Christ and the church. [33] Nevertheless let every one of you in particular so love his wife even as himself; and the wife see that she reverence her husband.*

Author Sharon James comments on God's purpose for marriage:

> *We are told today that "Families come in all shapes and sizes" — married or cohabiting, gay or straight. But these verses show that God designed one man to be joined to one woman in exclusive and faithful union. That is why they were originally one flesh, and then reunited. Jesus Christ quoted these verses and explained: "What therefore God has joined together, let not man separate." (Matt. 19:5-6) When Paul quotes this account, he explains the significance of marriage: it was planned to illustrate a more profound reality. From all eternity the triune God had a purpose for salvation for sinful humanity. Central to this plan was the self-giving love of the Lord Jesus Christ for his "bride", the church. Marriage was to be a signpost to point to this eternal reality. The husband's self-giving protection of, and provision for, his wife was to mirror Christ's love for his people. The wife's willing acceptance of the leadership of her husband was to reflect the church's submission to her Lord and Saviour.*[4]

I often share with couples who are getting married ten things that they should never do in a marriage. These "Ten Nevers," as I have called them, will make a profound difference in any marriage relationship, and help build a strong foundation for marriage.

Ten Things You Should Never Do in a Marriage

1. Never stop loving.
   a. The greatest example of this is Christ Himself.
   b. 1 Corinthians 13 tells us that true love is patient and kind. It is not jealous, envious, and does not keep score.

2. Never stop learning.
   a. Read, read, read.
   b. Read books that will change your life and have a positive impact on you and your family. Books on family, marriage, ethics, character, relationships, etc.

    c.   Of course, read the Bible, the greatest of all books.

    d.   Through the Bible we learn the greatest lessons in life.

3. Never stop listening.
    a.   This shows respect, compassion, and interest in others.
    b.   Slow your life down, and listen to one another.
    c.   Being a good listener is one of the kindest and most thoughtful things you can do.

4. Never stop living.
    a.   Enjoy life.
    b.   Get out of the ruts.
    c.   Life is short.
    d.   Do the things you enjoy doing (as long as they are moral, good, and ethical).
    e.   Try new things; go to new places; be adventurous and willing to explore new paths.

5. Never stop talking.
    a.   Communicate with each other.
    b.   Don't lecture, scold, nag, or be demeaning to one another.
    c.   Learn to enjoy sharing your most intimate and precious thoughts with one another.

6. Never stop forgiving.
    a.   The hardest thing for a man to say is, "I am sorry," or "Please forgive me."
    b.   Don't keep record or score on things that have hurt or offended you.

7. Never stop serving.
    a.   "How can I help?"
    b.   "What can I do?"
    c.   A true servant is always looking for ways to serve and make the other person happy.

8. Never stop dreaming.
   a. We were made by God to dream.
   b. It is in our very souls to aspire, to desire to achieve new goals.
   c. Always reach for new heights, set new records, look for new fields to conquer.
   d. Man always wants to run faster, jump higher, do better, etc.
   e. The person who stops dreaming is already dead before he died.

9. Never stop dying.
   a. This means dying to self.
   b. Man is by nature selfish, self-centered, and often only concerned for himself.
   c. Learn to think of others first.
   d. Put their needs and their interests in front of your own.

10. Never stop courting.
   a. "Have I told you how much I love you?"
   b. "Here, this is for you."
   c. "I planned this especially for you."
   d. "I wrote this for you."
   e. "I was thinking of you."
   f. When you were courting, you were thoughtful, considerate, and always looking for ways to make your partner happy, loved, and fulfilled. Never stop doing that.

Summary:

1. Never stop loving.
2. Never stop learning.
3. Never stop listening.
4. Never stop living.
5. Never stop talking.
6. Never stop forgiving.
7. Never stop serving.
8. Never stop dreaming.

9. Never stop dying to self.
10. Never stop courting.

Sex was designed by God for comfort and encouragement. What precious joys married couples enjoy when they share the intimacy of their sexual lives together. One night stands, prostitutes, and immoral people cannot satisfy the deep longings of the soul for comfort and encouragement. This thought is articulated in a famous Christian poem:

I Tried the Broken Cisterns Lord

O Christ, in Thee my soul hath found, and found in Thee alone The peace, the joy I sought so long, The bliss till now unknown. I sighed for rest and happiness, I yearned for them, not Thee; But while I passed my Saviour by, His love laid hold of me. I tried the broken cisterns, Lord, but ah! the waters failed! E'en as I stooped to drink they'd fled, And mocked me as I wailed. The pleasures lost I sadly mourned, But never wept for Thee, Till grace the sightless eyes received Thy loveliness to see. Now none but Christ can satisfy, None other name for me. There's love, and life, and lasting joy Lord Jesus found in Thee.

The British writer G. K. Chesterton once said, *"Every man who knocks on the door of a brothel is looking for God."*[5]

It is God who made man and gave him the desire for a meaningful sexual relationship with a woman. Every man who seeks sexual fulfillment is seeking to fulfill that God-given desire. In this sense, Chesterton realized that in seeking sexual fulfillment, men were seeking for the satisfaction that can only come from a right relationship with God and being fulfilled in the ways that God has ordained lawfully for him.

One author describes the proper boundaries for sexual fulfillment in this way:

As long as sex occurs within the bounds of marriage, it is neither wrong to desire it nor to take pleasure in it. This principle is reiterated in the New Testament where we frequently find the apostle Paul battling those who attempt to deny the satisfying of God-given desires such as the joy of eating certain foods and the joy of sex...sex is not dirty and to desire it is not wrong. Sexual desire only becomes wrong when it is misplaced or when it exceeds the parameters of God's word.[6]

Sex and marriage were designed to fulfill the creation mandate of Genesis 1:28, "*...Be fruitful and multiply...*" The fruit of our sexual love is the offspring such love produces. I look at each of my children and see them as a precious gift from God. But I also know that my children are the result of the special and intimate love that I have enjoyed with my wife. My children are therefore a double blessing to me. They are a gift from God, and they are the product of our marriage joy.

I have found that one reason why many marriages do not seem to grow and flourish spiritually is that most couples do not have a mission statement to guide them in their relationship together. Over the years I have used the Wedding Prayer by Louis Evans to help couples starting off in marriage to have a model and mission statement to focus on through the coming years. I committed this prayer to memory. Perhaps you might do this, as well, to enhance your understanding of what a Christian marriage should be like.

The Wedding Prayer

God of love, Thou hast established marriage for the welfare and happiness of mankind. Thine was the plan and only with Thee can we work it out with joy. Thou hast said, "It is not good for man to be alone. I will make a help meet for him." Now our joys are doubled since the happiness of the one is the happiness of the other. Our burdens now are halved, when we share them, we divide the load. Bless this husband. Bless him as provider of nourishment and raiment and sustain him in all the exactions and pressures of his battle for bread. May his strength be her protection, his character be her boast and her pride, and may he so live that she will find in him the haven for which the heart of woman truly longs.

Bless this loving wife. Give her a tenderness that will make her great, a deep sense of understanding and a great faith in Thee. Give her that inner beauty of soul that never fades, that eternal youth that is found in holding fast the things that never age.

Teach them that marriage is not living merely for each other; it is two uniting and joining hands to serve Thee. Give them a great spiritual purpose in life. May they seek the kingdom of God and His righteousness, and the other things shall be added unto them.

May they not expect that perfection of each other that belongs alone to Thee. May they minimize each other's weaknesses, be swift to praise and magnify each other's points of comeliness and strength, and see each other through a lover's kind and patient eyes.

Now make such assignments to them on the scroll of Thy will as will bless them and develop their characters as they walk together. Give them enough tears to keep them tender, enough hurts to keep them humane, enough of failure to keep their hands clenched tightly in Thine, and enough success to make them sure they walk with God. May they never take each other's love for granted, but always experience that breathless wonder that exclaims, 'Out of all this world you have chosen me.'

When life is done and the sun is setting, may they be found then as now hand in hand, still thanking God for each other. May they serve Thee happily, faithfully, together, until at last one shall lay the other into the arms of God.

This we ask through Jesus Christ, the great lover of our souls. Amen

Louis H. Evans, D.D., L.L.D.

A Christian worldview that prepares us to live for Christ must include a biblical view of our sexuality. One of the greatest challenges for every Christian is to learn to control his physical passions and bring them under the control of the Holy Spirit. Understanding the biblical purpose of sex and marriage is an important aspect of living for Jesus.

How to Get Started

1. Study carefully Genesis 1-3 and Ephesians 5 to understand the purpose of sex and marriage.
2. Make a commitment to God that you will only fulfill your sexual desires within the context of biblical marriage between a man and a woman.
3. If you are married, practice the "Ten Nevers."
4. Memorize *The Wedding Prayer* as the mission statement of your marriage.
5. If you are an older believer, take every opportunity to teach younger Christians the biblical purpose of sex and marriage.

Thoughts for Consideration

- *"There is no more lovely, friendly, and charming relationship, communion, or company than a good marriage."* Martin Luther

- *"God thought of sex before man did, and when man leaves God out of his sexual thinking he is in trouble."* John Blanchard

- *"All healthy men, ancient and modern, Eastern and Western, know that there is a certain fury in sex that we cannot afford to inflame, and that a certain mystery and awe must ever surround it if we are to remain sane."* G. K. Chesterton

- "The powerful sexual drives which are built into man's relationship with woman are not seen in Scripture as the foundation of marriage, but the consummation and physical expression of it." Sinclair Ferguson

- "The battle of life will probably not rise above the sex battle." E. Stanley Jones

- "God never intended that man could find the true meaning of his sexuality in any other relationship than that of the total self-giving involved in marriage." Al Martin

- "When sex is deformed, cheapened and exploited, then the potentiality of life and the whole social fabric of society deteriorates." Mary Whitehouse

- "No sinful act desecrates the body like fornication and sexual abuse. In this sense fornication has a deadly eminence." R. C. H. Lenski

- "Don't look around for a life partner, look up. Any other choice than God's will mean disaster." Anonymous

- "Marriage is more than finding the right person; it is being the right person." Anonymous

Questions for Discussion

1. What did God intend when He designed man and woman and brought them together in marriage?

2. What is the main lesson one learns from reading the warnings in Proverbs about the abuse of sex?

3. What is the difference between love and lust?

4. What is the biblical plan for husbands and wives as outlined by the Apostle Paul in Ephesians 5?

5. How many of the Ten Nevers can you remember?

6. What is your mission statement for your marriage?

7. How has "The Wedding Prayer" helped you with this idea of having a mission statement?

12
Becoming a Servant

"Let nothing be done through strife or vainglory; but in lowliness of mind let each esteem other better than themselves. Look not every man on his own things, but every man also on the things of others. Let this mind be in you, which was also in Christ Jesus: Who, being in the form of God, thought it not robbery to be equal with God: But made himself of no reputation, and took upon him the form of a servant, and was made in the likeness of men." Philippians 2:3-7

"True greatness, true leadership, is achieved not by reducing men to one's service but in giving oneself in selfless service of others."[1] J. Oswald Sanders

The key to a biblical worldview is to develop the attitude of a servant. It is to have a servant's heart. If we see ourselves as servants, we will have many opportunities to serve others and will know the blessing of God in a rich and bountiful way. The reason for this is that there are so few people today who really have a servant's heart. The absence of a humble and gracious heart to serve others is the reason the church is often perceived to be so cold and harsh. William Law, a great Christian leader, once said,

> Let every day be a day of humility; condescend to all the weaknesses and infirmities of your fellow-creatures, cover their frailties, love their excellencies, encourage their virtues, relieve their wants, rejoice in their prosperities, compassionate [alleviate] their distress, receive their

*friendship, overlook their unkindness, forgive their malice,
be a servant of servants, and condescend to do the lowliest
offices of the lowest of mankind.*[2]

Having the attitude of a servant is one of the things that will help
propel people on to greatness. The world is longing for true leaders to emerge somewhere in this darkened and selfish world that have a servant's heart. One of the great leaders in the American Civil Rights movement, Dr. Martin Luther King, Jr., once said,

> *Having the attitude of a servant is one of the things that will help propel people on to greatness.*

*Everybody can be great because anybody can serve.
You don't have to have a college degree to serve. You don't have to make your subject and verb agree to serve...You don't have to know the
second theory of thermodynamics in physics to serve. You
only need a heart full of grace. A soul generated by love.*[3]

One author, who understood the power of being a loyal servant,
quoted B. C. Forbes, journalist and the founder of Forbes Magazine:

> *Without loyalty nothing can be accomplished in any
> sphere. The person who renders loyal service in a humble
> capacity will be chosen for higher responsibilities, just as
> the biblical servant who multiplied the one pound given
> him by his master was made ruler over ten cities, whereas the servant who did not put his pound to use lost that
> which he had.*[4]

The problem with so many people today in all walks of life is
that they don't have this selfless attitude of serving others. Quite
often people today only engage themselves when there is something to be gained personally. The questions asked today often
are, "What's in it for me?" or "What will I get out of this?" Author

James Hunter was right on target when he said, *"There is an old saying that you can judge people's character by how they treat people who can do nothing for them."*[5]

There is an interesting story in 1 Kings 12. Solomon, the king of Israel, died. His son, Rehoboam, was going to be crowned the new king. Rehoboam did one of the wisest things that a new leader could possibly do. Rehoboam called together the wise old men who were his father's counselors and he asked for their advice and suggestions on how to be an effective leader to the people. The wise old men gave Rehoboam this answer: *"And they spake unto him saying, if thou wilt be a servant unto this people this day, and wilt serve them, and answer them, and speak good words to them, then they will be thy servants forever."* 1 Kings 12:7

This was great advice that every aspiring leader should pay attention to. Unfortunately, Rehoboam did not follow the counsel of his father's old friends. Instead, he consulted younger men who had grown up with him, and he followed their advice. This mistake proved to be a great disaster to Rehoboam and the kingdom. The young counselors advised Rehoboam to be a tough, mean-spirited tyrant, whom they said could accomplish more, not by leading the people with love and humility, but by driving them with fear and intimidation. The story ends in a tragic failure of leadership gone astray and wise counsel ignored. Just what was the advice that Solomon's old advisors gave to young Rehoboam? The advice contained these ideas:

1. Be a servant to the people.
2. Answer their questions, i.e. be available, approachable, and compassionate to them.
3. Speak kindly to them, i.e. respect them and avoid outbursts of temper, and making mean, disparaging, demeaning comments to them.

This would be wonderful advice for anyone to listen to and obey. If you want success in your life and walk with God, it is essential that you realize how important it is to be a true servant leader.

The Seven Characteristics of a Servant's Heart

There are a number of things that make up the servant's heart. Here are some of them.

1. Be a good listener. Oliver Wendell Holmes once said, *"To be able to listen to others in a sympathetic and understanding manner is, perhaps, the most effective mechanism in the world for getting along with people, and tying up their friendship for good. Too few people practice the 'white magic' of being good listeners."*[6]

2. Be sensitive to the hurts and sorrows of others. This means recognizing and sympathizing with others in their times of trial and suffering.

3. Take a sincere interest in the lives of others. This is the example of Jesus that Paul mentions in Philippians 2:3-7:

    > *Let nothing be done through strife or vainglory: but in lowliness of mind let each esteem other better than themselves. Look not every man on his own things, but every man also on the things of others. Let this mind be in you, which was also in Christ Jesus: Who, being in the form of God, thought it not robbery to be equal with God: But made himself of no reputation, and took upon him the form of a servant, and was made in the likeness of men.*

4. Be an encourager. I have used an analogy to teach my children about what kind of person they ought to be. I have said that they can be either a picture, a wet blanket, or a light. A person who is a picture is just that and nothing more. That person tends to come in a room and adds nothing to the conversation. They do not help, or encourage; in fact they don't do anything. The picture is just someone who is present but makes no significant contribution to the gathering. A wet blanket is the one who comes into a room with a bitter spirit or discouraged attitude. That person usually is quite negative. The only things they say tend to demoralize and discourage everyone that is present. This person is hard to be around. People tend

to grimace when they arrive, and secretly everyone wishes that they would either leave or shut up. But the light is the person who comes into a room and immediately lights everything up in a positive way. This person is an encourager, an edifier, and a person who blesses and makes everyone around them feel better and more positive. I have told my children you can be either a picture (someone who adds nothing significant to a gathering), a wet blanket (someone who discourages everyone else), or a light (someone who lights up the place by their presence with their comforting, positive words and by their attitude). Which person do you want to be?

5. Be a helper.
6. Be very slow to criticize others. If you must criticize, do your best to do it in a way that affirms, helps, encourages, and does not cut apart or destroy. And by the way, there is a secret to receiving criticism, too. Always remind yourself that if the one critiquing you knew your inner heart, there would be so much more they could really say. After receiving the criticism, take it to the Lord in prayer and ask if there might not be a kernel of truth in what has been said.
7. Be a minister. Every day when I get up, I remind myself that I am a minister of Christ. The word minister means one who serves. When I'm at home or traveling, I ask myself, "Who is my congregation today?" It may be my family, my neighbors, or someone with whom I am traveling. With these thoughts in mind, I pray to be filled with the Spirit so that I may indeed minister and serve those whom God has providentially placed in my presence that day. So I remind you that as you go through life, see yourself as a minister and servant to Christ. Your life has a purpose. You were designed to serve all whom you meet. In humility and with prayer, commit yourself

In humility and with prayer, commit yourself to being a blessing to others by serving them and ministering to their needs.

to being a blessing to others by serving them and ministering to their needs.

The secret and amazing power of a servant must not be overlooked in the framework of success. Servants who are unselfish and take a sincere interest in our lives are not easily forgotten.

The Law of the Harvest

The law of the harvest is from the Bible. This law teaches that you reap what you sow. If you sow (plant) corn, you'll reap (harvest) a crop of corn. If you sow wheat, you will harvest wheat. And so it goes. In our daily lives, if we sow hate, anger, bitterness, resentment, and ill-will, we will reap the same. If however, we sow love, kindness, patience and gentleness, we will reap the same. The old saying goes, "*What goes around comes around.*" Those who have discovered the secret of sowing a gracious Christian life and testimony to those they love, live, and work with will reap the joys of loyalty, respect, and love in return.

Most Mothers are True Servants

Another point that we should remember is that most women who are mothers have already learned the secret of being a servant-leader. Where would our world and culture be without the loving example of godly mothers who have devoted themselves to their children and families as servant-leaders preparing the next generation of great leaders by their examples. Consider with me the things that most mothers do instinctively, without a second thought, and without griping and complaining. Most mothers are servant-leaders who:

1. Care (They are great encouragers!)
2. Serve
3. Sacrifice
4. Listen
5. Inspire
6. Understand

7. Correct
8. Rebuke, if necessary
9. Love
10. Never give up on their children.

Every leader, every pastor, and every person seeking to develop a Christian worldview would be wise to consider the example of motherhood when seeking a model of servant-leadership to follow and emulate.

We must never forget that the greatest servant was Jesus Christ Himself. The more Christ-like we become, the more we will die to self and become a servant to others. True success in life is to be like Christ. Paul the apostle wrote of Jesus and described Him in this fashion in Philippians 2:5-8:

> [5] *Let this mind be in you, which was also in Christ Jesus:* [6] *Who, being in the form of God, thought it not robbery to be equal with God:* [7] *But made himself of no reputation, and took upon him the form of a servant, and was made in the likeness of men:* [8] *And being found in fashion as a man, he humbled himself, and became obedient unto death, even the death of the cross.*

This is the goal of being a servant. We should have in our biblical worldview the desire to be like Christ by being a servant to others. It is not easy at times to die to self and serve others selflessly. To be a true servant means that at times we must be willing to be second. We must be willing to put the concerns and needs of others above our own. Pastor John Kitchen says it so well:

> *It's hard to be happy being second. Someone once asked Arthur Fiedler, legendary conductor of the Boston Pops, what the most difficult instrument in the orchestra is to play. His reply: "Second fiddle." If you find a person willingly embracing obscurity to get God's work done, you'll find a person controlled by the Holy Spirit.*[7]

George Duncan also made this point when he said,

> Think for a moment how often we come across those
> whose worth is seldom recognized by men, but I am sure
> will never be overlooked by God, and will certainly not go
> unrewarded. Many are prepared to recognize the promi-
> nent part played by Simon Peter among the disciples, but
> forget that if there had not been an Andrew who "brought
> him to Jesus" there would never have been a Peter! The
> church universal gives thanks to God for Paul, the greatest
> Christian who ever lived, but forget that if there had not
> been a Barnabas there might never have been a Paul![8]

To become a servant, it is necessary to die to self. No one can
be a servant who does not learn what it means to die to self on
a daily basis. Jesus taught us by example and instruction the meaning of this Christian duty. Dying to self is the attitude of putting others first and yourself last. It is turning the other cheek and going the extra mile. It is the act of humbling yourself so that you can serve and lift others up. Jesus said, "He who saves his life will lose it and he who loses his life will save it." The great Baptist preacher C. H. Spurgeon understood and practiced this Christian duty. Spurgeon wrote:

> *No one can be a servant who does not learn what it means to die to self on a daily basis.*

> I am content to be criticized, misunderstood, and misrep-
> resented. The cost was counted long ago, and the estimate
> was so liberal that there is no fear of its being exceeded.
> "I know whom I have believed, and am persuaded that
> He is able to keep that which I have committed unto Him
> against that day."[9]

Years ago I came across these statements on dying to self. I have
used these thoughts to teach and inspire others in the Christian

duty of following the example of Jesus in being a servant who dies to self. Here are the statements:

Dying to Self

When you are forgotten, or neglected, or purposely set at naught, and you don't sting and hurt with the insult or the oversight, but your heart is happy, being counted worthy to suffer for Christ, THAT IS DYING TO SELF.

When your good is evil spoken of, when your wishes are crossed, your advice disregarded, your opinions ridiculed, and you refuse to let anger rise in your heart, or even defend yourself, but take in all in patient, loving silence, THAT IS DYING TO SELF.

When you lovingly and patiently bear any disorder, any irregularity, any impunctuality, or any annoyance; when you stand face-to- face with waste, folly, extravagance, spiritual insensibility-and endure it as Jesus endured, THAT IS DYING TO SELF.
When you are content with any food, any offering, any climate, any society, any raiment, any interruption by the will of God, THAT IS DYING TO SELF.

When you never care to refer to yourself in conversation, or to record your own good works, or itch after commendations, when you can truly love to be unknown, THAT IS DYING TO SELF.

When you can see your brother prosper and have his needs met and can honestly rejoice with him in spirit and feel no envy, nor question God, while your own needs are far greater and in desperate circumstances, THAT IS DYING TO SELF.

When you can receive correction and reproof from one of less stature than yourself and can humbly submit inwardly as well as outwardly, finding no rebellion or resentment rising up within your heart. THAT IS DYING TO SELF.

"That I may know Him, and the power of his resurrection, and the fellowship of his sufferings, being made conformable unto his death." Philippians 3:10[10]

The principle of dying to self is one of the most important aspects of servanthood that I know. I have prayed for grace over the years as a pastor to be a man who modeled this principle in my private and daily life. Not only have I aimed for this in my life, but I have also taught this to my flock and to my children. I believe all true and great leaders are those who are learning the secret of dying to self. Speaking of the importance of being a person who dies to self and who models the spirit of Christ in self sacrifice, Pastor John Kitchen made this remark:

> *Any local assembly of believers today needs those willing to care for the physical facilities the Lord has entrusted to them for furthering His purposes. It takes nothing less than the Spirit of God to enable a person to gladly embrace the obscurity of such a ministry for God's glory.*
>
> *How about your church? Chances are the grass is mowed in the summer, and in the winter the parking lot is plowed and the sidewalks shoveled. Enter the restrooms. Someone has scrubbed the toilets, washed the mirrors, and restocked the paper products. Light bulbs have been replaced, windows cleaned, carpets vacuumed, walls painted, flowerbeds weeded, shrubs trimmed. Someone has been active while you've been consumed with the rest of life. When God revives His people He raises up those who are willing to be servants.*[11]

A number of years ago, I wrote this description of what I wanted my life to be like as I served the Lord in the ministry. I have shared this with my family and friends to encourage them to be Christ-like in their everyday activities.

Take My Desires, Lord

Take my desire to be loved and enable me to love others.

Take my desire to have friends and enable me to befriend others.

Take my desire to be understood and enable me to understand others.

Take my desire to be comforted and enable me to comfort others.

Take my desire to be forgiven and enable me to forgive others.

Take my desire to be accepted and enable me to accept others.

Take my desire to be happy and enable me to make others happy.

Take my desire for honor and recognition and enable me to honor others.

Take my desire to be served and enable me to serve others.

Take my desire for praise and enable me to praise others.

Take my desire to be heard and enable me to listen to others.

Take my desire to be first and enable me to put others first and myself last.

Take my desire for revenge and enable me to show mercy to others.

Lord, take all of my desires, and in return, grant me the grace to be like Jesus, for in this alone shall I find true peace and happiness.

Robert L. Dickie
July 23, 1996

As we develop a worldview we need to make sure that we understand that it must contain the biblical concept of being a servant and dying to self. Author Steve Brown makes this comment on dying to self that should serve as a powerful reminder of the necessity of this important subject:

> When James Calvert went out to Fiji in 1838, he was told by the captain of the ship on which he sailed that he was going to a land of cannibals. The captain tried to dissuade Calvert from going by saying, "You are risking your life and all those with you if you go among such savages. You will all die." Calvert replied, "We died before we came here."[12]

How to Get Started

1. Remember that to be like Christ we must become servants.
2. Study carefully the seven characteristics of a servant's heart.
3. Practice dying to self every day.
4. Ask the Lord to enable you to live out the principles in the reading, "*Take My Desires, Lord.*"

Thoughts for Consideration

- *"My love for serving the Lord with my whole time and strength makes it a privilege to sacrifice other enjoyments."* J. B. Chapman

- *"It is not fitting, when one is in God's service, to have a gloomy face or a chilling look."* Saint Francis of Assisi

- *"I don't know what your destiny will be, but one thing I know: the only ones among you who will be really happy are those who have sought and found how to serve."* Albert Sweitzer

- *"Nothing liberates our greatness like the desire to help, the desire to serve."* Marianne Williamson

- *"God is not greater if you reverence him, but you are greater if you serve him."* St. Augustine

- *"Service to God through service to mankind is the only motivation acceptable to God for diligence and hard work in our vocational calling."* Jerry Bridges

- *"The highest honour in the church is not government but service."* John Calvin

- *"There are no trivial assignments in the work of the Lord."* Vance Havner

- *"It is better to be God's dog than the devil's darling."* C. H. Spurgeon

- *"The man who tries to do something and fails is infinitely better than the man who tries to do nothing and succeeds."* D. Martyn Lloyd-Jones

Questions for Discussion

1. How does the attitude of a servant propel people to greatness?

2. How does being a servant make one like Jesus Christ?

3. What are some of the things that make up a servant's heart?

4. What is meant by the law of the harvest?

5. How is it that most mothers are true servants?

6. What does it mean to die to self?

7. Give some examples of dying to self.

13
Striving for Success

"This book of the law shall not depart out of thy mouth; but thou shalt meditate therein day and night, that thou mayest observe to do according to all that is written therein: for then thou shalt make thy way prosperous, and then thou shalt have good success." Joshua 1:8

"Keep adding, keep walking, keep advancing, do not stop, do not turn back, do not turn from the straight road!" St. Augustine

In developing a Christian worldview, we must factor in the concept of striving for success. Just as holy living leads to peaceful dying, Christian living leads to success in life.

Of all people in this world, the one who believes in God should strive the most for success. Life is made up of discipline. And it is those who are disciplined who succeed in the challenges of life. Someone once said, *"Those who succeed are the efficient few. They are the few who have the ambition and will-power to develop themselves."*

> **Just as holy living leads to peaceful dying, Christian living leads to success in life.**

I once had the privilege of preaching at a pastor's conference in Kiev, Ukraine with Dr. John Blanchard. John is a gifted evangelist and author of many wonderful Christian books. One of the noticeable characteristics of this gracious man of God is his pursuit of excellence. John shared with me his motto for his life as the years were then beginning to wind down. He said to me, *"I try to do all that I can, as well as I can, for as long as I can."* This would be a good motto for every Christian to live by.

Sadly, this present generation has been marked by mediocrity. There are few people with the ambition and willpower to seek to improve themselves. We live in a time when we look to the government to give us what our forefathers worked so hard for. Winston Churchill's challenge to strive with *"Blood, sweat, and tears,"* would fall on deaf ears in most of the youth in our culture today. A study in 1983 reported the dismal failure of the American educational system. The failure of our schools to train and educate our youth is one of many reasons why so many people today are content with mediocrity. Here is a comment from that study: *"Each generation of Americans has outstripped its parents in education, in literacy and in economic attainment. For the first time in the history of our country, the educational skills of one generation will not surpass, will not equal, will not even approach, those of their parents."*[1]

When my son, Bob III, was a captain in the U. S. Air Force, he had this inscription on the wall in his office: *"Every morning in Africa a gazelle wakes up. It knows it must run faster than the fastest lion or it will be killed...every morning a lion wakes up. It knows it must outrun the slowest gazelle or it will starve to death. It doesn't matter whether you are a lion or a gazelle...when the sun comes up, you'd better be running."*

This quote just reminds us that there is hard work involved in achieving success. True success does not come to the lazy. It comes only to those who have the discipline and determination to set goals and strive for them. If we would be successful in life, then we must be those who have a passion for success. Of all people, Christians should be those with such a passion in their lives. As a matter of fact, it is a tragedy that so many people who profess to know and follow the Lord Jesus Christ have such poor testimonies when it comes to striving for excellence and success. Every night when I pray for my children, I always pray for each of them to strive for success. And every night they have heard me pray, "*O Lord, help my children strive for excellence in every area of their lives! Make them men and women of God. Help them in all that they do. Bless them spiritually, physically, mentally, and socially.*" Author and lecturer Ted W. Engstrom understood this idea of encouraging Christians to strive for excellence: "*Striving for excellence in our work, whatever it is, is not only our Christian duty, but a basic form of Christian witness. And our nonverbal communication speaks so loudly that people often cannot hear a single word we say.*"[2]

Again Engstrom writes:

> *Every truly worthwhile achievement of excellence has a price tag. The question you must answer for yourself is, How much am I willing to pay in hard work, patience, sacrifice, and endurance to be a person of excellence? Your answer is important, because the cost is great. But if you are willing to be the person you were meant to be, I think you will discover that for you the sky is the limit... Excellence is not restricted to sex, age, race, or occupation. This means a life of excellence is for you.*[3]

Every truly worthwhile achievement of excellence has a price tag.

If we are going to take seriously the call to follow Christ and to be His disciples, then we must remember that striving for excellence, success, and obedience to God is a costly matter. Bishop J. C. Ryle understood this and challenged his readers:

> *It does cost something to be a real Christian, according to the standard of the Bible. There are enemies to be overcome, battles to be fought, sacrifices to be made, an Egypt to be forsaken, a wilderness to be passed through, a cross*

to be carried, a race to be run. Conversion is not putting a man in an arm-chair and taking him easily to heaven. It is the beginning of a mighty conflict in which it costs much to win the victory.[4]

Striving for excellence is a God-given desire that is natural to all those who have known the grace of God in salvation. Excellence should be the distinguishing mark of a child of God. Author Bob Russell wrote: *"We all have a God-given desire, not just to work, but to excel and improve. Thorvaldsen, the famous sculptor, was once asked which of his works he considered to be the greatest. 'My next one,' he replied."*[5] To develop a Christian worldview that will enable us to strive for success in life will take courage, discipline, and tons of effort.

King Solomon wrote many proverbs that addressed these issues of hard work and laziness. Here are a few of them.

1. *"[6] Go to the ant, thou sluggard; consider her ways, and be wise: [7] Which having no guide, overseer, or ruler, [8] Provideth her meat in the summer, and gathereth her food in the harvest. [9] How long wilt thou sleep, O sluggard? When wilt thou arise out of thy sleep? [10] Yet a little sleep, a little slumber, a little folding of the hands to sleep: [11] So shall thy poverty come as one that travelleth, and thy want as an armed man."* Proverbs 6:6-11

2. *"He that gathereth in summer is a wise son: but he that sleepeth in harvest is a son that causeth shame."* Proverbs 10:5

3. *"The soul of the sluggard desireth, and hath nothing: but the soul of the diligent shall be made fat."* Proverbs 13:4

4. *"He also that is slothful in his work is brother to him that is a great waster."* Proverbs 18:9

5. *"Slothfulness casteth into a deep sleep; and an idle soul shall suffer hunger."* Proverbs 19:15

6. *"A slothful man hideth his hand in his bosom, and will not so much as bring it to his mouth again."* Proverbs 19:24

7. *"The desire of the slothful killeth him; for his hands refuse to labour."* Proverbs 21:25

8. *"The slothful man saith, There is a lion without, I shall be slain in the streets."* Proverbs 22:13
9. *"Seest thou a man diligent in his business? He shall stand before kings; he shall not stand before mean men."* Proverbs 22:29
10. *"[30] I went by the field of the slothful, and by the vineyard of the man void of understanding; [31] And, lo, it was all grown over with thorns, and nettles had covered the face thereof, and the stone wall thereof was broken down. [32] Then I saw, and considered it well: I looked upon it, and received instruction. [33] Yet a little sleep, a little slumber, a little folding of the hands to sleep: [34] So shall thy poverty come as one that travelleth; and thy want as an armed man."* Proverbs 24:30-34
11. *"He that tilleth his land shall have plenty of bread: but he that followeth after vain persons shall have poverty enough."* Proverbs 28:19

Years ago I read a quote about a man who was a communist. This quote revealed the passion and desire he had to achieve his dream of world communism. I have thought over the years how wonderful it would be if we all had that same burning desire and commitment to the things we believe and cherish. This young man went to Mexico and wrote to his fiancé, breaking off their engagement. He explained his involvement with communism. Here is the letter he sent to her.

We Communists don't have the time or the money for many movies or concerts or T-bone steaks or decent homes or new cars. We've been described as fanatics. We are fanatics. Our lives are dominated by one great overshadowing factor — the struggle for world Communism. We Communists have a philosophy of life, which no amount of money could buy. We have a cause to fight for, a definite purpose in life. We subordinate our petty, personal selves into a great movement of humanity, and if our personal lives seem hard or our egos appear to suffer through subordination to the Party, then we are adequately compensated by the thought that each of us in his small way is contributing to something new and true and better for mankind.

There is one thing in which I am dead in earnest about, and that is the Communist cause. It is my life, my business, my religion, my hobby, my sweetheart, my wife, and my mistress, my bread and meat. I work at it in the day time and dream of it at night. Its hold grows on me, not lessens, as time goes on. Therefore I cannot carry on a friendship, a love affair, or even a conversation without relating it to this force which both drives and guides my life. I evaluate people, books, ideas, and actions according to how they affect the Communist cause and by their attitude toward it. I've already been in jail because of my ideas and, if neces-sary, I'm ready to go before a firing squad.[6]

What made this man, and many others like him, able to bring a third of the earth under the sway of communist philosophy was his passion to be committed to his goal and dream. Communism, as history has shown us, is a bankrupt philosophy that was doomed for failure. While we reject the foolish ideas of this ideology, we can still learn much from those who were dedicated to its cause and ideals.

Over the years, I have tried to instill a philosophy of success and excellence into my children who were runners. I had printed a card that marked out for them the characteristics of a champi-on. These were self-evident truths that every good athlete should know. As I have repeated these things over and over to them in their training, I would say to them, *"Keep your ducks in order!"* They knew exactly what I meant.

The Characteristics of a Champion

1. Dedication
2. Determination
3. Concentration (consistency)
4. Vision (attainable goals)
5. Nutrition (proper diet)
6. Preparation
7. Rotation (performance/refuel/rest)
8. Imitation (following the example of others who have achieved)

9. Faith
10. Expectation (confidence that you have done all that you could to prepare)

I gave each of my children a laminated card with these characteristics of a champion on it. I continually remind them of the ingredients and marks of a winner. Champions, and those who achieve success, don't happen by luck, chance, or by fate. Great people, winners, and champions are those who learned by blood, sweat, and tears to do their best at all times. They are people driven by some unseen force to strive for success. This is what makes the difference in the lives of successful people.

Success does not come easily. Helen Keller, an American author who was deaf and blind, understood that success came only by hard work and discipline. She once made a statement that gives us insight into why she was able to achieve so much even though greatly handicapped. She said: *"I long to accomplish a great task; but it is my chief duty and joy to accomplish humble tasks as though they were great and noble. The world is moved along, not only by the mighty shoves of its heroes, but also by the aggregate of the tiny pushes of each honest worker."*[7]

...it is my chief duty and joy to accomplish humble tasks as though they were great and noble.

The late TV anchorwomen, Jessica Savitch, spoke to students at Columbia College in South Carolina. Her challenge to the graduates urged them to pursue excellence in all that they did. She said,

As a reporter, I have had a chance to observe people at the top of just about every field. And it makes no difference if they are male or female, black or white, old or young, the people I observed succeeding are those who have been taught or who teach themselves to strive for excellence. The pleasure comes from knowing you have done a job the best way you know how. It seems to me, however, in our modern society that there is very little done these days in pursuit of excellence. But whenever there is, it stands out for its rarity.[8]

This same thought was understood by Dr. Martyn Lloyd-Jones the great Welsh Preacher, who was in many ways a modern-day apostle to the evangelical world during the last century,

I defy you to read the life of any saint that has ever adorned the life of the Church without seeing at once that the greatest characteristic in the life of that saint was discipline and order. Invariably it is the universal characteristic of all the outstanding men and women of God...Obviously it is something that is thoroughly scriptural and absolutely essential.[9]

I was touched by reading the comments that Anglican Bishop Handley Moule wrote about his father. As I look back on my life, I have tried to be a father who has modeled the life of Christ before my children. I fear I have too often failed! But Handley Moule writes about his father in this way:

I can only look back upon him thankful that such a personality embodies to me the great word Father; a man so full of energy and capacity, so absolutely simple, so entirely fearless, so free from the seeking of his own glory, so ready both to bear and to do, a gentleman so true, a Christian so strong, so spiritual, so deep, such a pastor, such a parent, such a grandfather, such a friend.[10]

As we strive for success, it is important to heed this warning from the nineteenth-century English preacher, C. H. Spurgeon:

Success exposes a man to the pressures of people and this tempts him to hold on to his gains by means of fleshly methods and practices, and to let himself be ruled wholly by the dictatorial demands of incessant expansion. Suc-

cess can go to my head and will unless I remember that it is God who accomplishes the work, that he can continue to do so without my help, and that he will be able to make out with other means whenever he wants to cut me out.[11]

The Lost Art of Asking Good Questions

One further way to develop a worldview that leads to success in life is to learn the lost art of asking good questions. I can learn as much from a person by the questions they don't ask me, as by the ones they do. In Proverbs 13:20, *"He that walketh with wise men shall be wise: but a companion of fools shall be destroyed."* Whenever I have had the opportunity to spend time with an older minister or pastor, I have always found it a delight to ask questions that would instruct me and inspire me. In this way, I can find much to profit for my soul and walk with God. I would encourage every young man or woman to find a spiritual mentor with whom you can spend time, and not only observe their life, but also ask pertinent questions that will open up new worlds of thoughts and insights.

Martyn Lloyd-Jones made this comment about the importance of asking good questions. *"I sometimes think that the whole art of the Christian life is the art of asking questions."*[12] Every wise young person should make a list of important questions and either have it with them or know those questions so well, that when an opportunity arises, they will be able to use those questions to learn, grow, and become wiser by the asking.

Here are some of the questions that I have often asked older pastors and ministers when I had the opportunity:

* What books have you read that have changed your life?
* How do you read, and what is your method of mastering the contents of a good book?
* What is the most helpful book you have ever read next to the Bible itself?
* What books would you avoid reading?
* Who is your favorite author?
* How did you come to faith in Christ?
* How have you developed your spiritual life?

- What does it mean to be filled with the Spirit?
- How do you grow in grace?
- What preachers do you enjoy listening to?
- Who was the most powerful preacher you ever heard?
- What's your favorite verse in the Bible?
- What does it mean to you to walk with God?
- What does it mean to you to be a man of God?
- What are your greatest regrets in life?
- If you had it to do over again, how and what would you change in your life?
- How do you teach your wife and children the things of God?
- What things do you do to overcome temptation?
- What preachers or speakers have the most impact on your life?
- What is your favorite book of the Bible?
- How do you study Scripture?
- What is your favorite and most helpful commentary?
- What is your view of eschatology?
- What is your expectation for the future?
- How do you kill pride?
- How do you practice the presence of Christ?
- What does it mean to you to die to self?
- What advice would you give a young minister?
- What is the most important lesson you have learned in your life and ministry?
- What things do you do to stir up your love for God?
- How do you pray?
- When do you have your personal quiet time with the Lord?

Over the years, I have met very few people who seemed to be truly passionate about striving for success. But those individuals who did strive for success and excellence stirred my soul and ignited a fire in my heart to be the best I could be for the Lord. Years ago I read a book on prayer that had a quote in the forward that spoke to me of the need for Christians to be passionate in their quest for excellence. This quote still stirs me even though I first read it many years ago: *"The French Foreign Legion is world famous for* its **esprit de corps** and daredevil spirit. It has a motto: 'If I falter — push me on. If I stumble — pick me up. If I retreat — shoot me!' A far cry from the soft, silken ways of the average Christian of our day."[13]

A biblical worldview must be built on this foundational principle of knowing what success is and then working hard to achieve it in every area of one's life. *"This book of the law shall not depart out of thy mouth: but thou shalt meditate therein day and night, that thou mayest observe to do according to all that is written therein: for then thou shalt make thy way prosperous, and then thou shalt have good success."* Joshua 1:8 Be passionate in your pursuit of excellence and success.

How to Get Started

1. Memorize Joshua 1:8.
2. Have a goal and purpose for living, and then pursue it with all your heart.
3. Develop the heart of a champion.
4. Seek out a teacher or mentor and practice the lost art of asking them questions.

Thoughts for Consideration

* *"Show me a champion and I'll show you someone who has a deep devotion to obedience. Regardless of the sport or field, a person rises from obscurity to enjoy championship status by becoming fully obedient to his or her coach's training advice."* David Ireland

* *"By perseverance the snail reached the ark."* C. H. Spurgeon

* *"The will to persevere is often the difference between failure and success."* David Sarnoff, president of RCA

- *"Consider the postage stamp, its usefulness consists in the ability to stick to one thing till it gets there."* Josh Billings

- *"Preach, pray, and plug away."* Dr. Lehman Straus

- *"…it is a wretched waste to be gratified with mediocrity when the excellent lies before us."* Isaac D'Israeli

- *"The door to the room of success swings on the hinge of opposition"* Bob Jones, Sr.

- *"Success is more attitude than aptitude."* Anonymous

- *"The dictionary is the only place where you can find success before work."* Anonymous

- *"The man who is elated by success and cast down by failure is still a carnal man. At best, his fruit will have a worm in it."* A. W. Tozer

- *"Success without God only makes temporary friends and admirers."* Spiros Zodhiates

Questions for Discussion

1. Why of all people should Christians strive for success?

2. What is the price tag for excellence?

3. According to C. H. Spurgeon, what is the danger of success?

4. How does asking good questions prepare one for success?

5. What is your goal, purpose, or personal mission statement for your life?

6. Are you pursuing your goals with passion and discipline?

14
Building Character in the Christian Life

"Let no man despise thy youth; but be thou an example of the believers, in word, in conversation, in charity, in spirit, in faith, in purity. Till I come, give attendance to reading, to exhortation, to doctrine." 1 Timothy 4:12

"You can borrow brains, but you cannot borrow character!" Dr. Bob Jones, Sr.

A biblical worldview must contain a proper understanding of the importance and development of character.

What is character? Webster defines character as *"moral excellence and firmness. It is a person marked by notable and conspicuous traits."* Character can refer to certain qualities in our lives, or it can refer to honor and moral integrity. The antecedents of character are moral weaknesses, dishonor and dishonesty.

Speaking of the great need for leaders with character, author Les Csorba made these comments:

> *The leadership crisis in America is not a crisis of competence, but a crisis of character. A lack of character lies deep within the black box of every leadership disaster. Another clue recorded in the battered black box is the trust that was also shattered somewhere along the way. So consumed with performance and reputation, leaders neglect and compromise their high calling and forsake the character that can take them beyond any short term solution, applause, or victory. Character is like a tree, and reputation*

is like its shadow. President Lincoln said, "The shadow is what we think of it; the tree is the real thing." What we need are more sturdy trees and fewer shadows — more leaders and fewer ghosts.[1]

I like the verse in 1 Timothy 4:12 that the Apostle Paul uses for his young disciple, Timothy, to describe the qualities that he should emulate and pursue. These are things Paul mentions to Timothy that reveal our character. *"Let no man despise thy youth; but be thou an example of the believers, in word, in conversation, in charity, in spirit, in faith, in purity…"* Let's examine what each word in this verse means:

1. Word — i.e. the speech and the words we use in conversing with others
2. Conversation — i.e. the manner of life, the observable lifestyle we display
3. Charity — i.e. the love we demonstrate to others
4. Spirit — i.e. the attitude that others sense in us that makes us either contagious or repulsive
5. Faith — i.e. the trust and reliance that we have in the Lord
6. Purity — i.e. the kind of life that we live that is free from the pollutions of sin and flesh

Many people go though life without ever giving much thought or attention to the development of their character and soul. How tragic it is to live and strive for success while neglecting this great work of building character along the way. It is impossible to have true spiritual success if character is neglected. Christian author George MacDonald made this convicting remark: *"Foolish is the man, and there are many such men, who would rid himself and his fellows of discomfort by setting the world right, by waging war on the evils around him, while he neglects that integral part of the world where lies his business, his first business — namely his own character and conduct."*[2]

Author Oscar Wilde paid little attention to his inner life and the forming of character. This tragic mistake came back to haunt him.

As his life became a disappointment, he sadly made this confession:

> The gods had given me almost everything. But I let myself be lured into long spells of senseless and sensual ease... Tired of being on the heights, I deliberately went to the depths in search for new sensations. What the paradox was to me in the sphere of thought, perversity became to me in the sphere of passion. I grew careless of the lives of others. I took pleasure where it pleased me, and passed on. I forgot that every little action of the common day makes or unmakes character, and that therefore what one has done in the secret chamber, one has some day to cry aloud from the house-top. I ceased to be lord over myself. I was no longer the captain of my soul, and did not know it. I allowed pleasure to dominate me. I ended in horrible disgrace.[3]

These are haunting words. What we do in secret will one day be revealed when the righteous Judge of all the earth calls us to give an account of our sojourn here on earth. May we each so live that we will have boldness and joy in that great and awesome day. I have often exhorted my children to live with eternity in view. We cannot stress too often that a day of reckoning is approaching. Character in this life will help us prepare for the life to come. John Quincy Adams, the sixth president of the United States, once wrote a letter to his daughter to encourage her as she was seeking advice on the topic of choosing a husband. There are so many things that a father might say to his daughter when discussing that subject. I found it very pleasing that he shared this advice with his daughter confirming what I am saying to you here on the importance of character in life. "*Daughter! Get you an honest man for a husband and keep him honest. No matter whether he is rich, provided he be independent. Regard the honor and moral character of the man, more than all other circumstances. Think of no other greatness but that of the soul, no other riches but those of the heart.*"[4] John Quincy Adams is a man after my own heart. What better advice than that can we give our children?

Character is what makes a person do the little things in life well. It helps a man pay attention to the details that others often overlook.

When I think of a person's character, I associate it with a number of things. Character is what makes a person do the little things in life well. It helps a man pay attention to the details that others often overlook. I have stressed to my children that there are some things you cannot put a price tag on. If they have these qualities, they will be a very valuable asset to any business or company. These are the things that education alone can't give us.

1. Punctuality — Respect other's time by being on time yourself.
2. Loyalty — Strive to make those above you successful.
3. Quality — If a job is worth doing, it is worth doing well.
4. Cordiality — i.e. Be pleasant to be around, positive, and upbeat.
5. Enthusiasm — Be contagious.
6. Honesty — Tell the truth.
7. Humility — *"Seekest thou great things for thyself? Seek them not."* Jeremiah 45:5 (This does not mean we shouldn't seek to excel, be ambitious or do our best; it means that we are not seeking recognition so we can glory in ourselves and be puffed up with pride.)
8. Sincerity — Those people who convey to those whom they serve sincerity, that they really care, and that they have their best interest at heart, are those who win the affection and admiration of those around them. True sincerity is contagious and draws people to our side and cause.
9. Accountability — To develop character it is essential that we have a friend, wife, husband, partner, or associate to whom we can be accountable. Accountability just means that there is someone who is near to you who understands your goals and your dreams, who is helping to keep you on track. By being

accountable to a close friend or loved one, we are making sure that we are encouraging and being encouraged. The Scriptures give us insights into the importance of being accountable to others.

"Iron sharpeneth iron, so a man sharpeneth the countenance of his friend." Proverbs 27:17

"[9] Two are better than one because they have a good reward for their labour. [10] For if they fall, the one will lift up his fellow: but woe to him that is alone when he falleth; for he hath not another to help him up." Ecclesiastes 4:9-10

These are things that are priceless if found in employees. These qualities make a man more valuable than education or experience can ever make him.

Six Disciplines that Develop Character

As we think about the development of character, we should not forget or minimize the importance of adding these other disciplines to our lives.

1. Reading — Readers are leaders. Christian leader Harold J. Ockenga, who took a suitcase of books with him on his honeymoon said, *"Read to refill the wells of inspiration."*[4] The Christian author Dr. A. W. Tozer had this to say to Christians about the reading of good books:

    Why does today's Christian find the reading of great books always beyond him? Certainly intellectual powers do not wane from one generation to another. We are as smart as our fathers, and any thought they could entertain, we can entertain if we are sufficiently interested to make the effort. The major cause of the decline in the quality of current Christian literature is not intellectual but spiritual. To enjoy a great religious book requires a degree of consecration to God and detachment from the world that few modern Christians have. The early Christian Fathers, the Mystics, the Puritans, are not hard to understand, but they inhabit the highlands where the air is crisp and rarefied, and none but the God-enamored can come...One reason why people are unable to understand great Christian classics is that they are trying to understand without any intention of obeying them.[6]

The great Baptist preacher C. H. Spurgeon made this observation about the importance of reading in a person's life:

Master those books you have. Read them thoroughly. Bathe in them until they saturate you. Read and reread them; masticate them and digest them. Let them go into your very self. Peruse a good book several times and make notes and analysis of it. A student will find that his mental constitution is more affected by one book thoroughly mastered than by twenty books he has merely skimmed. Little learning and much pride come of hasty reading. Some men are disabled from thinking by their putting meditation away for the sake of much reading. In reading, let your motto be "much, not many."[7]

Reading builds and shapes our character. The famous poet Alexander Pope said,

A little learning is a dangerous thing;
Drink deep, or taste not the Pierian Spring;
There shallow draughts intoxicate the brain,
And drinking largely sobers us again.

(The Pierian Spring is poetic language that symbolizes learning and poetic interests)

Paul said in the Scriptures, *"The cloak that I left at Troas with Carpus, when thou comest bring with thee, and the books, but especially the parchments."* 2 Timothy 4:13 The Apostle Paul knew the value of diligent and continuous reading.

A student who studied under Vernon Grounds, the president of Denver Theological Seminary, recalls being in his study and noticing all the books that the professor had in his library. The student writes:

> *Books everywhere. Stacks and stacks of books, obviously in the process of being read. The bandwidth of the man's literary interests is staggering. Sitting in his book-strewn office, I think back to our orientation days at seminary more than forty years ago when the then-president, eyes twinkling, had said to the entering class, "Buy books until you have to mortgage your marital bed. And then keep on buying." Many of us believed him (and obeyed) then... and still do. He caused us to love books.*[8]

Gordon MacDonald, pastor and author, speaks of his own personal joy of reading:

> *My reading is first from the Scriptures and then from great classics of the Christian tradition. Augustine's Confessions, Thomas à Kempis's Imitation, Fenelon's letters, Catherine Booth's letters, and A. W. Tozer's books are all soul food for me. Repeatedly, I have returned to Bunyan's Pilgrim's Progress, and I take delight in attempting my own private modern-language translation of his Old English. Alexander Whyte's Bunyans's Characters has been a pleasant guide-book when I walk the path with Bunyan's Christian.*[9]

2. Prayer — Praying daily and often is absolutely essential to the development of character. Follow the Lord's Prayer as an example on how to pray, praying through the Psalms, and bringing our needs, hurts and all of our

Praying daily and often is absolutely essential to the development of character.

petitions to the Lord on a daily basis. By doing this, we grow and develop the character that God can use to impact the lives of all those around us. The Apostle Paul wrote to the people at Thessolonica, *"pray without ceasing."* 1 Thessalonians 5:17

Thomas à Kempis left this prayer as an example of how we should pray for the development of character in our lives:

> *Teach me to love, to be concealed and little esteemed, let me be truly humbled and heartily ashamed of my sin and folly. Teach me to bear reproaches evenly, for I have deserved them; to return all to Thee, for it is Thine alone; to suffer reproach thankfully; to amend my faults speedily, and when I have humbly, patiently, charitably, and diligently served Thee, change this habit into the shining garment of immortality, my confusion into glory, my folly into perfect knowledge, my weakness and dishonors into strength and beauties of the Sons of God. Amen.*[10]

Christian author E. M. Bounds has written extensively on the subject of prayer. In one of his books he made these comments on the connection between prayer and the development of character:

> *The office of prayer is to change the character and conduct of men...prayer produces cleanliness of heart and purity of life. It can produce nothing else. Unrighteous conduct is born of prayerlessness; the two go hand in hand. Prayer and sinning cannot keep company with each other. One or the other must, of necessity, stop. Get men to pray, and they will quit sinning...praying which does not result in right thinking and right living is a farce. We have missed the whole office of prayer if it fails to purge character and rectify conduct.*[11]

3. Meditation — This is the habit of talking within our soul about the things we are studying and learning from the Word. Meditation is a lost art. It is the asking of questions, of mulling things over, of giving serious and deep thought to things. David

wrote in Psalm 4:4, *"Stand in awe, and sin not: commune with your own heart upon your bed and be still."* Meditation is what keeps the fire of our devotion to Christ burning brightly. Nathanael Ranew describes the affects of meditation on our lives in this way: *"Meditation is that which keeps alive the fire on the altar, and helps to make it burn…meditation is a great heart warmer."* [12]

4. Worship — This is giving to God the glory that is due to His holy name. It involves praise, adoration, petition, thanksgiving, awe and wonder, and ascribing greatness to His name. I have often used the acrostic W-O-R-S-H-I-P to explain the meaning of true worship.

   W- Walk with God.
   O- Obey God.
   R- Repent before God.
   S- Surrender to God.
   H- Humble yourself before God.
   I- Intercede on behalf of others to God.
   P- Praise God.

5. Bible reading — this is the act of feeding our soul on a daily basis from the things we find in the Word of God. When Jesus was tempted, He answered Satan by saying, *"Man shall not live by bread alone, but by every word that proceedeth out of the mouth of God."* Matthew 4:4

6. Thirst — a thirst for knowledge and a deep hunger to learn is essential to developing character in one's life. William Barclay writes,

   It's possible to be a follower of Jesus without being a disciple; to be a camp-follower without being a soldier of the king; to be a hanger-on in some great work without pulling one's weight. Once someone was talking to a great scholar about a younger man. He said, "So and so tells me that he was one of your stu-

dents." The teacher answered devastatingly, "He may have attended my lectures, but he was not one of my students." There is a world of difference between attending lectures and being a student. It is one of the supreme handicaps of the Church that in the Church there are so many distant followers of Jesus and so few real disciples.[12]

These disciplines develop character in our lives and give depth to the soul. Those who have become great and impacted families, communities, and nations, have been men and women of great character. Christ-likeness is the best way to be sure we have the right kind of character in our lives. Aim to be like Christ in all things and you will have the assurance of developing true Christian character.

Let me remind you of how a lack of character can be damaging to your soul, marriage, and life's work. Being trustworthy is the core quality of every relationship. If we lack character and destroy the trust that others should have in us, we may never be able to recover and remove the damage. Author Pat Williams made this comment on the subject of trust and its importance: *"Get caught in one dishonest act — one lie, one theft, one fraud — and you have destroyed trust forever. Once trust has been damaged, It is very hard to restore."*[13]

> ## *Character development must be forged on the anvil of conviction.*

It must be remembered that character is not based on opinion polls, popularity, or determining which way the wind is blowing. Character development must be forged on the anvil of conviction. Pastor David Ireland states it very well:

To establish a lifestyle of integrity, you must not allow the opinion of the masses to dictate your choices of the heart. How far would Moses have gone if he had taken a poll in Egypt? What would Jesus Christ have preached if He had taken a poll in the land of Israel? What would have happened to the Reformation if Martin Luther had taken a poll? It isn't polls or public opinion of the moment that counts. It is right and wrong, and leadership that begins by possessing a heart for integrity.[14]

Teach Your Children Good Manners

Teaching our children how to behave in public and to have good manners is another aspect of character development. I believe that one of the greatest failures of this present generation is the failure of parents to teach their children manners. Having good manners is an important aspect of character development. What ever happened to chivalry? What ever happened to teaching young men to be gentlemen and young women to be ladies?

Ten Pet Peeves

I have a number of pet peeves. A pet peeve is something that causes continual, personal vexation. We usually find ourselves complaining about these little things that are so often annoying to us. Here are ten pet peeves that annoy many people. I pray that my children and grandchildren will grow up to be respectful ladies and gentlemen.

1. People who don't say "please" and "thank you."
2. People who are disrespectful to their parents.
3. People who let the door slam on those coming behind them.
4. People who don't stand up when a lady walks in the room.
5. People who use profanity in public. (I'm not too wild about those who use it in private as well!)
6. People who are sloppy and don't pick up after themselves.
7. People who blare their music in public.
8. People who are rude drivers.
9. People who dominate every conversation by talking about themselves.
10. People who do not practice good public hygiene — bad breath and body odor!

These ten pet peeves serve as a good measuring stick of how well-mannered a person has become.

One of the areas that most people have problems in is the subject of table manners. The occasion of eating together has always had a pleasant social significance. The word companion and company comes from the Latin *"com"* meaning "with" or "together" and the Latin *"panis"* meaning "bread" or "food." Therefore a companion is someone with whom you eat! How we behave or conduct ourselves at the dinner table, out in restaurants, and on special occasions is very important in the development of character in a person's life. I came across these twelve simple suggestions for children that may be of help to all of us when it comes to having proper table manners. I have slightly adapted these suggestions:

Twelve Basic Table Manners for Kids

1. Eat with a fork unless the food is meant to be eaten with fingers. Only babies eat with fingers.
2. Don't stuff your mouth full of food. It looks gross, and you could choke.
3. Chew with your mouth closed…This includes no talking with your mouth full.
4. Don't make any rude comments about food being served. It will hurt someone's feelings.
5. Always say thank you when served something. This shows appreciation.
6. If the meal is not buffet style, then wait until everyone is served before eating. This shows consideration. (Or until the hostess indicates when to start.)
7. Eat slowly; don't gobble up the food. Someone took a long time to prepare the food; enjoy it slowly. Slowly means to wait about five seconds after swallowing before getting another forkful.
8. When eating rolls, break off a piece of bread before buttering. Eating a whole piece of bread is inappropriate.
9. Don't reach over someone's plate for something; ask for the item to be passed to you. This shows consideration.

10. Do not pick anything out of your teeth. If it bothers you that badly, excuse yourself and go to the restroom to take care of it.
11. Always use a napkin to dab your mouth, which should be on your lap when not in use. Remember, dab your mouth only. Do not wipe your face or blow your nose with a napkin. Excuse yourself from the table and go to the restroom to do those things.
12. When eating at someone's home or as a guest of someone at a restaurant, always thank the host. Again, someone took time, energy, and expense to prepare the food; show your appreciation.[15]

Finally, let me add a few comments concerning those who bore others by talking about themselves. A necessary ingredient of true Christian character is humility. The humble soul is truly the noble soul. Humility is a rare trait in this self-centered narcissistic world. Humility is a product and result of the Spirit's work in our lives. Humility in a Christian's life is a reflection of the indwelling Christ. One habit that some people have is the annoying tendency of name dropping. Pastor Erwin W. Lutzer of Moody Memorial Church in Chicago, Illinois, describes this person well: *"Have you ever met a name dropper? You will recognize him when you do! He is the man who casually informs you that he met the President of the United States at a luncheon, that he is closely acquainted with outstanding athletes; and he calls celebrities by their first name. If he could write a book, he'd entitle it, Ten Famous Men Who Met Me."*[16]

As we seek success in life, let us never forget to work at building and developing true Christian character. Character is an integral part of a Christian worldview.

How to Get Started

1. To develop character, you must be able to define what character is. Write out a simple definition of character that you can memorize and quote to guide your life.

2. Practice the six disciplines that develop character in your life.
   - Reading good books
   - Prayer
   - Meditation
   - Worship
   - Bible reading
   - Thirst
3. Learn what it means to be a gentleman and a lady (the ten pet peeves!).
4. Develop the habit of being neat and orderly in your life. Work at keeping your living area clean and neat. Someone once said, "Cleanliness is next to godliness." This is a lesson all men need to learn when they get married!
5. Examine your personal life carefully to see how well you have learned the common courtesies and manners that belong to every lady and gentleman.
6. Make sure you have been born again. Only as God changes our natures can we change our daily habits and lifestyles.

Thoughts for Consideration

- *"The most important part of our lives is the part that only God sees."* Warren Wiersbe

- *"Let me be taught that the first great business on earth is the sanctification of my own soul."* Henry Martyn

- *"Nothing will more quickly rid us of laziness and coldness, of hypocrisy, cowardice and pride than the knowledge that God sees, hears and takes account."* John Stott

- *"A person's real character is revealed when no one else is looking."* David Ireland

- *"Let the words of my mouth, and the meditations of my heart, be acceptable in thy sight, O Lord, my strength, and redeemer."* Psalm 19:14

- *"Success is the product of character. The development of your character is in your own hands, and poverty plus honest ambition is the best environment for character-building."* Charlie "T" Jones

- *"Character is what God and the angels know of us; reputation is what men and women think of us."* Horace Mann

- *"Character is what you are in the dark."* Dwight L. Moody

- *"Character is something each one of us must build for himself, out of the laws of God and nature, the examples of others, and — most of all — out of the trials and errors of daily life. Character is the total of thousands of small daily strivings to live up to the best that is in us."* Alfred G. Trudeau

- *"A man shows his character by what he laughs at."* Anonymous

- *"Character is always lost when holy and lofty principles are sacrificed on the altar of expedience and compromise."* Anonymous

Questions for Discussion

1. What is character?

2. What things does the Apostle Paul say reveal our character in 1 Timothy 4:12?

3. What are some of the little things in life that reveal our character?

4. List the disciplines that develop character.

5. Discuss some of the consequences of a lack of character.

15
Making a Good First Impression

"The shew of their countenance doth witness against them..."
Isaiah 3:9

"I was not at all fascinated by the young orator's eloquence, while his countrified manner and speech excited more regret than reverence...the long badly trimmed hair and blue pocket handkerchief with white spots...these attracted my attention, and...awakened some feelings of amusement."[1] Susannah Thompson (The young lady who would eventually marry the man she critiqued — Charles Spurgeon!)

✿

The reason we seek to develop a Christian worldview is so that we can glorify God and serve Him better. By obeying God, we will have influence with those around us. Let us not forget, then, that the first impressions we make on those around us will either help us or hinder us in impacting others for Christ. Pastors, leaders, and all Christians should realize that they are the first message people receive. Before we ever open our mouths to speak to the people we are going to address and hope to influence, they have already drawn a conclusion about what we are going to say based on how we look and act. First impressions can be positive or negative. The great English preacher C. H. Spurgeon realized this and once, with twinkling eyes, said facetiously to the ministerial students studying under him, *"When you talk about heaven, let your facial expression reflect joy and excitement. When you talk about hell, your normal expression will do."*[2]

You never get a second chance to make a good first impression.

We should never minimize the importance of first impressions. Someone once said, *"You never get a second chance to make a good first impression."* People usually form their opinion of us within the first thirty seconds of meeting us. If we blow it during that little window of opportunity, we may never recover with that person. Right or wrong, first impressions are very hard to live down. To make a good impression requires that we show more interest in the other person than in ourselves.

When we first meet people, we can tell so much about them just by the countenance of their face. In Isaiah 3:9, the prophet Isaiah tells us that by simply examining the facial expression (countenance), we can many times determine what is going on inside a person. The word *countenance* in this verse is from the Hebrew word *"punim"* and refers to the facial expression that is seen on our face. It is also true of our dress. When we walk into a room, our very dress and attitude speaks volumes about our lives.

When we come to church, for example, I like to encourage people to dress accordingly. We are coming into the presence of Almighty God. Therefore, we should be mindful of this and not come too casually. If you were invited to the White House to meet the president of the United States, you would not go in jeans and a t-shirt. You would dress to show respect to the president. So it is that when we come to church, we should be mindful that we are in the presence of God. Therefore, I suggest that when we come to the Lord's house to worship, we should come reverently and dress respectfully.

Dressing properly for ministers and Christian leaders is also important. First impressions are a point that is often overlooked by many men who stand in the pulpit every week. One Christian leader made this comment about ministerial dress:

In connection with personality something should be said about appearance and dress. Though a dynamic personality may overcome a bad impression created by physical appearance, few men are dynamic enough to overcome such a handicap. Even a minister endowed with the strongest and most attractive personality will find that proper care in the matter of his personal appearance in the pulpit will be an asset in his dealing with the audience and increase the respect of his people for him and strengthen his leadership.[3]

When I size up a leader, there are four things that I believe are absolutely essential to make a good first impression.

1. A look of confidence
2. Good posture
3. A warm and contagious smile
4. Being dressed for success

A Smile is Contagious

Let me say a word here about the importance of greeting people with a warm and friendly smile. This is not always easy to do. We often find ourselves so busy, rushed, and distracted by schedules, meetings, and next appointments that we forget how important a smile can be to those who come in and out of our lives on a daily basis. Greeting people with a smile may be the single most important event of their day. A smile can change the entire outlook on a moment, a meeting, an hour, or even a day or week. We all know the power of a smile from a mate, lover, or friend. Here is what one author said about the power and the potential of a smile:

"A smile —
- *Costs nothing but creates much.*
- *Enriches those who receive without diminishing the wealth of those who give.*
- *Happens in a flash, but the memory of it can last a lifetime. None are so rich that they can get along without it and none so poor but are richer for it.*
- *Creates happiness in the home, fosters good will in a business, and is the countersign of friends.*

- *Is rest to the weary, daylight to the discouraged, and nature's best antidote for trouble.*
- *Cannot be bought, begged, or stolen, for it is of no earthly good to anybody until it is given away.*
- *And if any person should be too tired to give you a smile, why not give one of your own?*
- *For nobody needs a smile so much as one who has none to give."*[4]

Dress for Success!

Much has been said over the years about dressing for success. There is much truth to this. There is a time to be casual and a time to show respect to the position you occupy. Be wise in this area. First impressions are hard to live down. Make sure your first impression is a good one. Keep these simple points in mind:

1. Watch your posture. Stand up and be a person who exudes confidence. Don't slink around or sulk.
2. Always shake hands (if you are a man) with a firm handshake.
3. Dress appropriately. (Know when to dress down and when to dress up!) Dress for success. People of influence don't dress slovenly. Sometimes people tease me about dressing professionally when I am in public. What I have learned is that I am always on call and I always represent both my Lord and my church. When I meet people in public who know me, like it or not, I am going to influence them in one direction or another. A leader cannot afford to lose his influence by sloppiness, crude manners, or poor hygiene. I will get relaxed and casual at times, but a leader must pick and choose those times carefully. I have received many compliments over the years from people in the church that have said they always appreciated that when they or their friends ran into me in public they were always proud of the way I represented them and the church. They never had to be embarrassed by my dress!

Dressing for success also means we should be careful to avoid dressing in a manner that would bring reproach on our profession of faith in Christ. Christians cannot forget that they live in what has been called the "watching world." This means that we who profess faith and allegiance to Christ are always on display. People are watching our every move. People notice what we wear, where we go, what we say, how we react to things, and what our daily attitudes are. With this in mind, the believer must always be wise and careful not to live in a way that discredits the Lord we profess to love.

It is important that Christians dress modestly. This means that whether we are men or women, we should dress in a way that does not inadvertently give someone a reason to have impure and unrighteous thoughts. We have a holy obligation to be careful that our dress reflects the purity and modesty of Christian character. Speaking on this subject, author and pastor Joel Beeke said: "*We must also be modest about the way we dress, so that it does not encourage lust. Clothing that calls attention to our bodies arouses fleshly lusts that offend God. He blames those who provoke lust as much as those who lust after them.*"[5]

Here is a list of things that wise leaders would do well to follow.

1. Make sure your shirts and slacks are clean and pressed. (Clothes with the slept-in look will detract from one's influence and future promotion.)
2. Make sure your teeth are brushed and your breath is fresh.
3. Make sure your hair is combed.
4. Make sure your shoes are shined.
5. Make sure you are clean-shaven. (And wear aftershave or cologne!)
6. Make sure that if your slacks call for a belt, you have one on.
7. Make sure you always use deodorant.
8. Make sure that you bathe or shower every day. (Someone said that cleanliness is next to godliness.)

Ladies are no different. Every godly woman who desires to have influence with other people and other women must work on the way they look and present themselves. We have all been around special ladies who by spiritual life and warmth, and by the way they dressed and carried themselves, made us stop in our tracks and say, "That's a very special lady!"

In her book, *It Takes So Little to be Above Average*, Florence Littauer said that every woman who is leading and influencing other women should follow the ABC's of leadership:

> "**A**ttitude of a servant
> **B**earing of a Queen
> **C**lothing of a leader"[6]

Women should never wear immodest clothing in public. This is true of anyone who is a leader or married to a leader. Low-cut dresses, short tight skirts, bare midriffs, and suggestive clothing are never appropriate. Men are aroused physically by sight. Fathers and mothers need to teach their daughters that how they dress may cause men and young men to have impure thoughts towards them.   Teaching modesty is very needed in our culture today.

Here are some other suggestions for women while in public. A woman should always sit with her knees together whether she is wearing a skirt or slacks. When on stage or a platform, a woman should never cross her legs. Rather, she should turn her legs to one side and cross her ankles. No one should wear t-shirts, blouses, or sweaters that have offensive slogans or messages on them.

Non-Verbal Communication

Ninety-five percent of communication is non-verbal. Here is a list of things that we should seek to avoid if we are going to make a good first impression.

- Don't take the fig leaf stance in public. (Standing with your hands folded forming a v with straight arms in front)
- Don't be a "space invader." Give people some room! Getting too close to people is offensive and rude.
- Don't put up a road block by folding your arms when meeting and greeting people.
- Don't be a "back patter." Patting is for children and is patronizing to adults.

- Don't be a rocking chair. Rocking back and forth is distracting and gives the impression of insecurity.
- Don't be a fidgeter. Fidgeting is a sign of nervousness.

Here are some tips for making good first impressions:

- Pay attention.
- Listen!
- Smile.
- Look others in the eyes.
- Learn and use the other person's name.
- Give up the need to be right. (Don't correct, argue, debate, or confront; these things only alienate.)
- Learn to dress for the occasion.
- Show appreciation.

Making a good first impression is essential to success in life. We can greatly enhance our ability to make a good first impression by remembering some of the most common courtesies that are often forgotten in today's busy and selfish world. Author June Hines in her book, *The Etiquette Advantage* gave this list of courtesies that are helpful in making a good first impression.

- *Saying "Please," "Thank you," "Pardon me," "Excuse me," and "May I"* [I have always taught my sons to address people with "Yes Sir" or "No Sir," "Yes Ma'am" and "No Ma'am."]
- *Asking someone to be seated*
- *Showing a visitor or guest to the door*
- *Holding the door for someone coming behind you*
- *Writing thank-you notes promptly*[7]

There are also some negative habits and behaviors that are very destructive to good first impressions. Check your daily life habits and see if any of these negative habits are true of you.

- *Walking in front of someone*
- *Cracking your knuckles*
- *Backslapping*

- *Using toothpicks in public*
- *Chewing gum in public*
- *Coughing or sneezing uncovered*
- *Checking your watch while engaged in conversation with others*
- *Checking your email or mobile phone while engaged in a conversation without saying, "Pardon me for just a moment, I have an important call I need to check on."*
- *Interrupting*
- *Pointing*
- *Staring*
- *Whispering*
- *Fidgeting*
- *Laughing loudly*[8]

The Three C's of Success

Author and teacher June Hines Moore reminds us that successful people have three common traits: *"Successful people possess three common Characteristics: they are competent in their skills, confident in their demeanor, and considerate of others."*[9]

The Importance of Last Impressions

We should remember that last impressions are also lasting impressions. When you come to the end of your day, end it in a flurry. In high school, I ran cross country and track. Our coach always taught us to sprint in at the end of the race to the tape. He stressed to each of us that the last few steps in a race were crucial. Those who coasted in at the end of a race were often passed by other runners who were sprinting in and giving their all. If we are in a job and about to leave, we should remember that how we spend our last month, our last week, and even our last day will leave a lasting impression on those with whom we worked. For testimony's sake, if you take pride in your work and

> *...last impressions are also lasting impressions.*

person, do your best even at the last. You may have been a great worker, but if on the last day you did not do your best, you may be remembered by just that single event. First impressions are important, but so too are last impressions. Ask yourself right now, how do people see you? What thoughts do people have when they think of you? It would not be a bad thing to ask a trusted friend at work what kind of testimony you have with those around you. You might even ask your wife or husband what they think others think of you.

How to Get Started

1. Start dressing for success.
2. Know when to dress down and when to dress up.
3. Put on a smile!
4. Watch your posture in public.
5. Practice good personal hygiene.
6. Ask yourself, how do people see you?
7. Ask a good friend or your wife or husband what others think of you.

Thoughts for Consideration

*   *"First impressions are often the truest, as we find (not infrequently) to our cost, when we have been wheedled out of them by plausible professions or studied actions. A man's look is the work of years; it is stamped on his countenance by the events of his whole life, nay, more, by the hand of nature, and it is not to be got rid of easily."* William Hazlitt

*   *"The greatest way to make a positive first impression is to demonstrate immediately that the other person — not you — is the center of action and conversation."* Anonymous

- *"A bore is someone who talks so much about himself that you never get to talk about yourself."* Anonymous

- *"You'll make a superb initial impression when you demonstrate good listening skills."* Bill Lampton

- *"Few have strength of reason to overrule the perceptions of sense, and yet fewer have curiosity or benevolence to struggle long against the first impression: he who therefore fails to please in his salutation and address is at once rejected, and rarely obtains an opportunity of showing his latest excellences or essential qualities."* Samuel Johnson

- *"Etiquette rules are in our head. Manners are in our heart. Together they give us a two-way shield against embarrassment."* June Hines Moore

- *"In golf when we bungle the first tee shot, we get a free one called a mulligan. Unfortunately, there is never a second chance to make a good first impression."* June Hines Moore

- *"Your manners are always under examination by committees little suspected...awarding or denying you very high prizes when you least think of it."* Ralph Waldo Emerson

Questions for Discussion

1. What does it mean to dress for success?

2. In what contexts do we leave last impressions?

3. What are the three C's of success?

4. How much of our communication is non-verbal?

5. Why is is so hard to live down a bad first impression?

6. Do you know what others think of you?

7. Test yourself by examining the various lists of things to do or not do in this chapter. How well do you measure up?

16
Proclaiming the Gospel of Christ

"…I am not ashamed of the gospel of Christ for it is the power of God unto salvation…" The Apostle Paul, Romans 1:16

"The gospel is the good news of all that God has done through His Son Jesus Christ to bring His chosen people to heaven." Anonymous

∽

The development of a Christian worldview must include the gospel of Jesus Christ. What separates Christianity from all other religions and philosophies is the gospel that was proclaimed to us in the New Testament Scriptures. It is the precious gospel that makes the Christian worldview so wonderful and special. In fact, without the gospel of Jesus Christ the Christian worldview would be just another option that mattered little if it was accepted or rejected. Only because of the uniqueness and glory of the gospel is the Christian worldview superior to all other worldviews. In developing a Christian worldview the believer must understand what the gospel is and be involved in proclaiming that gospel to the generation in which he or she lives. To understand this gospel we need to do several things. We must define the gospel, defend the gospel, declare the gospel, and delight in the gospel.

> *It is the precious gospel that makes the Christian worldview so wonderful and special.*

Define the Gospel

The word *gospel* means "good news." The gospel is about the good news of all that God has done in and through His Son Jesus Christ to bring salvation to a world of unworthy sinners. In 1 Corinthians 15:3-4 the Apostle Paul gives us a concise summary of the gospel. Paul states, *"For I delivered unto you first of all that which I also received, how that Christ died for our sins according to the scriptures; And that he was buried, and that he rose again the third day according to the scriptures."* The Lord Jesus Christ in John 3:16 also gave us a brief statement that contains the gospel. Jesus said, *"For God so loved the world, that he gave his only begotten Son, that whosoever believeth in him should not perish, but have everlasting life."*

The gospel has been referred to by theologians as the Christ events of history. These events can be summarized as His coming from heaven to earth in the virgin birth, His living a holy life, His sacrificial death on the cross, His resurrection from the tomb, and His ascension back into Heaven. Robert H. Mounce defined the gospel in this manner: *"The English word 'gospel' (from the Anglo-Saxon god-spell, i.e., God-story) is the usual NT translation of the Greek euaggelion...The gospel is the joyous proclamation of God's redemptive activity in Christ Jesus on behalf of man enslaved in sin."*[1]

The gospel is about the life and death of Jesus Christ. First, Jesus lived a holy life and by it satisfied the laws of God that demanded obedience. Jesus then gives the repenting and believing sinner His own righteousness, enabling Him to be accepted in the presence of God. Secondly, Jesus died on the cross for our sins and thus satisfied God's justice that demands that all sin be punished. This is the great gospel of grace.

We must remember that Jesus Christ can redeem us because He is God. If Jesus was not God, then there would be no "good news" in the gospel. The fact that Jesus presented Himself as God, accepted the worship that was due God, and said and did the sort of things that only God could do, angered the religious leaders of His day. C. S. Lewis understood this and wrote:

Now unless the speaker is God, [forgiving sins] is really so preposterous as to be comic. We can all understand how a man forgives offences against himself. You tread on my toe and I forgive you, you steal my money and I forgive you. But what should we make of a man, himself unrobbed and untrodden on, who announced that he forgave you for treading on another man's toes and stealing other men's money? Asinine fatuity is the kindest description we should give of his conduct. Yet this is what Jesus did. He told people that their sins were forgiven, and never waited to consult all the other people whom their sins had undoubtedly injured. He unhesitatingly behaved as if He was the party chiefly concerned, the person chiefly offended in all offences. This makes sense only if He really was God whose laws are broken and whose love is wounded in every sin. In the mouth of any speaker who is not God, these words would imply what I can only regard as a silliness and conceit unrivalled by any other character in history.[2]

Defend the Gospel

The Christian who is developing a consistent worldview with his or her faith is also called upon to defend the gospel. The word *defend* comes from the Greek word *"apologia"* which means to defend. There are many people who not only reject the gospel but also have gone on the offensive to attack it and seek its destruction. It is therefore the responsibility of the believer to come to the defense of the gospel of Jesus Christ. For those who have come to understand the glory and the joy of the Christian faith it is their pleasure and privilege to defend this gospel. Failure to defend the gospel message would be tantamount to cowardice and betrayal. It is unthinkable for any believer not to rush to the defense of the great message of God's redeeming love for mankind as seen in the life and death of Jesus Christ, God's holy Son.

Believers defend the gospel by a number of ways. First, believers defend the gospel by their words. This means they study to know what the Bible teaches and they are prepared to give an answer or a defense to all and any who may raise questions about the content of the Bible or the nature of the Christian message.

A holy life is a great advertisement for the gospel.

Secondly, believers defend the gospel by their life. A holy life is a great advertisement for the gospel. When a believer is living a consistent life that is pure and holy it is a great defense against those who would attack and denigrate the gospel. Finally, believers defend the gospel by sharing it with others. When the gospel is preached, delivered, shared, explained, and discussed it is the power of God to bring men to salvation. The Apostle Paul wrote in Romans 1:16, *"For I am not ashamed of the gospel of Christ: for it is the power of God unto salvation to every one that believeth; to the Jew first, and also to the Greek."*

Declare the Gospel

Christians have a responsibility to declare the gospel. This means that they must share it, preach it, and deliver it to the people of their generation. A Christian worldview must have this at the very heart of its message. This is what Paul the apostle said in 1 Corinthians 15:1, *"Moreover, brethren, I declare unto you the gospel which I preached unto you, which also ye have received, and wherein ye stand."* John the apostle says something very similar in 1 John 1:3, *"That which we have seen and heard declare we unto you, that ye also may have fellowship with us: and truly our fellowship is with the Father, and with his Son Jesus Christ."* What Paul and John were delivering and declaring was the gospel of Jesus Christ. It is the believer's responsibility to proclaim this gospel to the entire world. As a matter of fact the last command that Jesus gave His church is referred to by the Christian church as the Great Commission. Matthew 28:19-20, *"Go ye therefore, and teach all nations, baptizing them in the name of the Father, and of the Son, and of the Holy Ghost: Teaching them to observe all things whatsoever I have commanded you: and, lo, I am with you always, even unto the end of the world. Amen."* This is the joy, duty, and responsibility of every Christian. This command is not just for those who have been called to be pastors, evangelists, or missionaries. This great command is for all the church at all times.

I would encourage everyone to find ways to proclaim this gospel to those whom you love, and to those whom you meet in life. There are a number of things that can be done to help deliver this message to the world in which we live. Here are a number of suggestions:

1. Pass out gospel booklets, tracts, and tapes or cds with a Christian message.
2. Invite people to the church where you worship.
3. Start a Bible study at home, or at work with those in your office or neighborhood.
4. Look for ways to do good works such as helping, serving, encouraging others so that you can have an opportunity to share Christ with them.
5. Visit people who are sick, shut in, or in the hospital so you can have an opportunity to share the gospel message with them.
6. Give to missions and volunteer to go on a missions trip to help your missionaries. This may give you a wonderful opportunity to share Christ with others.
7. Volunteer to teach Sunday School or work in your church in some capacity in order to have opportunities to share the gospel.
8. Certainly take every opportunity to share Christ with your own family, relatives, and loved ones.
9. Pray for people that the Lord would open up doors for you to witness to others.

Delight in the Gospel

The believer who has been saved by God's matchless grace needs to delight in the gospel of Christ. I can share my own testimony with you at this point. There is nothing in my life that thrills or stirs the emotions of my heart more than the gospel of Jesus Christ. When I consider what God has done for me in this wonderful good news I am at a loss as to how to express my gratitude and feelings. The other worldviews and world religions cannot even begin to compare to the gracious and wonderful things God has done for us in the person and work of His Son Jesus Christ.

When Paul the apostle wrote his letter to the church at Rome, in verse sixteen of the first chapter he said, *"For I am not ashamed of the gospel of Christ: for it is the power of God unto salvation to every one that believeth; to the Jew first, and also to the Greek."* The great expositor of the Word of God from Great Britain, Dr. Martyn Lloyd-Jones, made this interesting comment on this verse:

> *The kind of expression, the figure of speech, which he uses here — "I am not ashamed of…" is known as litotes — and litotes means "an assertion which is made in the form of the negative of a contrary assertion". Instead of saying here that he is "proud" of the gospel, the Apostle says that he is "not ashamed" of it. And to say that he is not ashamed of the gospel is another way of saying that he really glories in it, and that he boasts of it. He says, in writing to the Galatians, "God forbid that I should glory save in the cross of the Lord Jesus Christ". He did glory in it. He gloried in the preaching of the cross. But here he chooses to put it like this — "I am not ashamed of it".*[3]

Why did the Apostle Paul delight in the gospel? It was because he knew what the gospel had done for him. In the gospel he was:

1. Chosen in Christ.
2. Justified from his sins.
3. Given peace with God.
4. Accepted by God and had access into God's presence.
5. Given eternal life.
6. Given all the privileges of Sonship.

My friends, this is why we too should delight in the gospel of Jesus Christ. This gospel, this good news, is our only hope of salvation. This gospel is a precious gift from God given to all those whom God has chosen in Christ so that they might have eternal life. The songwriter put it well in poetic verse:

"O the love that drew salvation's plan,
O the grace that brought it down to man.
O the mighty gulf that God did span,
On Calvary."

How to Get Started

1. Make sure you can define the gospel. Write out in your own words what the meaning of the gospel of Jesus Christ really is.
2. Be committed to the defense of the gospel. By word, life, and sharing the gospel defend it for it has been committed into our hands for protection and publication.
3. Look for opportunities to share the message of the gospel with others. Look at the nine suggestions I gave you in this chapter on how to find a way to share the gospel. See if you can get involved in any of these activities.
4. Learn the joy of every day delighting in the gospel of Jesus. You can begin doing this by considering all that the gospel does for you in the person and work of Jesus Christ.

Thoughts for Consideration

* *"The gospel is a declaration, not a debate."* James S. Stewart

* *"God writes the gospel not in the Bible alone, but on trees, and flowers, and clouds, and stars."* Martin Luther

* *"The gospel is not so much a miracle as a marvel, and every line is suffused with wonder."* Roland Bainton

* *"The gospel is not a human plan for reaching up to God, but a divine plan for reaching down to man."* John Blanchard

* *"The whole gospel is contained in Christ."* John Calvin

- *"The gospel is the chariot wherein the Spirit rides victoriously when he makes his entrance into the hearts of men."* William Gurnall

- *"The man who does not glory in the gospel can surely know little of the plague of sin that is within him."* J. C. Ryle

- *"The heart of the gospel is redemption, and the essence of redemption is the substitutionary sacrifice of Christ."* C. H. Spurgeon

- *"When we preach Christ crucified, we have no reason to stammer, or stutter, or hesitate, or apologize; there is nothing in the gospel of which we have any cause to be ashamed."* C. H. Spurgeon

- *"The Trinity is the basis of the gospel, and the gospel is a declaration of the Trinity in action."* J. I. Packer

- *"The gospel begins and ends with what God is, not with what we want or think we need."* Tom Houston

Questions for Discussion

1. What is the gospel of Jesus Christ?

2. How can you tell a false gospel?

3. Do the other world religions have a gospel? If so, what is it, and how does it differ from the gospel of Jesus Christ?

4. How can a Christian defend the gospel?

5. What does it mean to you personally to delight and to glory in the gospel?

Part III: The Peace of Christian Living

17
Discovering the Peace of Romans 8:28

"I must confess that I am driven to my knees by the overwhelming conviction that I have no where else to go. My wisdom and that of all about me is insufficient to meet the demands of the day."
Abraham Lincoln

"And we know that all things work together for good to them that love God, to them who are the called according to his purpose."
Romans 8:28

One of the most comforting verses in the Bible is found in Paul's letter to the church at Rome. Romans 8:28 is one of the most well-loved and well-known verses in all of the Scriptures. This verse has been a great comfort to the people of God through the ages. I have made reference to this verse throughout this book. Here it is once again. *"And we know that all things work together for good to them that love God, to them who are the called according to his purpose."*

Often people will ask me, "How does this verse really work?" The phrase, *"All things"* refers to everything that may happen in our lives whether it is good or bad. How can all things be good for us? Does this mean that even disappointments, tragedies, failures, heartaches, and sorrows are good for us? The answer is yes. Romans 8:28 is essential to a biblical worldview. Let me share with you some of the lessons that I have learned over the years that relate to this precious promise from the Word of God. God uses *"all things"* good or bad:

1.　To get our attention and draw us into His arms.
2.　To develop patience in our lives.
3.　To teach us to pray and to trust Him.
4.　To teach us humility.
5.　To make us tender, sympathetic, and understanding of others when they too go through tough and difficult times.
6.　To teach us about God's patience and faithfulness.
7.　To prepare us for heaven. Most of us are too earthbound and content to be here below. Sufferings and trials shake us loose of time and life and create a longing to be home with the Lord.

The British author, Sharon James, understands that God often uses unusual circumstances and hard providences to teach His children some of their most important lessons. Here are some of her comments on this subject:

> *The Lord's priorities are so different from ours! God didn't just want to take the people to the land of milk and honey as quickly as possible. That was what they wanted, of course. No, God wanted them to increase in faith and trust. He wanted their holiness. It is just the same for us. God's priority is not for us to get through life as easily and comfortably as we can. Humanly speaking, that's just what we want! But his purpose is for us to become like Christ. Sometimes he leads us into hard places, where it may seem as if he has abandoned us. All too often we reason: "Because my life is so unbearable at the moment, the Lord must have forgotten me!" But sometimes the Lord does deliberately lead us to these hard places. We then learn to rely utterly on him.*[1]

> **God's priority is not for us to get through life as easily and comfortably as we can.**

Corrie Ten Boom, a woman who suffered intensely under Nazi rule in Germany, often quoted this wonderful poem that reminded her that God was involved in all the things that happen in our lives, whether good or bad, to mold us into the image of His Son.

My life is but a weaving between my Lord and me.
I cannot choose the colors, He weaveth steadily.
Oft times he weaveth sorrow, and I in foolish pride,
Forget He sees the upper, but I the underside.

Not till the looms are silent and the shuttles cease to fly,
Will God unroll the canvas and explain the reasons why.
The dark threads are just as needful in the Weaver's skillful hands
As the threads of gold and silver in the patterns He has planned.

Grant Colfax Tuller

Why is Romans 8:28 so important to us as we consider this subject of developing a biblical worldview for Christian living? It is for this one significant reason. We believe in the absolute sovereignty of God in all things. This great God, who chose, called, and regenerated us, also determines all things in our lives. We are to see ourselves as people of destiny. We should see ourselves as people who have been made in the image of God. Because of this, we should, of all people, strive for success. But having done all that we can to achieve our goals, we should then leave the results in His sovereign hands. Not everyone will win the race; not everyone will reach the target they are aiming for; not everyone can be the biggest or the best. But we will never achieve anything if we don't have a goal, if we don't set our sights on higher things. As I would train my children in their athletic competitions, I would ask them, "What is your goal? What do you want to accomplish?" Once we establish that, we can begin careful planning to seek to reach and achieve those goals. We first start by seeing what is our end or destination. Then we devise a plan. We set smaller achievable goals in front of us first. Then we see what sacrifices we need to make to reach these lesser goals. There is an old saying, "Rome was not built in a day." So, with hard work, sacrifice, and patience, we pursue our dreams. We may not always reach what we aimed at, but I'll tell you what — you will reach a lot higher and go a lot further if you set out to reach those goals, than if you don't do this at all. If you shoot for the moon, you may not hit the moon, but you will shoot a lot higher than if you only shot at the top of the trees.

Romans 8:28 brings peace to the lives of those who have followed Christ through the years of their lives with a passion to know and serve Him. How wonderful to come to the end of life and have that confidence that you have done your best to honor and serve God! E. Stanley Jones, the Methodist missionary and evangelist who spent over fifty years of his life serving God in the Indian sub-continent, came to the end of his life and wrote these inspiring words:

> *There are scars on my faith, but underneath those scars there are no doubts. [Christ] has me with the consent of all my being and with the cooperation of all my life. The song I sing is a lit song. Not the temporary exuberance of youth that often fades when middle and old age sets in with their disillusionment and cynicism...No, I'm 83, and I'm more excited today about being a Christian than I was at 18 when I first put my feet upon the way.*[2]

George Matheson expresses something very similar to this thought in his book *Thoughts for Life's Journey*. Matheson, like E. Stanley Jones, knew that God's hard providences provide the best school of preparation for His servants. Matheson writes:

> *My soul, reject not the place of thy prostration! It has ever been thy robbing-room for royalty. Ask the great ones of the past what has been the spot of their prosperity; they will say, "It was the cold ground on which I once was lying." Ask Abraham; he will point you to the sacrifice on Moriah. Ask Joseph; he will direct you to his dungeon. Ask Moses; he will date his fortune from his danger in the Nile. Ask Ruth; she will bid you build her monument in the field of her toil. Ask David; he will tell you that his songs come*

from the night. Ask Job; and he will remind you that God answered him out of the whirlwind. Ask Peter; he will extol his submersion in the sea. Ask John; he will give the palm to Patmos. Ask Paul; he will attribute his inspiration to the light which struck him blind. Ask one more — the Son of Man. Ask Him whence has come His rule over the world. He will answer, "From the cold ground on which I was lying — the Gethsemane ground; I received My scepter there." Thou too, my soul, shalt be garlanded by Gethsemane. The cup thou fain wouldst pass from thee will be thy coronet in the sweet by-and-by. The hour of thy loneliness will crown thee. The day of thy depression will regale thee. It is thy desert that will break forth into singing; it is the trees of thy silent forest that will clap their hands…The voice of God to thine evening will be this, "Thy treasure is hid in the ground where thou wert lying."[3]

As we grow old in life, we see so many things changing around us. The years come and go, good friends pass away and go to be with the Lord, and we find we have so many more aches and pains. Growing old can be a fearful and dreadful experience for many people. Yet this ought not to be the case for those who know the Lord of the universe as their Savior, Friend, and ever-present Comforter. Romans 8:28 brings us peace when we realize that God is with us, He has sustained us through all these many years and as we see the shadows of death approaching, He will surely see us through to the other side. What great peace belongs to the one who has trusted God and walked with Him through the years! No child of God should approach death and old age with fear and trepidation. Keep your eyes on the Lord. Remind yourself that He has never failed you. As you journey through life, never forget that at every stage, the best is always yet to come.

> **What great peace belongs to the one who has trusted God and walked with Him through the years!**

The great hymn writer John Newton understood this. John Newton is most famous for his writing the words to the beloved hymn Amazing Grace. In a letter to one of his friends Newton made this comment on Romans 8:28:

> ...If all things are in his hand, if the very hairs of our head are numbered; if every event, great and small, is under the direction of his providence and purpose; and if he has a wise, holy, and gracious end in view, to which everything that happens is subordinate and subservient — then we have nothing to do, but with patience and humility to follow as he leads, and cheerfully to expect a happy issue... How happy are they who can resign all to him, see his hand in every dispensation, and believe that he chooses better for them than they possibly could for themselves.[4]

I have not forgotten this as I have sought to walk with God and serve Him in my ministry. O friend, the best is always yet to come. When we are lying on our deathbed, and our loved ones and family gather around, remember that soon the angels themselves will carry you to your Lord and Savior Jesus Christ. What joy and happiness awaits those who have served Him faithfully through the years. And if you have many regrets, then carry these to the One who is full of love and mercy, whose invitation is always open to you, and He will forgive and wipe away all the stains, guilt, and regrets of your past life. Find the joy of being covered in the righteousness of Christ, and find the peace that comes from knowing that you have been washed pure and white in the precious blood of Jesus Christ your Lord.

Grow old along with me!
The best is yet to be,
The last of life, for which the first was made:
Our times are in His hand
Who saith, "A whole I planned,
Youth shows but half; trust God: see all nor be afraid!"

Robert Browning, from the poem *Rabbi Ben Ezra*

To Be Successful You Must Have a Dream

To be successful in living for Christ, you need to develop a Christian worldview. This worldview will be your map as you journey through life. This map will guide you and give you direction as you pursue your goals and dreams of living for the glory of God. To have success, you must have a dream, a goal, a target that you are aiming at. If you don't reach it, at least you can rest in the fact that you have done everything in your power to accomplish these things. Having done all that you can, you now leave the results in the hands of our sovereign God. Here is where God's peace comes in. We do our best but know that in the end everything is in our Lord's hands. If you prepare for the race, then at the starting line you will be filled with a sense of peace that you have done all that you could have done. The race begins, the contest is on, and whatever the results, you will not be tormented in the end by saying, "If I had only done this or that." Whether you win or finish last, if you have prepared well you will be at peace. I have often shared a quote with my children from American author John Greenleaf Whittier (1807-1892), *"Of all the sad words of tongue and pen, the saddest are these, it might have been."*

How to Get Started

1. Pursue your goals as if everything depends on you, but pray as if everything depends on God.
2. Never forget the lesson of Romans 8:28 that everything in life, good or bad, has a purpose.
3. If you are doing your best, then leave the results with God.
4. God's peace is sweet. The Scriptures teach us, *"Great peace have they which love thy law; and nothing shall offend them."* Psalm 119:165

Thoughts for Consideration

- *"Many men owe the grandeur of their lives to their tremendous difficulties."* C. H. Spurgeon

- *"All God's giants have been weak men who did great things for God, because they reckoned on God being with them."* J. Hudson Taylor

- *"There are no crown-wearers in heaven who were not cross bearers here below."* C. H. Spurgeon

- *"The Cross: God's way of uniting suffering with love."* Georgia Harkness

- *"We sleep in peace in the arms of God when we yield ourselves up to his providence."* Fenelon

- *"The peace of God will keep us from sighing under our troubles and from sinking under them."* Matthew Henry

- *"Peace comes not from the absence of trouble, but from the presence of God."* Alexander MacLaren

- *"We can sometimes see more through a tear than through a telescope."* Anonymous

- *"Without a doubt, what helps us most in accepting and dealing with suffering is an adequate view of God — learning who he is and knowing he is in control."* Joni Eareckson Tada

- *"There is a great want about all Christians who have not suffered. Some flowers must be broken or bruised before they emit any fragrance."* Robert Murray M'Cheyne

∞

Questions for Discussion

1. What is the Apostle Paul saying in Romans 8:28?

2. How can this text help us in times of trial and tribulation?

3. Have you found that there have been times you have been comforted by this passage?

4. What are some of the occasions where this promise has blessed and comforted you?

5. How could you use this to help comfort and encourage others?

18
Living in the Spirit of Praise

"In everything give thanks for this is the will of God in Christ Jesus concerning you." 1 Thessalonians 5:18

"The worst moment for an atheist is when he is genuinely thankful, but has nobody to thank." Dante Gabriel Rosetti

When we develop a Christian worldview with the purpose of living a life that is pleasing to God, we must take into account that that worldview is incomplete if the spirit of praise to God is missing. Although I have left this subject of praise towards the end of this book, it should be remembered that praising God is one of the most important aspects of Christian living.

Two men who could not speak the same language, met while traveling onboard a ship. They were both Christians but had no means of communicating their faith in the Lord to one another. One day, one of these men noticed the other was carrying a Bible. He could remain silent no longer. He approached his fellow traveler and pointing to the Bible he said, "Hallelujah!" The other man broke into a broad smile and said, "Amen!" The two men shook hands, and although they could not communicate verbally, their hearts had expressed a common bond and love in God through their praise! This story was told by F. W. Boreham. He tells how these two men had found a meeting place and a greeting place among the monumental untranslatables. *Hallelujah* is a word universally understood as meaning *"Praise the Lord."* Praise is the universal characteristic of all God's people.

Praise is an Activity and a Command

Praise is an activity. Praise is something that we do. Praise is a command that God gives to all of His children who have been born again. The commandment of God given in Scripture more than any other is the command to praise the Lord. I have often defined praise as, *"The verbal and heartfelt response of God's redeemed people in adoration for all that God is, and for all that God has done for them."* Author Sharon James makes this comment on praise: *"We naturally praise those things or people we admire or love; but God is far above them all, as the one who created all. And the best way to stir ourselves to praise him passionately is to remember all the wonderful things he has done."*[1]

> *The commandment of God given in Scripture more than any other is the command to praise the Lord.*

Let me expand on these comments. Christians should praise God for His greatness, sovereignty, mercy, love, grace, etc. Christians should also praise God for what He has done. We should praise God for His act in creating the world and all the beauty that it displays. We should praise God for His providence in maintaining this world and for protecting and providing for us. Perhaps most of all, we should praise God for His great salvation that is revealed to us through the person and work of His Son Jesus Christ. David says in Psalm 51:15, *"O Lord open thou my lips and my mouth shall show forth thy praise."* God opens our lips to praise Him when He saves us and gives us the gift of the new birth. When a baby is born, it cries. When a person is born again, they praise God. If praise and thankfulness are absent from the lives of those who claim to be Christians we must conclude that they have never known the wonders and the glory of God's saving grace.

The Apostle Paul describes the lostness of mankind in Ephesians 2:1-10:

> [1] *And you hath he quickened, who were dead in trespasses and sins;*[2] *Wherein in time past ye walked ac-*

cording to the course of this world, according to the prince of the power of the air, the spirit that now worketh in the children of disobedience: [3] Among whom also we all had our conversation in times past in the lusts of our flesh, fulfilling the desires of the flesh and of the mind; and were by nature the children of wrath, even as others. [4] But God, who is rich in mercy, for his great love wherewith he loved us, [5] Even when we were dead in sins, hath quickened us together with Christ, (by grace ye are saved;) [6] And hath raised us up together, and made us sit together in heavenly places in Christ Jesus: [7] That in the ages to come he might shew the exceeding riches of his grace in his kindness toward us through Christ Jesus. [8] For by grace are ye saved through faith; and that not of yourselves: it is the gift of God: [9] Not of works, lest any man should boast. [10] For we are his workmanship, created in Christ Jesus unto good works, which God hath before ordained that we should walk in them.

In the first few verses of this passage, the Apostle Paul is ruthlessly descriptive of how sinful and wretched all men are. But then he soars to great heights when he tells how God has reached down and saved each of us by His grace. Why does Paul do this? It is because he knows that if we see how low God had to stoop in order to save us and how high God has lifted us up, then we will be filled with the spirit of praise and adoration.

Praise is an Important Aspect of Christian Witness

When we praise God, we are conveying a message to all of those around us. To the world we are proclaiming that God is sovereign over every area of life. Psalm 135:6 tells us, "*Whatsoever the Lord pleased, that did he in heaven, and in earth, in the seas, and all deep places.*" We are proclaiming that God is God. Psalm 45:17 says, "*I will make thy name to be remembered in all generations: therefore shall the people praise thee for ever and ever.*" By praising God, we are directing the attention of those who do not know the grace of God to the Lord. When we praise God, we are also reminding ourselves that God is full of mercy. Psalm 145:1-8 says,

[1] *I will extol thee, my God, O king; and I will bless thy
name for ever and ever.* [2] *Every day will I bless thee;
and I will praise thy name for ever and ever.* [3] *Great is
the* LORD, *and greatly to be praised; and his greatness is
unsearchable.* [4] *One generation shall praise thy works to
another, and shall declare thy mighty acts.* [5] *I will speak
of the glorious honor of thy majesty, and of thy wondrous
works.* [6] *And men shall speak of the might of thy terrible
acts: and I will declare thy greatness.* [7] *They shall abun-
dantly utter the memory of thy great goodness, and shall
sing of thy righteousness.* [8] *The* LORD *is gracious, and full
of compassion; slow to anger, and of great mercy.*

When we praise God we are reminding ourselves that God has
not forgotten us, that He will meet all of our physical and spiritual
needs. Praising God reveals our love, adoration, and worship to
Him. Praise also serves as a testimony to other believers that we
are thankful and trust the God who saved us and brought us out
of darkness.

Praise Makes Our Joy Complete

Most of all, praise is that activity and response of the soul that fills
us with our greatest joy and peace. Sometimes when people hear
that God commands men to praise Him, they conclude that this
is a major flaw in the God who is revealed to us in the Scriptures.
They draw the wrong conclusion that this is a sign of arrogance
and pride that should be inconsistent with the biblical concept of
God. But such reasoning is incorrect. It is true that if I commanded
men to praise or worship me it would indeed be a sign of tremendous arrogance and pride. I am just a man with many faults and
flaws in my life and character. But God is far superior to me and
to every person. When God commands men to praise Him, He is
not acting out of character with Himself. We must not forget that
although men are not worthy of worship and adoration, God is.
God is the Creator of all life. God is the only One who is transcen-
dent, holy, infinitely great, and wondrous beyond our comprehension. God alone in this universe is worthy of worship and praise.
But when God commands men to praise Him, He also knows that

this is not just for His benefit, but for ours, as well. Let me explain it in this way. When I fell in love with my wife, I had a deep affection for her. The love that I had for the woman that I had set my affections on could never be complete or satisfied as long as I remained anonymous in my relationship with her. There was an intense desire burning in my heart to tell her openly and sincerely that I was in love with her. When I finally had the opportunity to express my feelings, there was not only a great relief but a joy and satisfaction that went beyond anything that I had ever known before. Similarly, God knows that our joy and satisfaction will never be complete until we pour out our hearts to Him in adoration and praise. Praise is not just for God; it is also for our benefit.

Hosea the prophet, speaking to the children of Israel, said that we should "...*render the calves of our lips.*" Hosea 14:2 True worship is giving the sacrifice of praise to the God we love. When developing a Christian worldview, we must not forget the importance of living in the spirit of praise. There is tremendous joy and peace to those who are redeemed by the Lord Jesus Christ. No matter what trials or tribulations befall the people of God, they are sustained by the gracious promises and wonderful presence of God. Therefore, the Apostle Paul said, "*In everything give thanks for this is the will of God in Christ Jesus concerning you.*" 1 Thessalonians 5:16

The Christian life is a great adventure. The author of the book of Hebrews reminds us that we are merely strangers and pilgrims in this world here below. (Hebrews 11:13) We are strangers and sojourners in this world. But in spite of this we have great joy and peace.

One hymn writer captured the joy of living in praise when he wrote this wonderful hymn and gospel song:

How Wonderful

I walk at night beneath majestic skies,
And know behind them is a God all-wise,
Who pinned all stars each in a lonely place,
Then wrapped them in the darkened robe of space.

I scan the heavens with rapture in my soul,
And wonder how the God who made the whole,
Could ever fix His thoughts on one like me,
Or give His Son to die upon a tree.

When I awake I know that God has not slept,
For watch or'e me so faithfully was kept;
A fuse of lonely color blinds my eye,
And fills my heart with love for Him on high.

I walk at noon am warmed by shining sun,
And know the earth's true light my love has won;
I watch the flowers, the tender blade of grass,
The stately trees as on my way I pass.

The glorious sunset draws me close to Heaven,
I think on Him whose life for me was given;
Great longing comes to me when twilight falls,
For Heavens home, from there my Savior calls.

Refrain: O Lord, my God how wonderful thou art,
To make our world and satisfy man's heart;
With humbled pride before my God I bow,
How wonderful, how glorious art Thou.

Ester D. Eden

Praise and Edification is Essential to Christian Ministry

One final aspect of praise that is essential for Christians to under-stand is the importance of praising other Christians. This is some-times referred to as edification or giving recognition to those who deserve it. The principle of edifying others is not only taught in the Bible; it was also practiced by our Lord and Savior Jesus Christ. First, let me explain what edification means. To edify someone is to give them praise, honor, and recognition for what they have accomplished. This is taught us in the Bible in such passages as Proverbs 3:27, "*Withhold not good from them to whom it is due, when it is in the power of thine hand to do it.*" Romans 13:7 says,

"Render therefore to all their dues: tribute to whom tribute is due; custom to whom custom; fear toe whom fear; honour to whom honour." Galatians 6:10 says, *"As we have therefore opportunity, let us do good unto all men, especially unto them who are of the household of faith."* We may have a difficult time doing this for we think that praise only belongs to God. The idea of giving honor to or edifying someone is not an unscriptural concept as I have shown. Jesus gave honor to John the Baptist when He spoke of him to his disciples and said he was the greatest of all the prophets. Matthew 11:11 reads, *"Verily I say unto you, Among them that are born of women there hath not risen a greater than John the Baptist: notwithstanding he that is least in the kingdom of heaven is greater than he."* I have observed that in many Christian circles we tend to edify and honor our dead Christian leaders while crucifying and criticizing our living Christian leaders. This is a tragic mistake. If churches would learn the secret of edifying their pastors and Christian leaders it would lead to greater respect and possibly greater potential for outreach. I have tried to practice this concept of edification whenever I go and speak to another church. If people leave their church on Sunday and throughout the week go out and tell with excitement and enthusiasm what good things they are learning in church and how much they love and respect their pastors, people might be encouraged to come and see for themselves. This is exactly what the disciples did when they first met Jesus. They were so excited that they went out and told all of their friends to come and see what they had found. Andrew, the brother of Peter, was one who was so excited about Jesus that he went home and told his brother about Him. John 1:41: *"He first findeth his own brother Simon, and saith unto him, We have found the Messias, which is, being interpreted, the Christ."* The woman who met Jesus at the well in

> *...in many Christian circles we tend to edify and honor our dead Christian leaders while crucifying and criticizing our living Christian leaders.*

John 4 did the same thing. When she was overwhelmed by the presence of Christ she dropped her water pot, ran into town, and told all the men about the amazing person that she had just met. She raised the question to all of them that this person might be the Messiah. John 4:28-29 states, *"The woman then left her water-pot, and went her way into the city, and saith to the men, Come, see a man, which told me all things that ever I did: is not this the Christ?"* We should follow this example.

What Edification Does for Those That Are Edified

1. It encourages the one edified.
2. It inspires the one edified to keep working harder and to strive to excel in what they are doing.
3. It strengthens the one edified.
4. It gives the one edified credibility with those outside the church or organization.
5. It sets an example to others to edify and show respect to their leaders.
6. It creates loyalty and cements the church together in a spirit of love and appreciation.
7. It comes back to the one who did the edifying. If we edify others it shows that we are truly Christ-like, for Jesus was the chief encourager to His disciples.

In his book, *Six Battles Every Man Must Win*, Bill Perkins shares three ways that parents can bless their children. These three suggestions also fit the subject of edification. Whether people are seeking to bless their children or honor their pastor and Christian leaders, these three simple suggestions are excellent points to remember:

1. Verbal affirmation: words of affection and approval. We should speak many more words of support than words of correction or criticism.
2. Physical affirmation: a hand on the shoulder, a pat on the back, or a hug.
3. Predictive affirmation: words that foresee a bright future that is consistent with their personal strengths.[2]

As you live for the glory of God, may He be pleased to fill your soul to overflowing with joyful praise. The believer who lives in the spirit of praise will know a joy and peace that all the storms of hell can never shake.

How to Get Started

1. Make a list of things for which you can be thankful and praise God.
2. Begin to praise God everyday.
3. Keep a journal and write down the answers to prayers and any other things that will be a source of praise for you when you recall them in the days to come, God's gracious dealings in your life.
4. Learn to praise God for even the things that normally would have caused you pain and sorrow. We should praise God for everything in our lives, good or bad.
5. Begin to encourage your pastors and spiritual leaders with sincere heartfelt edification.

Thoughts for Consideration

- *"Bless the Lord today; he blesses you every day."* Anonymous

- *"I have never sufficiently praised the Lord, and never can."* Andrew Bonar

- *"Praise is the best of all sacrifices and the true evidence of godliness."* John Calvin

- *"In commanding us to glorify Him, God is inviting us to enjoy Him."* C. S. Lewis

- *"Praising and adoring God is the noblest part of the saint's work on earth, as it will be his chief employ in heaven."* A. W. Pink

- *"Praise is the rent which God requires for the use of His mercies."* C. H. Spurgeon

- *"Oh, how I wish I could adequately set forth the glory of that One who is worthy to be the object of our worship!"* A. W. Tozer

- *"In prayer we act like men; in praise we act like angels."* Thomas Watson

- *"Come thou fount of every blessing, Tune my heart to sing Thy grace; Streams of mercy, never ceasing, Call for sings of loudest praise. Teach me some melodious sonnet, Sung by flaming tongues above; Oh the vast, the boundless treasure of my Lord's unchanging love!"* Robert Robinson

- *"A hammer sometimes misses its mark — a bouquet never."* Monta Crane

- *"I praise loudly; I blame softly."* Catherine II of Russia

Questions for Discussion

1. How often do you praise God?

2. What does it mean to praise God?

3. Why is praising God an important aspect of Christian living?

4. Have you learned to praise God for even the hard and difficult things that have entered your life?

5. Do others see you as a person who is filled with praise for God or as a grumbler and complainer?

6. What does it mean to edify another person or Christian leader?

7. Does the Bible teach edification?

8. What are the results of edification?

19
Preparing for Death

"Remember me as you pass by,
As you are now so once was I.
As I am now so you shall be,
Prepare for death and follow me."
Anonymous
Found on a gravestone in Lancaster, Pennsylvania

"It is appointed unto men once to die and after this the judge-
ment." Hebrews 9:27

A biblical worldview must include instructions of how to prepare for death. Perhaps the most helpful example of how to
die well comes from Jesus Himself. Pastor Kirk Neely, who wrote
a very helpful book on facing death and grief, said, *"As Jesus*
came to the end of his life at the hands of Roman executioners, he
blessed others: a dying thief, his own mother, the beloved disciple
John, even those who put him to death. His word of forgiveness
from the cross is a word of blessing for all people in all times."[1]

We all know that we are going to die someday. How sobering
this thought can be. Yet most people live as though they think they
will live forever. When thoughts of death arise in their minds, they
dismiss them as quickly as possible. This is not only foolish, but it
is also dangerous. The Bible tells us that when death comes for us,
we will be ushered either into God's immediate presence or into a
place of judgment and torment. It would then seem prudent that
we should make sure that we are ready for death. Let me share

with you some things that everyone should do to prepare for that great and terrible day when death claims and ushers us into our eternal destiny.

Make Your Calling and Election Sure

The Apostle Peter said, *"Wherefore the rather, brethren, give diligence to make your calling and election sure: for if ye do these things, ye shall never fall."* 2 Peter 1:10 The Bible speaks of unconditional election. This simply means that God has chosen a people to give to His Son the Lord Jesus Christ. Peter Jeffrey explains the meaning and mystery of election in this way:

> *The subject of election and predestination is undoubtedly one of the most controversial among Christians. Some believers love and treasure it as the most thrilling and humbling of doctrines; other believers will not tolerate it at any price and regard it as totally wrong. Let us first of all define what the Bible means by election.*
>
> *All men and women are sinners, all are guilty of breaking God's law, therefore all deserve judgement and hell. No one deserves salvation, but election is God saving by his grace some guilty sinners whom he has chosen.*
>
> *The elect are no better than anyone else. They are not chosen because they deserve something. So they can never feel superior to any who are not elect. The non-elect only get what their sin deserves so they can never complain that they are being treated unfairly.*[2]

All those whom God has chosen will eventually come to Christ in salvation. Whenever I discuss the doctrine of election with people, one of the questions that always comes up is this: "How do I know if I am one of the elect?" This is an important question. If we would prepare for death, this is one of the most important questions for which to find the answer. Let me share some of the ways we can approach this subject to determine if we are among the elect.

First, I would say that if you are asking this question — that in itself is a good sign. I have found that most non-Christians have little or no interest in these kinds of things at all. It is a good sign for a person to be concerned if he or she is one of the elect or not.

Secondly, I would ask if you understand the gospel. If a person has a clear understanding and comprehension of the basic truths of the gospel, this will be absolutely essential to their salvation. The Scripture says, *"Faith cometh by hearing, and hearing by the word of God."* Romans 10:17 We know this — the elect are those who know what the gospel is and how it applies to their lives. If a person lives and dies in ignorance of the gospel, we can be sure that person was not one of the elect of God. Those who are among the elect will come to know the gospel and obey the gospel commands to repent of sin and put faith in the Lord Jesus Christ.

Thirdly, ask yourself if there has been any change in your life since the time you put your faith in Jesus Christ. The elect are those who have been born again and as a result of that new birth have new longings and desires that are spiritual in nature. The fruit of the Spirit is, *"Love, joy, peace, longsuffering, gentleness, goodness, faith, meekness, temperance..."* Galatians 5:22-23 We do not expect perfection out of those who are the elect of God, but we do expect to see a change of heart and nature that will be evidenced by the presence of this spiritual fruit in their lives. If there is no fruit in a person's life, then we can assume there is also no grace. It's as simple as that. *"No fruit, no grace."*

Fourthly, we should ask ourselves if we have a desire to be with Christ and obey Him in every area of our lives. The elect will be those who have such desires. Those who have no interest in Christ or any desires to love and obey Him are certainly not showing any signs of being the elect of God. Over the years I have used the acrostic wolf to explain what a true Christian is. Perhaps this little thought will be of help to you as you consider if you are one of the elect or not.

W—Worship
O—Obedience
L—Love
F—Follow

A Christian is one who worships, obeys, loves, and follows Jesus Christ. The elect of God will be known as the people who fit this pattern in their lives. If a person does not worship, obey, love, or follow Christ, we can assume that at the least, they have not come to a saving knowledge of God in salvation. All of the elect, having come to Christ by faith, will give evidence of the four things that are seen in the acrostic W-O-L-F.

Fifthly, to determine if we are the elect of God we should evaluate the witness of God's Spirit. Does the Holy Spirit bear witness with our spirit that we are the children of God? Assurance of salvation is a gift from the Holy Spirit. If a person is one of the elect, the Holy Spirit will draw them to Christ. The person being drawn to the Lord will be convicted of his or her sin and given the gifts of repentance and faith. After repenting of sin and putting faith in the Lord Jesus Christ, the believer will have the inner witness of the Spirit in his or her life. The Spirit will give us a sense or the knowledge that we are the children of God. Assurance of salvation can depart from us if we sin, fall into a period of disobedience, or neglect the disciplines of reading the Word of God and prayer. But those who are the elect of God will know in their heart of hearts that they have had an encounter with the living God. Pastor Vernon Higham of Cardiff, Wales, who is one of the godliest men I have ever known, wrote a little book titled *The Unsearchable Riches of Christ*. In this book Pastor Higham reveals that the doctrine of election is often used by God to give a sweet assurance to believers that their salvation is in the hands of a wise and sovereign God. Pastor Higham writes:

> *There begins to grow in us the realization of an assurance and a security that no one is able to shake.*

> *I've found a Friend, O such a Friend;*
> *He loved me ere I knew Him;*
> *He drew me with the cords of love,*
> *And thus He bound me to Him;*
> *And round my heart still closely twine*
> *Those ties which nought can sever,*

For I am His, and He is mine,
For ever and for ever.

With all the assurance that this brings, we know that our salvation is not dependent upon our feelings, but upon God's will. With such knowledge, even when Satan assails us with fearful doubts as to whether there has been a work of grace in our hearts, we rest upon God's immutable will. Those whom the Father has chosen in Christ from eternity will come to the Saviour, and can never be separated from the Lord.[3]

Sixthly, Jesus taught His disciples that the one distinguishing mark of a true believer was love. "*A new commandment I give unto you, That ye love one another; as I have loved you, that ye also love one another, By this shall all men know that ye are my disciples, if ye have love one to another.*" John 13:34-35 Those who are the elect of God not only love God but will also love other believers. It may not always be easy to love other people who profess faith in the Lord Jesus Christ. Sometimes people can be annoying, difficult to live with, and even rude or unkind. But the one true mark of a believer is that they have been taught to love one another. Christians worldwide are known for their love. They strive to be like their Master. If you have love in your heart for others who profess to be the people of God, that is a good sign. If you are struggling to love some other Christian, you would be wise to remember that Christ loves you in spite of all your sins, flaws, and imperfections. Since God has been so loving, gracious, and patient with us, it would seem a small thing for us to do the same towards those whom we have a hard time living with or being around. The Scripture teaches us that love covers a multitude of sins. The ability to love as Christ loved is what really makes us Christ-like.

From all of these things, we can learn to make our calling and election sure, as Peter the apostle tells us to do. In developing a Christian worldview, we must know how to prepare for death. A worldview that neglects this last great event of human experience is defective and deficient in the most vital area of our life's experience.

Come Boldly to the Throne of Grace

In preparing for death we need to do what the apostle tells us to do in Hebrews 4:16: *"Let us therefore come boldly unto the throne of grace, that we may obtain mercy, and find grace to help in time of need."* My friends, death is going to come. For some of us it will come suddenly and sever that thin cord that separates us from eternity. For others, death will come with the advance of years, the slow aging process, the decaying of our bodies, and the loss of our youth, vigor, and health. We will not be caught unawares by the approach of death. Death is looming on the distant horizon and every day its approach is nearer than the day before.

Death is looming on the distant horizon and every day its approach is nearer than the day before.

As pastor Vernon Higham wrote, *"Sooner or later it dawns upon us that we do not live here forever. The stark reality confronts us that relatives, friends and neighbors die. It does not take much thought on our part to conclude that one day we too shall die."*[4]

As we see the moment coming upon us when we shall be called to stand before the God of the universe to give an account of our earthly life and labors here, we would be wise to listen to what the apostle told us in Hebrews. I know of no better way to prepare for death than to find my comfort and safety in running to that marvelous throne of grace where Jesus sits at the right hand of His Father. O what mercy, grace, peace, and love we find when we meet with our God there. John Calvin, commenting about this throne said it, *"...is not marked by a naked majesty which overpowers us, but is adorned with a new name, that of grace."*[5]

This is the Father's throne. This is a throne where we can come with boldness. We need not fear or hesitate to come to this throne, for God Himself has invited us to draw near. The Father does not merely invite us to draw near — He commands us to do so and to come without any hesitation. Come boldly! This is how we are to come. Come confessing your sins. Come with the knowledge of all your failures. Come knowing that you are not perfect, but come anyway. Come because God invites you to come. Come because He already knows your weaknesses, fears, and doubts. This is a gracious throne and promise from the Lord. This is the way to prepare for death. Come to the God who sits on that throne and pour your heart out to Him there. Tell Him about fears of death, worries, doubts, and concerns. One poet wrote verses on this precious text to explain the kinds of things we might seek from the Lord when we draw near with boldness to His throne of grace. Perhaps these verses will stir your heart to seek the Lord for similar needs in your own soul.

> *"Deep regret for follies past,*
> *Talents wasted, time misspent*
> *Hearts debased by worldly cares,*
> *Thankless for the blessings lent.*
>
> *Foolish fears and fond desires,*
> *Vain regrets for things as vain;*
> *Lips too seldom taught to praise,*
> *Oft to murmur and complain;*
>
> *These and every secret fault,*
> *Filled with grief and shame we own;*
> *Humbled at thy feet we lie,*
> *Seeking pardon from thy throne."*

Jeremy Taylor

How precious is this invitation to each of us as Christians. We have a throne of grace to approach when we sin, fail, are filled with fears and doubts, and are about to die. There is no throne mentioned in any other major world religion that offers the riches of God's grace and mercy to those in need and who fear death.

Dr. Edgar Andrews of London, England described this throne in this fashion:

> *The writer bids us come "boldly", or "with boldness". The words mean "confidently", "frankly" and "without conceal-ment". We should not seek to hide our sins and our weak-ness, however much we are ashamed of them. Our very frailty in these matters constitutes a claim upon the great High Priest. Is this really so? Yes, because we come first of all to "obtain mercy", and only sinners need that...But the Saviour's throne affords more than mercy. We may also "find grace to help in time of need" (4:16). After all, it is a throne of grace!...In almost every instance of the use of "grace" in the Old Testament, the word is coupled with the verb "to find". "Noah found grace in the eyes of the Lord" (Gen. 6:8; see also Moses in Exod. 33:12)...It is clear that "to find" grace is a Hebrew idiom — "to be looked upon with favour by one who owes nothing to the person fa-voured". We cannot earn grace; we can only "find" it at the footstool of the God of grace.*[6]

When I think of approaching death, Hebrews 4:16 is such a com-fort. We can run into the loving arms of our great High Priest the Lord Jesus Christ and find peace, pardon, grace, and mercy in the time of our greatest need — death.

Consider Dying a Great Gain

Most of the people with whom I have spoken concerning death have never viewed death as something to which one should look forward. It is not uncommon for many to fear death. With this in mind, we can see why death is not a popular and pleasant subject. But this should not be true of those who know the Lord. A Christian worldview should teach us not only to not fear death but to actually look forward to death as the day of our greatest promotion. This attitude towards death does not come easily. Like many other things in the Christian's life, we must be taught to embrace death as the gateway to heaven and being with Christ. The Apostle Paul wrote, *"For to me to live is Christ, and to die* is gain." Philippians 1:21 Pastor John Piper gave wise advice concerning death: *"It is good to ponder our death. We should live well that we might die well. Part of living well is learning why death is gain."*[7]

> *We should live well that we might die well. Part of living well is learning why death is gain.*

John Piper goes on to list five reasons why death is gain to a believer. We should remember these five things when we see death approaching our door.

- At the moment of death, spirits will be made perfect. All sin, fears, sorrows, and tears will be removed forever.
- At the moment of death, we will be relieved of the pain of this world.
- At the moment of death, we will be given profound rest in our souls.
- At the moment of death, we will experience a deep at-home-ness. When the believer is with Christ, there will be contentment and peace that we have never known.
- At the moment of death, we will be with Christ.

Here is what Piper had to say about being with Christ:

> *Christ is a more wonderful person than anyone on earth. He is wiser, stronger, and kinder than anyone you enjoy spending time with. He is endlessly interesting. He knows exactly what to do and what to say at every moment to make his guests as glad as they can possibly be. He overflows with love and infinite insight into how to use that love to make his loved ones feel loved. Therefore Paul said, "For to me, to live is Christ, and to die is gain. But if I am to live on in the flesh, this will mean fruitful labor for me; and I do not know which to choose. But I am hard-pressed from both directions, having the desire to depart and be with Christ, for that is very much better." (Philippians 1:21-23)*[8]

We are going to die. Never forget this. Live with your eyes on the throne room of heaven. The Latin phrase *"Momento Mori"* means "Remember that you must die." The way to prepare for death is to embrace with all your heart the gospel of Jesus Christ. There is no preparation for death apart from this. For those who know the Lord, preparing for death is absolutely essential if we would have a joyful entrance into the presence of God. In a sense, my entire life is preparation for that great moment, when by the plan and will of God, I am called home to be with the Lord. The German Reformer, Martin Luther, understood the importance of preparing for death and wrote: *"Life is a constant and daily journey toward death. One after another dies, and the living must merely engage in the miserable business of carrying one another to the grave. All of us are traveling the same road together."*[9]

Life is a constant and daily journey toward death.

May God enable all of us who are developing a Christian worldview the desire and determination to make ourselves ready for that precious day when we take our journey home!

How to Get Started

1. Make sure that you understand the gospel. This is the place to begin. Do you understand the doctrine of justification by faith alone?
2. Make your calling and election sure. Review the steps that I have outlined for you in this chapter.
3. Take some time to think on the glory of heaven as John Piper has reminded us.
4. Learn the secret of living well so that you can die well.
5. The time to prepare for death begins with each new day.

Thoughts for Consideration

- *"He whose head is in heaven need not fear to put his feet into the grave."* Matthew Henry

- *"If we remember that by death we are called back from exile to home, to our heavenly fatherland, shall we then not be filled with comfort?"* John Calvin

- *"A believer's last day is his best day."* Thomas Brooks

- *"Has this world been so kind to you that you would leave it with regret? There are better things ahead than any we leave behind."* C. S. Lewis

- *"When death strikes the Christian down, he falls into heaven."* John Blanchard

- *"Death is but a passage out of a prison into a palace."* John Bunyan

- *"It is never too soon to begin to make friends with death."* Anonymous

- *"If a philosophy of life cannot help me to die, then in a sense it cannot help me to live."* D. Martyn Lloyd-Jones

- *"He who does not prepare for death is more than an ordinary fool. He is a madman."* C. H. Spurgeon

- *"Our people die well."* John Wesley

- *"He may look on death with joy who can look on forgiveness with faith."* Thomas Watson

Questions for Discussion

1. Why do you think people fear death?

2. What steps can people take to make their calling and election sure?

3. How can Hebrews 4:16 help us when it comes time to die?

4. Why should death be a great gain for the Christian?

5. What is the most important thing you can do to prepare for death?

6. Why should a Christian worldview include preparing for death?

Conclusion

The principles in this book are based on the Judeo-Christian Scriptures. These things give us a grid through which we can filter all of our life's experiences. If we keep these things in mind, they will help us on our way to success. By developing a Christian worldview, we will be equipped with a map, a set of directions and instructions that will greatly aid us in our walk with God.

The main thing is to keep working on your private life. Implement these ideas and principles into your daily living. Aim high and work at it every day. Success does not come in a moment, but rather in a lifetime of hard work and discipline. Do you have a dream? Go for it. Do you have a vision? Pray for it. Do you long for a greater meaning in life? Seek God with all your heart. You will find Him, for that is what He promised. *"And ye shall seek me and find me, when ye shall seek me with all of your heart."* Jeremiah 29:13

Don't give up or be discouraged at how hard the way may be. C. H. Spurgeon once told his people, *"The way may be rough, but it cannot be long."* Don't listen to the negative voices that say that you cannot achieve your dreams. What if Edison gave up working on the light bulb because some of his co-workers and associates told him he was crazy? They did, but he did not give up. What if Jackie Robinson, the first black man to play professional baseball, quit playing ball because there were those who said he would never be allowed to play in the Big Leagues? They did, but he did not listen to those voices. What if Martin Luther gave up and buckled under the pressure and fear of the times of the Reformation when people said he would be burned at the stake as a heretic? He did not quit, even though the church leaders were against him. My friends, life is made up of dreams. What is your dream? What is your goal? What is your vision? Never give up; never quit; never stop working. With a biblical worldview, you can achieve those dreams and rise higher than anyone ever imagined you could. Listen to these powerful and inspiring words:

> *History is replete with examples of men and women who changed their world because they dared to accept the challenge of a dream — a goal — of a Mt. Everest...a four minute mile...a symphony...a Pilgrim's Progress...a walk on the moon...a city reached for God...a slum beautified. Augustine, Savonarola, Martin Luther, John Calvin, John Wesley, D. L. Moody, George Washington Carver, Martin Luther King — they all had a dream, a goal. Large ambitions, high goals, great dreams are free to all of us.*[1]

Let me summarize the timeless and priceless principles that make up a Christian worldview and enable us to live for Christ. These nineteen principles and concepts are the foundation upon which a life pleasing to God is built.

1. Receiving the instructions from God known as the Creation Mandate.
2. Remembering that we are a people of destiny with a purpose in life to fulfill God's will for our lives.
3. Knowing that we must discover our main purpose which is to live for the glory of God.
4. Learning the joy and the blessing that the fear of God adds to our lives.
5. Remembering the importance of loving the Word of God. This is priceless.
6. Remembering the joys of walking with God. This is the stuff that life is made of.
7. Making wise use of our time, knowing that we must give an account to God one day for how we have used it.
8. Understanding the biblical view of wealth, that it is to be used for God's kingdom to have influence in the earth.
9. Making sure we have a biblical self image of ourselves. We have been made in the image of God and therefore have great significance in all that we are and do.

10. Practicing the art of friendship. This makes us truly like Christ.
11. Developing a healthy view of our sexuality. Fulfill this wonderful gift within the context of marriage.
12. Understanding the importance of being a servant to others.
13. Being passionate about excellence and striving for success in everything that we do. This pleases the Lord!
14. Building character in the Christian life. Character is one of the missing ingredients of most leaders today.
15. Remembering the importance of making a good first impression. Success and influence can be destroyed in a few careless and thoughtless moments that may never be recovered.
16. Proclaiming the gospel of Christ.
17. Resting in the peace of Romans 8:28.
18. Learning to praise God continually.
19. Preparing for death.

Those who make an effort to build upon this foundation will live their life in the framework of a Christian worldview. They have every reason to expect God's blessing on all that they do.

No life is ever wasted if it is spent on the one supreme goal of living for Jesus. A biblical worldview will enable us to live our lives in a way that is pleasing to God. After all, this is what is most important for all of us to do.

Living for Jesus

Living for Jesus a life that is true;
striving to please him in all that I do,
yielding allegiance, gladhearted and free,
this is the pathway of blessing for me.

Refrain:
O Jesus, Lord and Savior,
I give myself to thee;
for thou, in thy atonement,
didst give thyself for me;
I own no other master,
my heart shall be thy throne,

My life I give, henceforth to live,
O Christ for thee alone.

Living for Jesus who died in my place,
bearing on Calvary my sin and disgrace,
such love constrains me to answer his call,
follow his leading and give him my all.
(Refrain)

Living for Jesus wherever I am,
doing each duty in his holy name,
willing to suffer affliction or loss,
deeming each trial a part of my cross.
(Refrain)

Living for Jesus through earth's little while,
my dearest treasure, the light of his smile,
seeking the lost ones he died to redeem,
bringing the weary to find rest in him.

Endnotes

Preface

1. Philip E. Johnson, Quoted in the forward of *Total Truth* by Nancy Pearcey, (Crossway Books, 2004), p. 11.
2. Chuck Colson, *How Now Shall We Then Live?* (Tyndale House, 1999), p. 17.
3. Os Guinness, *The Long Journey Home* (Zondervan Publishers, 2003), p. 16.

Introduction

1. Bob Briner, *The Management Methods of Jesus*, (Nelson Business, 1996), p. 1-2.

Part I: The Purpose of Christian Living

Chapter 1: Following the Instructions

1. Nancy Pearcey, *Total Truth*, (Crossway Books, 2004), p. 47.
2. Francis Schaeffer, *Death in the City*, p. 80.
3. Charles Colson, *How Now Shall We Live*.
4. Nancy Pearcey, *Total Truth*, (Crossway Books, 2004), p. 19.
5. Doug Sherman and William Hendricks, *Your Work Matters to God* (NavPress, 1987), p.7, 77, 87.
6. Abraham Kuyper, quoted on http://en.thinkexist.com/keyword/square_inch/.
7. Abraham Kuyper, *You Can Do Greater Things Than Christ*, trans. Jan H. Boer (Jos, Nigeria: Institute of Church and Society, 1991), p. 74.
8. D. James Kennedy, *Lord of All, Developing a Christian Word-and-Life View*, (Crossway Books, 2005), p. 204.
9. D. James Kennedy, *Lord of All, Developing a Christian World-and-Life View*, (Crossway Books, 2005), p. 117.

10. John J. Dunphy, *"Religion for a New Age,"* The Humanist, January/February 1983, p. 26.
11. Martin Luther, quoted in *The Rebirth of America* (Philedelphia: Arthur S. Demoss Foundation, 1986), p. 127.
12. Mark Steyn, *America Alone,* (Regnery Publishing, Inc. 2006), p. 156.
13. Ibid. p. 160.
14. Os Guinness, *The Call: Finding and Fulfilling the Central Purpose of Your Life* (W Publishing Group, 1998) p. 4.

Chapter 2: Being a People of Destiny

1. Ken Ham, *How Could A Loving God...?* (Master Books, 2007), p. 125.
2. M. Basis Pennington, *Thomas Merton: Brother Monk* (Harper & Row, 1987)
3. Ayatollah Ruhollah Khomeini of Iran, quoted by Hal Lindsey, *The Everlasting Hatred — The Roots of Jihad,* (Oracle House Publishing, 2002), p. 2.
4. Kirk H. Neely, *When Grief Comes,* (Baker Book House, 2007), p. 109-110.
5. J Campbell White, 1909, secretary of the Layman's Missionary Movement.
6. Charles Swindoll, *Jesus the Greatest Life of All,* (Thomas Nelson Publishers, 2008) p. 142.
7. James Russell Lowell, "The Present Crises" in *Poems by James Russell Lowell,* vol. 2 (Ticknor, Reed, and Fields, 1849) p. 57.
8. C. H. Spurgeon, *An All Round Ministry,* (Banner of Truth Trust, 1978) p. 228-229.

Chapter 3: What is Our Main Purpose in Life?

1. Quote by Eric Liddell
2. J. Oswald Sanders, *Enjoying Intimacy with God* (Discovery House, 2000), p. 139.
3. John Piper, *Desiring God: Meditations of a Christian Hedonist* (Multnomah, 1986), p. 201-202.

4. Gordon MacDonald, *A Resilient Life*, (Nelson Publishers, 2004), p. 76.
5. John Milton, from his poem, *On His Blindness*, http://www.sonnets.org/milton.html
6. Nancy Pearcey, *Total Truth*, (Crossway Books, 2004), p. 66.
7. James C. Hunter, *The World's Most Powerful Leadership Principle*, (WaterBrook Press, 2004), p. 119.
8. Jim Berg, *Changed into His Image*, (Bob Jones University Press, 1999) p. 68-69.
9. C. S. Lewis, *Mere Christianity*, p. 54.
10. C. S. Spurgeon and Harald, *C. H. Spurgeon's Autobiography*, vol. 3 (Passmore & Alabaster, 1899) p. 49.
11. Newsweek Magazine, December 14, 1981, *"Thinking: A Neglected Art."*

Chapter 4: The Fear of the Lord

1. Dr. David D. Ireland, *Perfecting Your Purpose*, (Warner Faith, 2005), p. 220-221.
2. Pat Williams, *The Paradox of Power*, (Warner Faith Publishers, 2002), p. 126.
3. John C. Maxwell, *Talent Is Never Enough*, (Thomas Nelson Publishers, 2007), p. 204-205.
4. John Kitchen, *Revival in the Rubble*, (CLC Publications, 2006), p. 192.
5. Ibid. p. 230-231.
6. Ken Collier and Matt Williams, *Biblical Leadership*, (Ambassador Publications, 2004), p. 83.
7. Charles Swindoll, *Living Above the Level of Mediocrity*, (Word Publishers, 1987), p. 246.
8. Joel Beeke and Randall Pederson, *"Philip Henry,"* in *Meet the Puritans*, (Reformation Heritage Books, 2006).
9. Arnold Dallimore, *George Whitefield: The Life and Times of the Great Evangelist of the Eighteenth-century Revival* (Crossway Books, 1979), p. 80.
10. Bruce Larson, *There's a Lot More to Health Than Not Being Sick* (Word Books Publisher), p. 61.
11. Edmund Burke, quoted by Mark Steyn in *America Alone*, (Regnery Publishing, Inc. 2006), p. 150.

Chapter 5: Loving the Word of God

1. B. B. Warfield, *The Inspiration and Authority of the Bible*, (Presbyterian and Reformed, 1964), p. 160.
2. Gideon's International (Slightly adapted).
3. Robert L. Peterson & Alexander Strauch, *Agape Leadership — Lessons in Spiritual Leadership from the Life of R. C. Chapman*, (Lewis and Roth Publishers, 1991), p. 15-16.
4. John Piper, *Desiring God*, (Multnomah Publishers, 2001), p. 356-357.
5. Quoted in Daniel Fuller, "*I Was Just Thinking,*" in *Today's Christian*, September 1977.
6. C. H. Spurgeon, *Lectures to My Students*, (Zondervan Publishing House, 1954), p. 206.
7. Quoted from his *Autobiography* in Iain Murray, *The Forgotten Spurgeon*, (Banner of Truth Trust, 1973), p. 34.
8. David D. Ireland, *Journey to the Mountain of God*, (Warner Faith Publishers, 2006), p. 173.
9. D. James Kennedy, *Lord of All, Developing a Christian World-and-Life View*, (Crossway Books, 2005), p. 247.

Chapter 6: Walking with God

1. C. H. Spurgeon, *The Metropolitan Tabernacle Pulpit*, vol. 35 "*Faith Essential to Pleasing God*, (Banner of Truth Trust, 1969), p. 577.
2. C. H. Spurgeon, *The Metropolitan Tabernacle Pulpit*, no. 681, March 18, 1866, "*And God Opened Her Eyes...*" (Banner of Truth Trust, 1969), p.199-200.
3. Herbert Butterfield, *Christianity and History* (Charles Scribner's Sons, 1949), p. 115.
4. Elton Trueblood, *While it is Yet Day*, (Harper & Row, 1974), p. 67.
5. David D. Ireland, *Journey to the Mountain of God*, (Time Warner, 2006), p. 177.
6. Jim Berg, *Changed into His Image*, (Bob Jones University Press, 1999), p. 142.

7. Howard Rutledge and Phyllis Rutledge with Mel White and Lyla White, *In the Presence of Mine Enemies*, (Fleming Revell, 1973), p. 34.
8. Stuart Olyott, *Alive in Christ*, (Evangelical Press, 1994), p. 120.
9. C. S. Lewis, *The Weight of Glory and Other Addresses*, (Eerdmans, 1965), p. 2.
10. Harry Lauder, quoted in G. B. F. Hallock, *Five Thousand Best Modern Illustrations*, (George H. Doran Company, 1972), p.256.
11. Bob Russell, *Money, A User's Manual*, (Multnomah Press), p. 54.
12. Charles Swindoll, *Jesus, the Greatest Life of All*, (Thomas Nelson Publishers, 2008) p. 147.
13. A. W. Tozer, *God's Pursuit of Man*, (WingSpread Publishers, 1978).

Part II: The Practical Aspects of Christian Living

Chapter 7: Using Our Time Wisely

1. J. Oswald Sanders, *Paul the Leader*, (Nav Press, 1984), p. 62.
2. Os Guinness, *The Long Journey Home*, (Zondervan Publishers, 2001), p. 49.
3. J. Oswald Sanders, *Spiritual Leadership*, (Moody Press, 1967), p. 88.
4. William Barclay, *The Gospel of Matthew*, (Westminster, 1975), p. 280.
5. J. Oswald Sanders, *Paul the Leader*, (Nav Press, 1984), p. 155-156.
6. Donald S. Whitney, *Spiritual Disciplines for the Christian Life*, (Nav Press, 1991), p. 131-132.
7. J. Oswald Sanders, *Spiritual Leadership*, (Moody Press), p. 85.
8. Gordon MacDonald, *Ordering Your Private World*, (Thomas Nelson Publishers, 1985), p. 17-18.

9. Ibid. p. 36.
10. Bob Russell, *Money, A User's Manual*, (Multnomah Press), p. 39.
11. Dr. David D. Ireland, *Perfecting Your Purpose*, (Warner Faith, 2005), p. 130-131.

Chapter 8: Developing a Biblical View of Wealth

1. Lewis C. Henry, *Five Thousand Quotations for all Occasions*, (Doubleday and Company, Inc., 1945), p. 178.
2. R. C. Sproul, *Now That's a Good Question*, (Tyndale House Publishers, 1996), p. 436.
3. J.C. Ryle, *Practical Religion* (James Clarke, 1959), p. 216.
4. A. W.Tozer, *The Pursuit of God* (Christian Publications, 1948), p. 21.
5. Elizabeth Elliot, *Discipline: The Glad Surrender*, (Revell, 1982), p. 112.
6. James Montgomery Boice, *Christ's Call to Discipleship*, (Kregel Publications, 1998), p. 88-89.
7. John Kitchen, *Revival in the Rubble*, (CLC Publications, 2006), p. 129.
8. A. W. Pink, *Tithing*, (Reiner Publications), p. 3.
9. J. Oswald Sanders, *Enjoying Intimacy with God*, (Discovery House, 2000), p. 137-138.
10. Larry Burkett, *Giving and Tithing*, (Moody Press, 1998), p. 17.
11. J. C. Ryle, *Walking with God*, (Grace Publications, 2005), p. 87.
12. Bob Russell, *Money, A User's Manual*, (Multnomah Press), p. 93-94.

Chapter 9: Nurturing a Biblical Self-image

1. Roousas John, Rushdooney, *Biblical Institutes*, Vol. 1, (Presbyterian and Reformed Publishing Company, 1973), p. 343.
2. Ted W. Engstrom, *The Pursuit of Excellence*, (Zondervan

Publishing House, 1982), p. 57.

3. Larry J. Michael, *"Responding to Personal Attacks,"* available online at www.churchcentral.com/nw/template/Article.html/id/16051.

4. A. W. Tozer, *The Pursuit of God*, (Christian Publications, 1948), p. 112.

5. Florence, Littauer, *It Takes So Little to be Above Average*, (Harvest House Publishers, 1983), p. 38.

6. Erwin W. Lutzer, *Failure the Back Door to Success*, (Moody Press, 1976), p. 72.

7. *Apocalypse? No!* Australia's Commission for the Future, p. 14.

Chapter 10: Being a True Friend

1. Dr. Karl Menninger, quoted by James C. Hunter, *The World's Most Powerful Leadership Principle*, (Waterbrook Press, 2004), p. 213.

2. Florence Littauer, *It Takes So Little to be Above Average,* (Harvest House Publishers, 1983), p. 167-168.

3. Dietrich Bonhoeffer, *Life Together*, trans. John W. Doberstein (Harper & Row, 1954), p. 97.

4. James Montegomery Boice, *Christ's Call to Discipleship*, (Kregel Publishers, 1998), p. 63.

5. Gordon MacDonald, *A Resilient Life*, (Nelson Publishers, 2004), p. 84.

6. Tana Reiff, *"If There's Anything I Can Do...,"* McCall's Magazine, February, 1983.

7. Florence, Littauer, *It Takes So Little to be Above Average*, (Harvest House Publishers, 1983), p. 169.

8. Gordon MacDonald, *A Resilient Life*, (Nelson Publishers, 2004), p. 223.

9. C. H. Spurgeon, "The Influence of Company," *The Sword and the Trowel* (1884) from the C. H. Spurgeon Collection, version 2.0 (AGES Software, 2001).

Chapter 11: Understanding the Biblical Purpose of Sex and Marriage

1. J. Steven Lang, http://cbn.com/Spirituallife/CBNTeaching sheets/promises_sexuality.aspx
2. Nancy Pearcey, *Total Truth*, (Crossway Books, 2004), p. 146.
3. Sharon James, *Gentle Rain on Tender Grass*, (Evangelical Press, 2006), p. 69.
4. Ibid., p. 4.
5. Anthony Selvaggio, *What the Bible Teaches About Marriage*, (Evangelical Press, 2007), p. 191.
6. Ibid., p. 193-194.

Chapter 12: Becoming a Servant

1. J. Oswald Sanders, *Spiritual Leadership*, (Chicago, Moody Press, 1967), p.13.
2. Ibid., p. 57.
3. James Hunter, *The World's Most Powerful Leadership Principle*, (WaterBrook Press, 2004), p. 78.
4. Charlie Jones, *Life is Tremendous*, (Tyndale House Publishers, 1996), p. 33.
5. James Hunter, *The World's Most Powerful Leadership Principle*, (WaterBrook Press, 2004), p. 145.
6. John Kitchen, *Revival in the Rubble*, (CLC Publications, 2006), p. 220.
7. George Duncan, *Marks of Christian Maturity*, (Marshall Pickering, 1986), p. 145-146.
8. J. Oswald Sanders, *Paul the Leader*, (Nav Press, 1984) p. 55.
9. C. H. Spurgeon, *An All Round Ministry*, (Banner of Truth Trust, 1978), p. 375.
10. Found online at http://www.ecoin.net/bc/fm_dts.html
11. John Kitchen, *Revival in the Rubble*, (CLC Publications, 2006), p. 222.
12. Stephen Brown, *No More Mr. Nice Guy!* (Nelson Publishers, 1986), p. 166-167.

Chapter 13: Striving for Success

1. Newsweek Magazine, May 9, 1983, "Can Schools Be Saved?"
2. Ted W. Engstrom, *The Pursuit of Excellence*, (Zondervan

Publishing Company, 1982), p. 22.

3. Ibid, p. 17.
4. J. C. Ryle, *Holiness, Its Nature and Hindrances*, (James Clarke, 1959), p. 71.
5. Bob Russell, *Money, A User's Manual*, (Multnomah Books), p. 37.
6. Billy Graham, *A Call to Commitment*, (Billy Graham Evangelistic Association, 1960), p. 1-2.
7. Dr. David D. Ireland, *Perfecting Your Purpose*, (Warner, Faith, 2005), p. 29.
8. Time Magazine, June 20, 1983.
9. Martyn Lloyd-Jones, *Spiritual Depression*, (Eerdman's Publishing Company, 1965), p. 34.
10. John Battersby Harford and Frederick Charles MacDonald, *Handley Carr Glyn Moule: Bishop of Durham*, (Hodder and Stroughton, 1992).
11. J. Oswald Sanders, *Spiritual Leadership*, (Moody Press, 1967), p. 23.
12. D. Martyn Lloyd-Jones, *Spiritual Depression: Its Causes and Cure*, (Eerdman's Publishing Company, 1965), p. 224.
13. David Otis Fuller, *A Treasury of Prayer* compiled by Leonard Ravenhill, (Bethany Fellowship, Inc. 1961), p. 7.

Chapter 14: Building Character in the Christian Life

1. Les T. Csorba, *Trust*, (Thomas Nelson, Inc. 2004), p. 231-232.
2. Quoted by Jay Kessler, *Growing* (out of print), p. 41.
3. William Barclay, *The Letters to the Galatians and Ephesians*, (Westminster, 1976), p. 100.
4. Dorothie Bobbe, *Abigail Adams*, (Putnam, 1966), p. 206.
5. Christianity Today, March 1966, p. 36.
6. The Alliance Weekly, February, 1956, p. 2.
7. H. Thielecke, *Encounter with Spurgeon*, p. 197.
8. Gordon MacDonald, *A Resilient Life*, (Nelson Publishers, 2004), p. 31.
9. Ibid., p. 192.
10. Warren Wiersbe, *In Praise of Plodders*, (Kregel Publications, 1994), p. 33.

11. E. M. Bounds, Quoted in *A Treasury of Prayer*, edited by Leonard Ravenhill, (Bethany Fellowship, Inc. 1961), p. 138-139.
12. Nathanael Ranew, *Solitude Improved by Divine Meditation*, (1839, reprinted by Soli Deo Gloria, 1995), p. 72-73.
13. Charles Swindoll, *Living Above the Level of Mediocrity*, (Word Publishers, 1987), p. 122.
14. Dr. David D. Ireland, *Perfecting Your Purpose*, (Warner, Faith, 2005), p. 67.
15. Found online at: http://www.drdaveanddee.com/elbows.html
16. Pat Williams, *The Paradox of Power*, Warner Faith Publishers, 2002, p. 101.
17. Erwin W. Lutzer, *Failure the Back Door to Success*, (Moody Press, 1976), p. 22.

Chapter 15: The Importance of First Impressions

1. Susannah Thompson, quoted by Ian Murray, *The Early Years* (Banner of Truth, 1962), p. 280.
2. C. H. Spurgeon, Quoted by Steve Brown in *How to Talk So People Will Listen*, (Baker Book House, 1993), p. 62-63.
3. Bob Jones Jr. *How to Improve Your Preaching*, (Bob Jones University Press, 1960), p. 94-95.
4. Ted W. Engstrom, *The Pursuit of Excellence*, (Zondervan Publishing House, 1982), p. 56-57.
5. Joel Beeke, *Overcoming the World*, (Presbyterian and Reformed Publishing Company, 2005), p. 24.
6. Florence Littauer, *It Takes So Little to be Above Average*, (Harvest House Publishers, 1983), p. 110.
7. June Hines Moore, *The Etiquette Advantage*, (Broadman and Holman Publishers, 1998), p. 9.
8. Ibid. p. 10.
9. Ibid. p. 10.

Chapter 16: Proclaiming the Gospel

1. Robert Mounce, Quoted in *Baker's Dictionary of Theology*, (Baker Book House, 1975), p. 254-255.

2. C. S. Lewis, *Mere Christianity*, Quoted by Charles Swindoll, *Jesus, the Greatest Life of All,* (Thomas Nelson Publishers, 2008) p. 4.
3. Martyn Lloyd-Jones, *Romans, The Gospel of God, vol. 1,* (Zondervan Publishing House, 1986), p. 258-259.

Part III: The Peace of Christian Living

Chapter 17: Discovering the Peace of Romans 8:28

1. Sharon James, *Gentle Rain on Tender Grass*, (Evangelical Press), p. 54.
2. E. Stanley Jones, *A Song of Ascents* (Abingdon Press, 1968), p. 20.
3. George Matheson, *Thoughts for Life's Journey*, (Hodder & Stoughton, 1908) p. 266-267.
4. John Newton, *Letters of John Newton* (The Banner of Truth Trust, 1960), p. 137.

Chapter 18: Living in the Spirit of Praise

1. Sharon James, *Gentle Rain on Tender Grass* (Evangelical Press), p. 121.
2. Bill Perkins, *Six Battles Every Man Must Win*, (Tyndale House Publishers, 2004), p. 69.

Chapter 19: Preparing for Death

1. Kirk H. Neely, *When Grief Comes*, (Baker Book House, 2007), p. 69.
2. Peter Jeffery, *Bitesize Theology*, (Evangelical Press, 2002), p. 87.
3. Vernon Higham, *Unsearchable Riches*, (Christian Focus Publications, 2003), p. 52-53.
4. Ibid, p. 155.
5. John Calvin, *Commentary on Hebrews*, p. 57.
6. Dr. Edgar Andrews, *A Glorious High Throne*, (Evangelical Press, 2003), p. 144-145.
7. John Piper, *A Godward Life*, (Multnomah Publishers, 1997), p. 50.

8. Ibid., p. 50-52.
9. Martin Luther, quoted by Roger Ellsworth, *What the Bible Teaches About Heaven*, (Evangelical Press, 2007, p. 24.

Conclusion

1. Ted W. Engstrom, *The Pursuit of Excellence*, (Zondervan Publishing Company, 1982), p. 31-32.

Scripture References

Bibliography

1. Jim Berg, *Changed into His Image*, Bob Jones University Press

2. John Calvin, *Golden Booklet of the True Christian Life*, Baker Books

3. Robert L. Dickie, *What the Bible Teaches about Worship*, Evangelical Press

4. Elizabeth Elliot, *The Shadow of the Almighty*, Harper Collins Publishers

5. Dr. Martyn Lloyd-Jones, *Spiritual Depression*, Eerdmans Publishing Company

6. J. I. Packer, *Evangelism and the Sovereignty of God*, InterVarsity Press

7. John MacArthur, *Ashamed of the Gospel*, Crossway Books

8. J. C. Ryle, *Holiness*, Hendrickson Publishers

9. J. Oswald Sanders, *Spiritual Leadership*, Moody Press

10. A. W. Tozer, *The Pursuit of God*, Wing Spread Publishers

11. Donald Whitney, *Spiritual Disciplines for the Christian Life,* NavPress Publishing Group

Other Titles by the Author

Authentic Christianity 101 (published by Evangelical Press)

What the Bible Teaches About Worship (published by Evangelical Press)

A Biblical Perspective of Wealth (published by the TEAM)

All available through Emmaus Road Publishing, Inc.